At Good old Siwash

AT GOOD OLD SIWASH

.

Twenty-five yards with four Muggledorfer men hanging
on his legs

AT

GOOD OLD SIWASH

BY

GEORGE FITCH

ILLUSTRATED

BOSTON

LITTLE, BROWN, AND COMPANY

1911

THE UNIVERSITY PRESS, CAMBRIDGE, U.S.A.

PREFACE

LITTLE did I think, during the countless occasions on which I have skipped blithely over the preface of a book in order to plunge into the plot, that I should be called upon to write a preface myself some day. And little have I realized until just now the extreme importance to the author of having his preface read.

I want this preface to be read, though I have an uneasy premonition that it is going to be skipped as joyously as ever I skipped a preface myself. I want the reader to toil through my preface in order to save him the task of trying to follow a plot through this book. For if he attempts to do this he will most certainly dislocate something about himself very seriously. I have found it impossible, in writing of college days which are just one deep-laid scheme after another, to confine myself to one plot. How could I describe in one plot the life of the student who carries out an average of three plots a day? It is unreasonable. So I have done the next best thing. There is a plot in every chapter. This requires the use of upwards of a dozen villains, an almost equal number of heroes, and a whole bouquet of heroines.

But I do not begrudge this extravagance. It is necessary, and that settles it.

Then, again, I want to answer in this preface a number of questions by readers who kindly consented to
become interested in the stories when they appeared in
the *Saturday Evening Post*. Siwash is n't Michigan
in disguise. It is n't Kansas. It is n't Knox. It
is n't Minnesota. It is n't Tuskegee, Texas, or Tufts.
It is just Siwash College. I built it myself with a
typewriter out of memories, legends, and contributed
tales from a score of colleges. I have tried to locate
it myself a dozen times, but I can't. I have tried to
place my thumb on it firmly and say, " There, darn
you, stay put." But no halfback was ever so elusive
as this infernal college. Just as I have it definitely
located on the Knox College campus, which I myself
once infested, I look up to find it on the Kansas
prairies. I surround it with infinite caution and attempt to nail it down there. Instead, I find it in
Minnesota with a strong Norwegian accent running
through the course of study. Worse than that, I often
find it in two or three places at once. It is harder to
corner than a flea. I never saw such a peripatetic
school.

That is only the least of my troubles, too. The
college itself is never twice the same. Sometimes I
am amazed at its size and perfection, by the grandeur
of its gymnasium and the colossal lines of its stadium.
But at other times I cannot find the stadium at all, and
the gymnasium has shrunk until it looks amazingly

like the old wooden barn in which we once built up
Sandow biceps at Knox. I never saw such a college
to get lost in, either. I know as well as anything that
to get to the Eta Bita Pie house, you go north from
the old bricks, past the new science hall and past
Browning Hall. But often when I start north from
the campus, I find my way blocked by the stadium,
and when I try to dodge it, I run into the Alfalfa Delt
House, and the Eatemalive boarding club, and other
places which belong properly to the south. And when
I go south I frequently lose sight of the college altogether, and can't for the life of me remember what
the library tower looks like or whether the theological
school is just falling down, or is to be built next year;
or whether I ought to turn to my right, and ask for
directions at Prexie's house, or turn to my left and
crawl under a freight train which blocks a crossing on
the Hither, Yonder and Elsewhere Railroad. If you
think it is an easy task to carry a whole college in your
head without getting it jumbled, just try it a while.

Then, again, the Siwash people puzzle me. Professor Grubb is always a trial. That man alternates a
smooth-shaven face with a full beard in the most
startling manner. Petey Simmons is short and flaxen-
haired, long and black-haired, and wide and hatchet-
faced in turns, depending on the illustrator. I never
know Ole Skjarsen when I see him for the same reason. As for Prince Hogboom, Allie Bangs, Keg
Rearick and the rest of them, nobody knows how they
look but the artists who illustrated the stories; and

as I read each number and viewed the smiling faces of these students, I murmured, " Goodness, how you have changed!"

So I have struggled along as best I could to administer the affairs of a college which is located nowhere, has no student body, has no endowment, never looks the same twice, and cannot be reached by any reliable route. The situation is impossible. I must locate it somewhere. If you are interested in the college when you have read these few stories, suppose you hunt for it wherever college boys are full of applied deviltry and college girls are distractingly fair; where it is necessary to win football games in order to be half-way contented with the universe; where the spring weather is too wonderful to be wasted on College Algebra or History of Art; and where, whatever you do, or whoever you like, or however you live, you can't forget it, no matter how long you work or worry afterward.

There! I can't mark it on the map, but if you have ever worried a college faculty you 'll know the way.

GEORGE FITCH.

July, 1911.

CONTENTS

ix

ILLUSTRATIONS

AT GOOD OLD SIWASH

CHAPTER I

OLE SKJARSEN'S FIRST TOUCHDOWN

AM I GOING to the game Saturday? Am I? Me? Am I going to eat some more food this year? Am I going to draw my pay this month? Am I going to do any more breathing after I get this lungful used up? All foolish questions, pal. Very silly conversation. Pshaw!

Am I going to the game, you ask me? Is the sun going to get up to-morrow? You could n't keep me away from that game if you put a protective tariff of seventy-eight per cent ad valorem, whatever that means, on the front gate. I came out to this town on business, and I 'll have to take an extra fare train home to make up the time; but what of that? I 'm going to the game, and when the Siwash team comes out I 'm going to get up and give as near a correct imitation of a Roman mob and a Polish riot as my throat will stand; and if we put a crimp in the large-footed, humpy-shouldered behemoths we 're going up against this afternoon, I 'm going out to-night and burn the City Hall. Any Siwash man who is a gentleman would do it. I'll probably have to run like thunder to beat some of them to it.

You know how it is, old man. Or maybe you don't, because you made all your end runs on the Glee Club. But I played football all through my college course and the microbe is still there. In the fall I think football, talk football, dream football, even though I haven't had a suit on for six years. And when I go out to the field and see little old Siwash lining up against a bunch of overgrown hippos from a university with a catalogue as thick as a city directory, the old mud-and-perspiration smell gets in my nostrils, and the desire to get under the bunch and feel the feet jabbing into my ribs boils up so strong that I have to hold on to myself with both hands. If you've never sat on a hard board and wanted to be between two halfbacks with your hands on their shoulders, and the quarter ready to sock a ball into your solar plexus, and eleven men daring you to dodge 'em, and nine thousand friends and enemies raising Cain and keeping him well propped up in the grandstands — if you haven't had that want you wouldn't know a healthy, able-bodied want if you ran into it on the street.

Of course, I never got any further along than a scrub. But what's the odds? A broken bone feels just as grand to a scrub as to a star. I sometimes think a scrub gets more real football knowledge than a varsity man, because he doesn't have to addle his brain by worrying about holding his job and keeping

his wind, and by dreaming that he has fumbled a
punt and presented ninety-five yards to the hereditary
enemies of his college.   I played scrub football five
years, four of 'em under Bost, the greatest coach who
ever put wings on the heels of a two-hundred-pound
hunk of meat;   and while my ribs never lasted long
enough to put me on the team, what I did n't learn
about the game you could put in the other fellow's
eye.

Say, but it's great, learning football under a good
coach.   It's the finest training a man can get anywhere on this old globule.   Football is only the
smallest thing you learn.   You learn how to be
patient when what you want to do is to chew somebody up and spit him into the gutter.   You learn
to control your temper when it is on the high speed,
with the throttle jerked wide open and buzzing like
a hornet convention.   You learn, by having it told
you, just how small and foolish and insignificant you
are, and how well this earth could stagger along without you if some one were to take a fly-killer and mash
you with it.   And you learn all this at the time of
life when your head is swelling up until you mistake
it for a planet, and regard whatever you say as a
volcanic disturbance.

I suppose you think, like the rest of the chaps who
never came out to practice but observed the game
from the dollar-and-a-half seats, that being coached
in football is like being instructed in German or
calculus.   You are told what to do and how to do

it, and then you recite. Far from it, my boy! They
don't bother telling you what to do and how to do
it on a big football field. Mostly they tell you what
to do and how you do it. And they do it artistically,
too. They use plenty of language. A football coach
is picked out for his ready tongue. He must be a
conversationalist. He must be able to talk to a
greenhorn, with fine shoulders and a needle-shaped
head, until that greenhorn would pick up the ball and
take it through a Sioux war dance to get away from
the conversation. You can't reason with football
men. They 're not logical, most of them. They are
selected for their heels and shoulders and their leg
muscles, and not for their ability to look at you
with luminous eyes and say: " Yes, Professor, I
think I understand." The way to make 'em understand is to talk about them. Any man can understand
you while you are telling him that if he were just
a little bit slower he would have to be tied to the
earth to keep up with it. That hurts his pride.
And when you hurt his pride he takes it out on
whatever is in front of him — which is the other
team. Never get in front of a football player when
you are coaching him.

But this brings me to the subject of Bost again.
Bost is still coaching Siwash. This makes his 'steenth
year. I guess he can stay there forever. He 's
coached all these years and has never used the same
adjective to the same man twice. There 's a record
for you! He 's a little man, Bost is. He played end

on some Western team when he only weighed one
hundred and forty.   Got his football knowledge
there.   But where he got his vocabulary is still a
mystery.   He has a way of convincing a man that
a dill pickle would make a better guard than he is,
and of making that man so jealous of the pickle
that he will perform perfectly unreasonable feats
for a week to beat it out for the place.   He has a
way of saying " Hurry up," with a few descriptive
adjectives tacked on, that makes a man rub himself
in the stung place for an hour; and oh, how mad
he can make you while he is telling you pleasantly
that while the little fellow playing against you is
only a prep and has sloping shoulders and weighs
one hundred and eleven stripped, he is making you
look like a bale of hay that has been dumped by mistake on an athletic field.   And when he gets a team
in the gymnasium between halves, with the game
going wrong, and stands up before them and sizes
up their insect nerve and rubber backbone and hereditary awkwardness and incredible talent in doing the
wrong thing, to say nothing of describing each indi-
vidual blunder in that queer nasal clack of his —
well, I 'd rather be tied up in a great big frying-pan
over a good hot stove for the same length of time,
any day in the week.   The reason Bost is a great
coach is because his men don't dare play poorly.
When they do he talks to them.   If he would only
hit them, or skin them by inches, or shoot at them,
they would n't mind it so much; but when you get

on the field with him and realize that if you miss a tackle he is going to get you out before the whole gang and tell you what a great mistake the Creator made when He put joints in your arms instead of letting them stick out stiff as they do any other sign-post, you 're not going to miss that tackle, that 's all.

When Bost came to Siwash he succeeded a line of coaches who had been telling the fellows to get down low and hit the line hard, and had been showing them how to do it very patiently. Nice fellows, those coaches. Perfect gentlemen. Make you proud to associate with them. They could take a herd of green farmer boys, with wrists like mules' ankles, and by Thanksgiving they would have them familiar with all the rudiments of the game. By that time the season would be over and all the schools in the vicinity would have beaten us by big scores. The next year the last year's crop of big farmer boys would stay at home to husk corn, and the coach would begin all over on a new crop. The result was, we were a dub school at football. Any school that could scare up a good rangy halfback and a line that could hold sheep could get up an adding festival at our expense any time. We lived in a perpetual state of fear. Some day we felt that the normal school would come down and beat us. That would be the limit of disgrace. After that there would be nothing left to do but disband the college and take to drink to forget the past.

But Bost changed all that in one year. He did n't

care to show any one how to play football. He was
just interested in making the player afraid not to
play it. When you went down the field on a punt
you knew that if you missed your man he would
tell you when you came back that two stone hitching-
posts out of three could get past you in a six-foot
alley. If you missed a punt you could expect to be
told that you might catch a haystack by running with
your arms wide open, but that was no way to catch
a football. Maybe things like that don't sound jabby
when two dozen men hear them! They kept us catching punts between classes, and tackling each other
all the way to our rooms and back. We simply had
to play football to keep from being bawled out. It's
an awful thing to have a coach with a tongue like
a cheese knife swinging away at you, and to know
that if you get mad and quit, no one but the dear
old coll. will suffer — but it gets the results. They
use the same system in the East, but there they only
swear at a man, I believe. Siwash is a mighty proper
college and you can't swear on its campus, whatever
else you do. Swearing is only a lazy man's substitute
for thinking, anyway; and Bost wasn't lazy. He
preferred the descriptive; he sat up nights thinking
it out.

We began to see the results before Bost had been
tracing our pedigrees for two weeks. First game of
the season was with that little old dinky Normal
School which had been scaring us so for the past five
years. We had been satisfied to push some awkward

halfback over the line once, and then hold on to the enemy so tight he could n't run; and we started out that year in the same old way. First half ended 0 to 0, with our boys pretty satisfied because they had kept the ball in Normal's territory. Bost led the team and the substitutes into the overgrown barn we used for a gymnasium, and while we were still patting ourselves approvingly in our minds he cut loose:

"You pasty-faced, overfed, white-livered beanbag experts, what do you mean by running a beauty show instead of a football game?" he yelled. "Do you suppose I came out here to be art director of a statuary exhibit? Does any one of you imagine for a holy minute that he knows the difference between a football game and ushering in a church? Don't fool yourselves. You don't; you don't know anything. All you ever knew about football I could carve on granite and put in my eye and never feel it. Nothing to nothing against a crowd of farmer boys who have n't known a football from a duck's egg for more than a week! Bah! If I ever turned the Old Folks' Home loose on you doll babies they 'd run up a century while you were hunting for your handkerchiefs. Jackson, what do you suppose a half-back is for? I don't want cloak models. I want a man who can stick his head down and run. Don't be afraid of that bean of yours; it has n't got anything worth saving in it. When you get the ball you 're supposed to run with it and not sit around trying to hatch it. You, Saunders! You held that other guard just like a sweet-pea vine. Where did you ever learn that sweet, lovely way of falling down on your nose when a real man sneezes at you? Did you ever hear of sand? Eat it! Eat it! Fill yourself up with it. I want you to get in that line this half and stop something or I'll make you play left end in a fancy-work club. Johnson, the only way to get you around the field is to put you on wheels and haul you. Next time you grow fast to the ground I'm going to violate some forestry regulations and take an axe to you. Same to you, Briggs. You'd make the All-American boundary posts, but that's all. Vance, I picked you for a quarterback, but I made a mistake; you ought to be sorting eggs. That ball isn't red hot. You don't have to let go of it as soon as you get it. Don't be afraid, nobody will step on you. This isn't a rude game. It's only a game of post-office. You need n't act so nervous about it. Maybe some of the big girls will kiss you, but it won't hurt."

Bost stopped for breath and eyed us. We were a sick-looking crowd. You could almost see the remarks sticking into us and quivering. We had come in feeling pretty virtuous, and what we were getting was a hideous surprise.

"Now I want to tell this tea-party something," continued Bost. "Either you're going out on that field and score thirty points this last half or I'm going to let the girls of Siwash play your football for you. I'm tired of coaching men that are n't good at anything but falling down scientifically when they 're tackled. There is n't a broken nose among you. Every one of you will run back five yards to pick out a soft spot to fall on. It 's got to stop. You 're going to hold on to that ball this half and take it places. If some little fellow from Normal crosses his fingers and says ' naughty, naughty,' don't fall on the ball and yell ' down ' until they can hear it uptown. Thirty points is what I want out of you this half, and if you don't get 'em — well, you just dare to come back here without them, that 's all. Now get out on that field and jostle somebody. Git! "

Did we git? Well, rather. We were so mad our clothes smoked. We would have quit the game right there and resigned from the team, but we did n't dare to. Bost would have talked to us some more. And we did n't dare not to make those thirty points, either. It was an awful tough job, but we did it with a couple over. We raged like wild beasts. We scared those gentle Normalites out of their boots. I can't imagine how we ever got it into our heads that they could play football, anyway. When it was all over we went back to the gymnasium feeling righteously triumphant, and had another hour with Bost in which he took us all apart without anæs-thetics, and showed us how Nature would have done a better job if she had used a better grade of lumber in our composition.

That day made the Siwash team. The school went wild over the score. Bost rounded up two or three more good players, and every afternoon he lashed us around the field with that wire-edged tongue of his. On Saturdays we played, and oh, how we worked! In the first half we were afraid of what Bost would say to us when we came off the field. In the second half we were mad at what he had said. And how he did drive us down the field in practice! I can remember whole cross sections of his talk yet:

"Faster, faster, you scows. Line up. Quick! Johnson, are you waiting for a stone-mason to set you? Snap the ball. Tear into them. Low! Low! Hi-i! You end, do you think you're the quarter pole in a horse race? Nine men went past you that time. If you can't touch 'em drop 'em a souvenir card. Line up. Faster, faster! Oh, thunder, hurry up! If you ran a funeral, center, the corpse would spoil on your hands. Wow! Fumble! Drop on that ball. Drop on it! Hogboom, you'd fumble a loving-cup. Use your hand instead of your jaw to catch that ball. It is n't good to eat. That's four chances you've had. I could lose two games a day if I had you all the time. Now try that signal again — low, you linemen; there's no girls watching you. Snap it; snap it. Great Scott! Say, Hogboom, come here. When you get that ball, don't think we gave it to you to nurse. You're supposed to start the same day with the line. We give you that ball to take forward. Have you got to get a legal permit to start those legs of yours? You'd make a good vault to store footballs in, but you're too stationary for a fullback. Now I'll give you one more chance — "

And maybe Hogboom would n't go some with that chance!

In a month we had a team that would n't have used past Siwash teams to hold its sweaters. It was mad all the time, and it played the game carnivorously. Siwash was delirious with joy. The whole school turned out for practice, and to see those eleven men snapping through signals up and down the field as fast as an ordinary man could run just congested us with happiness. You 've no idea what a lovely time of the year autumn is when you can go out after classes and sit on a pine seat in the soft dusk and watch your college team pulling off end runs in as pretty formation as if they were chorus girls, while you discuss lazily with your friends just how many points it is going to run up on the neighboring schools. I never expect to be a Captain of Industry, but it could n't make me feel any more contented or powerful or complacent than to be a busted-up scrub in Siwash, with a team like that to watch. I 'm pretty sure of that.

But, happy as we were, Bost was n't nearly content. He had ideals. I believe one of them must have been to run that team through a couple of brick flats without spoiling the formation. Nothing satisfied him. He was particularly distressed about the fullback. Hogboom was a good fellow and took signal practice perfectly, but he was no fiend. He lacked the vivacity of a real, first-class Bengal tiger. He would n't eat any one alive. He 'd run until he was pulled down, but you never expected him to explode in the midst of seven hostiles and ricochet down the field for forty yards. He never jumped over two men and on to another, and he never dodged two ways at once and laid out three men with stiff arms on his way to the goal. It was n't his style. He was good for two and a half yards every time, but that did n't suit Bost. He was after statistics, and what does a three-yard buck amount to when you want 70 to 0 scores?

The result of this dissatisfaction was Ole Skjarsen. Late in September Bost disappeared for three days and came back leading Ole by a rope — at least, he was towing him by an old carpet-bag when we sighted him. Bost found him in a lumber camp, he afterward told us, and had to explain to him what a college was before he would quit his job. He thought it was something good to eat at first, I believe. Ole was a timid young Norwegian giant, with a rick of white hair and a reënforced concrete physique. He escaped from his clothes in all directions, and was so green and bashful that you would have thought we were cannibals from the way he shied at us — though, as that was the year the bright hat-ribbons came in, I can't blame him. He was n't like anything we had ever seen before in college. He was as big as a cart-horse, as graceful as a dray and as meek as a missionary. He had a double width smile and a thin little old faded voice that made you think you could tip him over and shine your shoes on him with impunity. But I would n't have tried it for a month's allowance. His voice and his arms did n't harmonize worth a cent. They were as big as ordinary legs — those arms, and they ended in hands that could have picked up a football and mislaid it among their fingers.

No wonder Ole was a sensation. He did n't look exactly like football material to us, I 'll admit. He seemed more especially designed for light derrick work. But we trusted Bost implicitly by that time and we gave him a royal reception. We crowded around him as if he had been a T. R. capture straight from Africa. Everybody helped him register third prep, with business-college extras. Then we took him out, harnessed him in football armor, and set to work to teach him the game.

Bost went right to work on Ole in a businesslike manner. He tossed him the football and said: "Catch it." Ole watched it sail past and then tore after it like a pup retrieving a stick. He got it in a few minutes and brought it back to where Bost was raving.

"See here, you overgrown fox terrier," he shouted, "catch it on the fly. Here!" He hurled it at him.

"Aye ent seen no fly," said Ole, allowing the ball to pass on as he conversed.

"You cotton-headed Scandinavian cattleship ballast, catch that ball in your arms when I throw it

to you, and don't let go of it!" shrieked Bost, shooting it at him again.

"Oll right," said Ole patiently. He cornered the
ball after a short struggle and stood hugging it
faithfully.

"Toss it back, toss it back!" howled Bost, jumping up and down.

"Yu tal me to hold it," said Ole reproachfully,
hugging it tighter than ever.

"Drop it, you Mammoth Cave of ignorance!"
yelled Bost. "If I had your head I'd sell it for
cordwood. Drop it!"

Ole dropped the ball placidly. "Das ban fule
game," he smiled dazedly. "Aye ent care for it.
Eny faller got a Yewsharp?"

That was the opening chapter of Ole's instruction.
The rest were just like it. You had to tell him to
do a thing. You then had to show him how to do it.
You then had to tell him how to stop doing it. After
that you had to explain that he wasn't to refrain
forever — just until he had to do it again. Then you
had to persuade him to do it again. He was as good-
natured as a lost puppy, and just as hard to reason
with. In three nights Bost was so hoarse that he
couldn't talk. He had called Ole everything in the
dictionary that is fit to print; and the knowledge that
Ole didn't understand more than a hundredth part
of it, and didn't mind that, was wormwood to his
soul.

For all that, we could see that if any one could

teach Ole the game he would make a fine player.
He was as hard as flint and so fast on his feet that
we could n't tackle him any more than we could have
tackled a jack-rabbit. He learned to catch the ball
in a night, and as for defense — his one-handed
catches of flying players would have made a National
League fielder envious. But with all of it he was
perfectly useless. You had to start him, stop him,
back him, speed him up, throttle him down and run
him off the field just as if he had been a close-
coupled, next year's model scootcart. If we could have
rigged up a driver's seat and chauffeured Ole, it
would have been all right. But every other method of
trying to get him to understand what he was expected
to do was a failure. He just grinned, took orders,
executed them, and waited for more. When a two-
hundred-and-twenty-pound man takes a football,
wades through eleven frantic scrubs, shakes them all
off, and then stops dead with a clear field to the goal
before him — because his instructions ran out when
he shook the last scrub — you can be pardoned for
feeling hopeless about him.

That was what happened the day before the Muggledorfer game. Bost had been working Ole at fullback all evening. He and the captain had steered
him up and down the field as carefully as if he had
been a sea-going yacht. It was a wonderful sight.
Ole was under perfect control. He advanced the ball
five yards, ten yards, or twenty at command. Nothing
could stop him. The scrubs represented only so

many doormats to him. Every time he made a play
he stopped at the latter end of it for instructions.

When he stopped the last time, with nothing before him but the goal, and asked placidly, " Vere
skoll I take das ball now, Master Bost ? " I thought
the coach would expire of the heat. He positively
steamed with suppressed emotion. He swelled and
got purple about the face. We were alarmed and
were getting ready to hoop him like a barrel when
he found his tongue at last.

" You pale-eyed, prehistoric mudhead," he spluttered, " I 've spent a week trying to get through that
skull lining of yours. It 's no use, you field boulder.
Where do you keep your brains ? Give me a chance
at them. I just want to get into them one minute
and stir them up with my finger. To think that I
have to use you to play football when they are paying
five dollars and a half for ox meat in Kansas City.
Skjarsen, do you know anything at all ? "

" Aye ban getting gude eddication," said Ole
serenely. " Aye tank I ban college faller purty sune,
I don't know. I like I skoll understand all das har
big vorts yu make."

" You 'll understand them, I don't think," moaned
Bost. " You could n't understand a swift kick in
the ribs. You are a fool. Understand that, muttonhead ? "

Ole understood. " Vy for yu call me fule ? " he
said indignantly. " Aye du yust vat you say."

" Ar-r-r-r ! " bubbled Bost, walking around himself

three or four times. " You do just what I say! Of
course you do. Did I tell you to stop in the middle
of the field? What would Muggledorfer do to you
if you stopped there? "

" Yu ent tal me to go on," said Ole sullenly. " Aye
go on, Aye gass, pooty qveek den."

" You bet you 'll go on," said Bost. " Now, look
here, you sausage material, to-morrow you play fullback. You stop everything that comes at you from
the other side. Hear? You catch the ball when it
comes to you. Hear? And when they give you the
ball you take it, and don't you dare to stop with it.
Get that? Can I get that into your head without a
drill and a blast? If you dare to stop with that
ball I 'll ship you back to the lumber camp in a cattle
car. Stop in the middle of the field — Ow!"

But at this point we took Bost away.

The next afternoon we dressed Ole up in his armor
— he invariably got it on wrong side out if we did n't
help him — and took him out to the field. We confidently expected to promenade all over Muggledorfer
— their coach was an innocent child beside Bost —
and that was the reason why Ole was going to play.
It did n't matter much what he did.

Ole was just coming to a boil when we got him
into his clothes. Bost's remarks had gotten through
his hide at last. He was pretty slow, Ole was, but
he had begun getting mad the night before and had
kept at the job all night and all morning. By afternoon he was seething, mostly in Norwegian. The

injustice of being called a muttonhead all week for
not obeying orders, and then being called a mudhead
for stopping for orders, churned his soul, to say nothing of his language. He only averaged one English
word in three, as he told us on the way out that to-day
he was going to do exactly as he had been told or
fill a martyr's grave — only that was n't the way he
put it.

The Muggledorfers were a pruny-looking lot. We
had the game won when our team came out and
glared at them. Bost had filled most of the positions
with regular young mammoths, and when you dressed
them up in football armor they were enough to make
a Dreadnought a little nervous. The Muggleses
kicked off to our team, and for a few plays we
plowed along five or ten yards at a time. Then
Ole was given the ball. He went twenty-five yards.
Any other man would have been crushed to earth
in five. He just waded through the middle of the
line and went down the field, a moving mass of wrig-
gling men. It was a wonderful play. They dis-
interred him at last and he started straight across
the field for Bost.

"Aye ent mean to stop, Master Bost," he shouted.
"Dese fallers har, dey squash me down — "

We hauled him into line and went to work again.
Ole had performed so well that the captain called his
signal again. This time I hope I may be roasted in
a subway in July if Ole did n't run twenty-five yards
with four Muggledorfer men hanging on his legs.

We stood up and yelled until our teeth ached. It took about five minutes to get Ole dug out, and then he started for Bost again.

" Honest, Master Bost, Aye ent mean to stop," he said imploringly. " Aye yust tal you, dese fallers ban devils. Aye fule dem naxt time — "

" Line up and shut up," the captain shouted. The ball was n't over twenty yards from the line, and as a matter of course the quarter shot it back to Ole. He put his head down, gave one mad-bull plunge, laid a windrow of Muggledorfer players out on either side, and shot over the goal line like a locomotive.

We rose up to cheer a few lines, but stopped to stare. Ole did n't stop at the goal line. He did n't stop at the fence. He put up one hand, hurdled it, and disappeared across the campus like a young whirlwind.

" He does n't know enough to stop! " yelled Bost, rushing up to the fence. " Hustle up, you fellows, and bring him back! "

Three or four of us jumped the fence, but it was a hopeless game. Ole was disappearing up the campus and across the street. The Muggledorfer team was nonplussed and sort of indignant. To be bowled over by a cyclone, and then to have said cyclone break up the game by running away with the ball was to them a new idea in football. It was n't to those of us who knew Ole, however. One of us telephoned down to the *Leader* office where Hinckley, an old team man, worked, and asked him to head off Ole and send him

back. Muggledorfer kindly consented to call time,
and we started after the fugitive ourselves.

Ten minutes later we met Hinckley downtown.
He looked as if he had had a slight argument with a
thirteen-inch shell. He was also mad.

"What was that you asked me to stop?" he
snorted, pinning himself together. "Was it a gorilla
or a high explosive? When did you fellows begin
importing steam rollers for the team? I asked him
to stop. I ordered him to stop. Then I went around
in front of him to stop him — and he ran right over
me. I held on for thirty yards, but that's no way
to travel. I could have gone to the next town just
as well, though. What sort of a game is this, and
where is that tow-headed holy terror bound for?"

We gave the answer up, but we could n't give up
Ole. He was too valuable to lose. How to catch him
was the sticker. An awful uproar in the street gave
us an idea. It was Ted Harris in the only auto in
town — one of the earliest brands of sneeze vehicles.
In a minute more four of us were in, and Ted was
chiveying the thing up the street.

If you 've never chased an escaping fullback in
one of those pioneer automobiles you 've got something coming. Take it all around, a good, swift man,
running all the time, could almost keep ahead of one.
We pumped up a tire, fixed a wire or two, and
cranked up a few times; and the upshot of it was
we were two miles out on the state road before we
caught sight of Ole.

He was trotting briskly when we caught up with him, the ball under his arm, and that patient, resigned expression on his face that he always had when Bost cussed him. "Stop, Ole," I yelled; "this is no Marathon. Come back. Climb in here with us."

Ole shook his head and let out a notch of speed.

"Stop, you mullethead," yelled Simpson above the roar of the auto — those old machines could roar some, too. "What do you mean by running off with our ball? You're not supposed to do hare-and-hounds in football."

Ole kept on running. We drove the car on ahead, stopped it across the road, and jumped out to stop him. When the attempt was over three of us picked up the fourth and put him aboard. Ole had tramped on us and had climbed over the auto.

Force wouldn't do, that was plain. "Where are you going, Ole?" we pleaded as we tore along beside him.

"Aye ent know," he panted, laboring up a hill; "das ban fule game, Aye tenk."

"Come on back and play some more," we urged. "Bost won't like it, your running all over the country this way."

"Das ban my orders," panted Ole. "Aye ent no fule, yentlemen; Aye know ven Aye ban doing right teng. Master Bost he say 'Keep on running!' Aye gass I run till hal freeze on top. Aye ent know why. Master Bost he know, I tenk."

"This is awful," said Lambert, the manager of

the team. "He's taken Bost literally again — the chump. He'll run till he lands up in those pine woods again. And that ball cost the association five dollars. Besides, we want him. What are we going to do?"

"I know," I said. "We're going back to get Bost. I guess the man who started him can stop him."

We left Ole still plugging north and ran back to town. The game was still hanging fire. Bost was tearing his hair. Of course, the Muggledorfer fellows could have insisted on playing, but they were n't anxious. Ole or no Ole, we could have walked all over them, and they knew it. Besides, they were having too much fun with Bost. They were sitting around, Indian-like, in their blankets, and every three minutes their captain would go and ask Bost with perfect politeness whether he thought they had better continue the game there or move it on to the next town in time to catch his fullback as he came through.

"Of course, we are in no hurry," he would explain pleasantly; "we're just here for amusement, any-way; and it's as much fun watching you try to catch your players as it is to get scored on. Why don't you hobble them, Mr. Bost? A fifty-yard rope would n't interfere much with that gay young Percheron of yours, and it would save you lots of time rounding him up. Do you have to use a lariat when you put his harness on?"

Fancy Bost having to take all that conversation,

with no adequate reply to make. When I got there he was blue in the face. It did n't take him half a second to decide what to do. Telling the captain of the Siwash team to go ahead and play if Muggledorfer insisted, and on no account to use that 32 double-X play except on first downs, he jumped into the machine and we started for Ole.

There were no speed records in those days. Would n't have made any difference if there were. Harris just turned on all the juice his old double-opposed motor could soak up, and when we hit the wooden crossings on the outskirts of town we fellows in the tonneau went up so high that we changed sides coming down. It was n't over twenty minutes till we sighted a little cloud of dust just beyond a little town to the north. Pretty soon we saw it was Ole. He was still doing his six miles per. We caught up and Bost hopped out, still mad.

"Where in Billy-be-blamed are you going, you human trolley car?" he spluttered, sprinting along beside Skjarsen. "What do you mean by breaking up a game in the middle and vamoosing with the ball? Do you think we 're going to win this game on mileage? Turn around, you chump, and climb into this car."

Ole looked around him sadly. He kept on running as he did. "Aye ent care to stop," he said. "Aye kent suit you, Master Bost. You tal me Aye skoll du a teng, den you cuss me for duing et. You tal me not to du a teng and you cuss

me some more den. Aye tenk I yust keep on a-run-
ning, lak yu tal me tu last night. Et ent so hard
bein' cussed ven yu ban running."

"I tell you to stop, you potato-top," gasped Bost.
By this time he was fifteen yards behind and losing
at every step. He had wasted too much breath on
oratory. We picked him up in the car and set him
alongside of Ole again.

"See here, Ole, I'm tired of this," he said, sprinting up by him again. "The game's waiting. Come
on back. You're making a fool of yourself."

"Eny teng Aye du Aye ban beeg fule," said Ole
gloomily. "Aye yust keep on runnin'. Fallers
ent got breath to call me fule ven Aye run. Aye
tenk das best vay."

We picked Bost up again thirty yards behind.
Maybe he would have run better if he had n't choked
so in his conversation. In another minute we landed
him abreast of Ole again. He got out and sprinted
for the third time. He wabbled as he did it.

"Ole," he panted, "I've been mistaken in you.
You are all right, Ole. I never saw a more intelligent fellow. I won't cuss you any more, Ole. If
you'll stop now we'll take you back in an automobile
— hold on there a minute; can't you see I'm all out
of breath?"

"Aye ban gude faller, den?" asked Ole, letting
out another link of speed.

"You are a" — puff-puff — "peach, Ole," gasped
Bost. "I'll" — puff-puff — "never cuss you again.

Please " — puff-puff — " stop!　Oh, hang it, I 'm all in."　And Bost sat down in the road.

A hundred yards on we noticed Ole slacken speed. " It 's sinking through his skull," said Harris eagerly. In another minute he had stopped.　We picked up Bost again and ran up to him.　He surveyed us long and critically.

" Das ban qveer masheen," he said finally.　" Aye tenk Aye lak Aye skoll be riding back in it.　Aye ent care for das futball game, Aye gass.　It ban tu much running in it."

We took Ole back to town in twenty-two minutes, three chickens, a dog and a back spring.　It was close to five o'clock when he ran out on the field again. The Muggledorfer team was still waiting.　Time was no object to them.　They would only play ten minutes, but in that ten minutes Ole made three scores.　Five substitutes stood back of either goal and asked him with great politeness to stop as he tore over the line.　And he did it.　If any one else had run six miles between halves he would have stopped a good deal short of the line.　But as far as we could see, it had n't winded Ole.

Bost went home by himself that night after the game, not stopping even to assure us that as a team we were beneath his contempt.　The next afternoon he was, if anything, a little more vitriolic than ever — but not with Ole.　Toward the middle of the signal practice he pulled himself together and touched Ole gently.

He pulled himself together
and touched Ole gently

Page 26

"My dear Mr. Skjarsen," he said apologetically, " if it will not annoy you too much, would you mind running the same way the rest of the team does? I don't insist on it, mind you, but it looks so much better to the audience, you know."

"Jas," said Ole; "Aye ban fule, Aye gass, but yu ban tu polite to say it."

CHAPTER II

WERE you ever Hamburgered by a real, live
college fraternity? I mean, were you ever
initiated into full brotherhood by a Greek-letter society with the aid of a baseball bat, a sausage-making
machine, a stick of dynamite and a corn-sheller?
What's that? You say you belong to the Up-to-Date
Wood-choppers and have taken the josh degree in the
Noble Order of Prong-Horned Wapiti? Forget it.
Those aren't initiations. They are rest cures. I went
into one of those societies which give horse-play initiations for middle-aged daredevils last year and was
bored to death because I forgot to bring my knitting.
They are stiff enough for fat business men who never
do anything more exciting than to fall over the lawn
mower in the cellar once a year; but, compared with
a genuine, eighteen-donkey-power college frat initiation with a Spanish Inquisition attachment, the little
degree teams, made up of grandfathers, feel like a
slap on the wrist delivered by a young lady in frail
health.

Mind you, I'm not talking about the baby-ribbon
affairs that the college boys use nowadays. It does n't

seem to be the fashion to grease the landscape with freshmen any more. Initiations are getting to be as safe and sane as an ice-cream festival in a village church. When a frat wants to submit a neophyte to a trying ordeal it sends him out on the campus to climb a tree, or makes him go to a dance in evening clothes with a red necktie on. A boy who can roll a peanut half a mile with a toothpick, or can fish all morning in a pail of water in front of the college chapel without getting mad and trying to thrash any one is considered to be lion-hearted enough to orna- ment any frat. These are mollycoddle times in all departments. I'm glad I'm out of college and am catching street cars in the rush hours. That is about the only job left that feels like the good old times in college when muscles were made to jar some one else with.

Eight or ten years ago, when a college fraternity absorbed a freshman, the job was worth talking about. There was no half-way business about it. The freshman could tell at any stage of the game that something was being done to him. They just ate him alive, that was all. Why, at Siwash, where I was lap-welded into the Eta Bita Pies, any fra- ternity which initiated a candidate and left enough of him to appear in chapel the next morning was the joke of the school. Even the girls' fraternities gave it the laugh. The girls used to do a little quiet initiating themselves, and when they received a sister into membership you could generally follow her mad career over the town by a trail of hairpins, "rats" and little fragments of dressgoods.

Those were the days when the pledgling of a good high-pressure frat wrote to his mother the night before he was taken in and telegraphed her when he found himself alive in the morning. There used to be considerable rivalry between the frats at Siwash in the matter of giving a freshman a good, hospitable time. I remember when the Sigh Whoopsilons hung young Allen from the girder of an overhead railroad crossing, and let the switch engines smoke him up for two hours as they passed underneath, there was a good deal of jealousy among the rest of us who had n't thought of it. The Alfalfa Delts went them one better by tying roller skates to the shoulders and hips of a big freshman football star and hauling him through the main streets of Jonesville on his back, behind an automobile, and the Chi Yi's covered a candidate with plaster of Paris, with blow-holes for his nose, sculptured him artistically, and left him before the college chapel on a pedestal all night. The Delta Kappa Sonofaguns set fire to their house once by shooting Roman candles at a row of neophytes in the cellar, and we had to turn out at one A.M. one winter morning to help the Delta Flushes dig a freshman out of their chimney. They had been trying to let him down into the fireplace, and when he got stuck they had poked at him with a clothes pole until they had mussed him up considerably. This just shows you what a gay life the young scholar led in the days

when every ritual had claws on, and there was no
such thing as soothing syrup in the equipment of a
college.

Of all the frats at Siwash the Eta Bita Pies, when
I was in college, were preëminent in the art of near-
killing freshmen. We used to call our initiation " A
little journey to the pearly gates," and once or twice
it looked for a short time as if the victim had mislaid his return ticket. Treat yourself to an election
riot, a railway collision and a subway explosion, all
in one evening, and you will get a rather sketchy
idea of what we aimed at. I don't mean, of course,
that we ever killed any one. There is no real danger
in an initiation, you know, if the initiate does exactly
as he is told and the members don't get careless and
something that was n't expected does n't happen — as
did when we tied Tudor Snyder to the south track
while an express went by on the north track, and then
had the time of our young lives getting him off ahead
of a wild freight which we had n't counted on. All
we ever aimed at was to make the initiate so thankful
to get through alive that he would love Eta Bita Pie
forever, and I must say we usually succeeded. It is
wonderful what a young fellow will endure cheerfully for the sake of passing it on to some one else
the next year. I remember I was pretty mad when
my Eta Bita Pie brethren headed me up in a barrel and
rolled me downhill into a creek without taking the
trouble to remove all the nails. It seemed like wanton
carelessness. But long before my nose was out of

splints and my hide would hold water I was perfecting our famous " Lover's Leap " for the next year's bunch. That was our greatest triumph. There was an abandoned rock quarry north of town with thirty feet of water in the bottom and a fifty-foot drop to the water. By means of a long beam and a system of pulleys we could make a freshman walk the plank and drop off into the water in almost perfect safety, providing the ropes did n't break. It created a sensation, and the other frats were mad with jealousy. We took every man we wanted the next fall before the authorities put a stop to the scheme. That shows you just how repugnant the idea of being initiated is to the green young collegian.

Of course, fraternity initiations are supposed to be conducted for the amusement of the chapter and not of the candidate. But you can't always entirely tell what will happen, especially if the victim is husky and unimpressionable. Sometimes he does a little initiating himself. And that reminds me that I started out to tell a story and not to give a lecture on the polite art of making veal salad. Did I ever tell you of the time when we initiated Ole Skjarsen into Eta Bita Pie, and how the ceremony backfired and very nearly blew us all into the discard? No? Well, don't get impatient and look in the back of the book. I 'll tell it now and cut as many corners as I can.

As I have told you before, Ole Skjarsen was a little slow in grasping the real beauties of football science.

There wasn't a college anywhere around us that didn't have
Ole's hoofmarks all over its pride

It took him some time to uncoil his mind from the principles of woodchopping and concentrate it on the full duty of man in a fullback's position. He nearly drove us to a sanitarium during the process, but when he once took hold, mercy me, how he did progress from hither to yon over the opposition! He was the wonder fullback of those times, and at the end of three years there was n't a college anywhere that did n't have Ole's hoofmarks all over its pride. Oh, he was a darling. To see him jumping sideways down a football field with the ball under his arm, landing on some one of the opposition at every jump and romping over the goal line with tacklers hanging to him like streamers would have made you want to vote for him for Governor. Ole was the greatest man who ever came to Siwash. Prexy had always been considered some personage by the outside world, but he was only a bump in the background when Ole was around.

Of course we all loved Ole madly, but for all that he did n't make a frat. He did n't, for the same reason that a rhinoceros does n't get invited to garden parties. He did n't seem to fit the part. Not only his clothes, but also his haircuts were hand-me-down. He regarded a fork as a curiosity. His language was a sort of a head-on collision between Norwegian and English in which very few words had come out undamaged. In social conversation he was out of bounds nine minutes out of ten, and it kept three men busy changing the subject when he was in full

swing. He could dodge eleven men and a referee
on the football field without trying, but put him in a
forty by fifty room with one vase in it, and he could n't
dodge it to save his life.

No, he just naturally did n't fit the part, and up
to his senior year no fraternity had bid him. This
grieved Ole so that he retired from football just before the Kiowa game on which all our young hearts
were set, and before he would consent to go back
and leave some more of his priceless foot-tracks on
the opposition we had to pledge him to three of our
proudest fraternities. Talk of wedding a favorite
daughter to the greasy villain in the melodrama in
order to save the homestead! No crushed father,
with a mortgage hanging over him in the third act,
could have felt one-half so badly as we Eta Bita Pies
did when we had pledged Ole and realized that all
the rest of the year we would have to climb over him
in our beautiful, beamed-ceiling lounging-room and
parade him before the world as a much-loved brother.

But the job had to be done, and all three frats took
a melancholy pleasure in arranging the details of the
initiation. We decided to make it a three-night
demonstration of all that the Siwash frats had learned
in the art of imitating dynamite and other disinte-
grants. The Alfalfa Delts were to get first crack at
him. They were to be followed on the second night
by the Chi Yi Sighs, who were to make him a brother,
dead or alive. On the third night we of Eta Bita
Pie were to take the remains and decorate them with

our fraternity pin after ceremonies in which being
kicked by a mule would only be considered a two-
minute recess.

We fellows knew that when it came to initiating
Ole we would have to do the real work. The other
frats could n't touch it. They might scratch him up a
bit, but they lacked the ingenuity, the enthusiasm —
I might say the poetic temperament — to make a
good job of it. We determined to put on an initiation which would make our past efforts seem like the
effort of an old ladies' home to start a rough-house.
It was a great pleasure, I assure you, to plan that
initiation. We revised our floor work and added some
cellar and garret and ceiling and second-story work
to it. We began the program with the celebrated third
degree and worked gradually from that up to the
twenty-third degree, with a few intervals of simple
assault and battery for breathing spells. When we
had finished doping out the program we shook hands
all around. It was a masterpiece. It would have
made Battenberg lace out of a steam boiler.

Ole was initiated into the Alfalfa Delts on a
Wednesday night. We heard echoes of it from our
front porch. The next morning only three of the
Alfalfa Delts appeared at chapel, while Ole was out
at six A. M., roaming about the campus with the
Alfalfa Delt pin on his necktie. The next night the
Chi Yi Sighs took him on for one hundred and seventeen rounds in their brand new lodge, which had a
sheet-iron initiation den. The whole thing was a

fizzle. When we looked Ole over the next morning
we could n't find so much as a scratch on him. He
was wearing the Chi Yi pin beside the Alfalfa Delt
pin, and he was as happy as a baby with a bottle of
ink. There were nine broken window-lights in the
Chi Yi lodge, and we heard in a roundabout way
that they called in the police about three A. M. to
help them explain to Ole that the initiation was over.
That 's the kind of a trembling neophyte Ole was.
But we just giggled to ourselves. Anybody could
break up a Chi Yi initiation, and the Alfalfa Delts
were a set of narrow-chested snobs with automobile
callouses instead of muscles. We ate a hasty dinner
on Friday evening and set all the scenery for the big
scrunch. Then we put on our old clothes and waited
for Ole to walk into our parlor.

He was n't due until nine, but about eight o'clock
he came creaking up the steps and dented the door
with his large knuckles in a bashful way. He looked
larger and knobbier than ever and, if anything, more
embarrassed. We led him into the lounging-room in
silence, and he sat down twirling his straw hat. It
was October, and he had worn the thing ever since
school opened. Other people who wore straw hats in
October get removed from under them more or less
violently; but, somehow, no one had felt called upon
to maltreat Ole. We hated that hat, however, and
decided to begin the evening's work on it.

"Your hat, Mr. Skjarsen," said Bugs Wilbur in
majestic tones.

Ole reached the old ruin out. Wilbur took it and tossed it into the grate. Ole upset four or five of us who could n't get out of the way and rescued the hat, which was blazing merrily.

"Ent yu gat no sanse?" he roared angrily. "Das ban a gude hat." He looked at it gloomily. "Et ban spoiled now," he growled, tossing the remains into a waste-paper basket. "Yu ban purty fallers. Vat for yu do dat?"

The basket was full of papers and things. In about four seconds it was all ablaze. Wilbur tried to go over and choke it off, but Ole pushed him back with one forefinger.

"Yust stay avay," he growled. "Das basket ent costing some more as my hat, I gass."

We stood around and watched the basket burn. We also watched a curtain blaze up and the finish on a nice mahogany desk crack and blister. It was all very humorous. The fire kindly went out of its own accord, and some one tiptoed around and opened the windows in a timid sort of way. It was a very successful initiation so far — only we were the neophytes.

"This won't do," muttered "Allie" Bangs, our president. He got up and went over to Ole. "Mr. Skjarsen," he said severely, "you are here to be initiated into the awful mysteries of Eta Bita Pie. It is not fitting that you should enter her sacred boundaries in an unfettered condition. Submit to the brethren that they may blindfold you and bind you for the ordeals to come." Gee, but we used to use hand-picked language when we were unsheathing our claws!

Ole growled. " Ol rite," he said. " But Aye tal yu ef yu fallers burn das har west lak yu burn ma hat I skoll raise ruffhaus like deekins! "

We tied his hands behind him with several feet of good stout rope and hobbled him about the ankles with a dog chain. Then we blindfolded him and put a pillowslip over his head for good measure. Things began to look brighter. Even a demon fullback has to have one or two limbs working in order to accomplish anything. When all was fast Bangs gave Ole a preliminary kick. " Now, brethren," he roared, " bring on the Macedonian guards and give them the neophyte! "

Now I 'm not revealing any real initiation secrets, mind you, and maybe what I 'm telling you did n't exactly happen. But you can be perfectly sure that something just as bad did happen every time. For an hour we abused that two hundred and twenty pounds of gristle and hide. It was as much fun as roughhousing a two-ton safe. We rolled him downstairs. He broke out sixty dollars' worth of balustrade on the way and he did n't seem to mind it at all. We tried to toss him in a blanket. Ever have a two-hundred-and-twenty-pound man land on you coming down from the ceiling? We got tired of that. We made him play automobile. Ever play automobile? They tie roller skates and an automo-

bile horn on you and push you around into the
furniture, just the way a real automobile runs into
things. We broke a table, five chairs, a French window, a one-hundred-dollar vase and seven shins. We
did n't even interest Ole. When a man has plowed
through leather-covered football players for three
years his head gets used to hitting things. Also his
heels will fly out no matter how careful you are.
We took him into the basement and performed our
famous trick of boiling the candidate in oil. Of
course we wanted to scare him. He accommodated
us. He broke away and hopped stiff-legged all over
the room. That was n't so bad, but, confound it, he
hopped on us most of the time! How would you like
to initiate a bronze statue that got scared and hopped
on you?

. We got desperate. We threw aside the formality
of explaining the deep significance of each action and
just assaulted Ole with everything in the house. We
prodded him with furnace tools and thumped him
with cordwood and rolling-pins and barrel-staves and
shovels. We walked over him, a dozen at a time.
And all the time we were getting it worse than he
was. He did n't exactly fight, but whenever his elbows
twitched some fellow's face would happen to be in
the way, and he could n't move his knee without getting it tangled in some one's ribs. You could hear
the thunders of the assault and the shrieks of the
wounded for a block.

At the end of an hour we were positively all in.

There were n't three of us unwounded. The house was a wreck. Wilbur had a broken nose. "Chick" Struthers' kneecap hurt. "Lima" Bean's ribs were telescoped, and there was n't a good shin in the house. We quit in disgust and sat around looking at Ole. He was sitting around, too. He happened to be sitting on Bangs, who was yelling for help. But we did n't feel like starting any relief expedition.

Ole was some rumpled, and his clothes looked as if they had been fed into a separator. But he was intact, as far as we could see. He was still tied and blindfolded, and I hope to be buried alive in a branch-line town if he was n't getting bored.

"Vat fur yu qvit?" he asked. "It ent fun setting around har."

Then Petey Simmons, who had been taking a minor part in the assault in order to give his wheels full play, rose and beckoned the crowd outside. We left Ole and clustered around him.

"Now, this won't do at all," he said. "Are we going to let Eta Bita Pie be made the laughing-stock of the college? If we can't initiate that human quartz mill by force let's do it by strategy. I've got a plan. You just let me have Ole and one man for an hour and I'll make him so glad to get back to the house that he'll eat out of our hands."

We were dead ready to turn the job over to Petey, though we hated to see him put his head in the lion's mouth, so to speak. I hated it worse than any of the others because he picked me for his assistant. We

went in and found Ole dozing in the corner. Petey
prodded him. " Get up! " he said.

Ole got up cheerfully. Petey took the dog chain
off of his legs. Then he threw his sub-cellar voice
into gear.

" Skjarsen," he rumbled, " you have passed right
well the first test of our noble order. You have faced
the hideous dangers which were in reality but shams
to prove your faith, and you have borne your suffer-
ings patiently, thus proving your meekness."

I let a couple of grins escape into my sweater-sleeve.
Oh, yes, Ole had been meek all right.

" It remains for you to prove your desire," said
Petey in curdled tones. " Listen! " He gave the Eta
Bita Pie whistle. We had the best whistle in college.
It was six notes — a sort of insidious, inviting thing
that you could slide across two blocks, past all manner
of barbarians, and into a frat brother's ear without
disturbing any one at all. Petey gave it several times.
" Now, Skjarsen," he said, " you are to follow that
whistle. Let no obstacle discourage you. Let no bar-
rier stop you. If you can prove your loyalty by following that whistle through the outside world and back
to the altar of Eta Bita Pie we will ask no more of
you. Come on! "

We tiptoed out of the cellar and whistled. Ole followed us up the steps. That is, he did on the second
attempt. On the first he fell down with melodious
thumps. We hugged each other, slipped behind a
tree and whistled again.

Ole charged across the yard and into the tree. The line held. I heard him say something in Norwegian that sounded secular. By that time we were across the street. There was a low railing around the parking, and when we whistled again Ole walked right into the railing. The line held again.

Oh, I 'll tell you that Petey boy was a wonder at getting up ideas. Think of it! Benjamin Franklin, Thomas Edison, Christopher Columbus, old Bill Archimedes and all the rest of the wise guys had overlooked this simple little discovery of how to make a neophyte initiate himself. It was too good to be true. We held a war dance of pure delight, and we whistled some more. We got behind stone walls, and whistled. We climbed embankments, and whistled. We slid behind blackberry bushes and ash piles and across ditches and over hedge fences, and whistled. We were so happy we could hardly pucker. Think of it! There was Ole Skjarsen, the most uncontrollable force in Nature, following us like a yellow pup with his dinner three days overdue. It was as fascinating as guiding a battleship by wireless.

We slipped across a footbridge over Cedar Creek, and whistled. Ole missed the bridge by nine yards. There is n't much water in Cedar Creek, but what there is is strong. It took Ole fifteen minutes to climb the other bank, owing to a beautiful collection of old barrel-hoops, corsets, crockery and empty tomato cans which decorated the spot. Did you ever see a blindfolded man, with his hands tied behind his back,

trying to climb over a city dump? No? Of course
not, any more than you have seen a green elephant.
But it's a fine sight, I assure you. When Ole got
out of the creek we whistled him dexterously into a
barnyard and right into the maw of a brindle bull-
pup with a capacity of one small man in two bites
— we being safe on the other side of the fence, beyond the reach of the chain. Maybe that was mean,
but Eta Bita Pie is not to be trifled with when she
is aroused. Anyway, the bull got the worst of it.
He only got one bite. Ole kicked in the barn door
on the first try, and demolished a corn sheller on
the second; but on the third he hit the pup squarely
abeam and dropped a beautiful goal with him. We
went around to see the dog the next day. He looked
quite natural. You would almost think he was
alive.

It was here that we began to smell trouble. I had
my suspicions when we whistled again. There was
a pretty substantial fence around that barnyard, but
Ole did n't wait to find the gate.

He came through the fence not very far from us.
He was conversing under that mangled pillowslip,
and we heard fragments sounding like this:

"Purty soon Aye gat yu — yu spindle-shank, vite-
face, skagaroot-smokin' dudes! Ugh — ump!" —
here he caromed off a tree. "Ven Aye gat das blindfold off, Aye gat yu — yu Baked-Pie galoots! —
Ugh! Wow!" — barbed-wire fence. "Vistle sum
more, yu vide-trousered polekats. Aye make yu

vistle, Aye bet yu, rite avay! Up — pllp — pllp!"
That's the kind of noise a man makes when he
walks into a horse-trough at full speed.

"Gee!" said Petey nervously. "I guess we've
given him enough. He's getting sort of peevish. I
don't believe in being too cruel. Let's take him back
now. You don't suppose he can get his hands loose,
do you?"

I did n't know. I wished I did. Of course, when
you watch a lion trying to get at you from behind
a fairly strong cage you feel perfectly safe, but you
feel safer when you are somewhere else, just the
same. .We got out on the pavement and gave a gentle
whistle.   .

"Aye har yu!" roared Ole, coming through a
chicken yard. "Aye har yu, you leetle Baked Pies!
Aye gat yu purty soon. Yust vait."

We did n't wait. We put on a little more gasoline
and started for the frat house. We did n't have to
whistle any more. Ole was right behind us. We
could hear him thundering on the pavement and
pleading with us in that rich, nutty dialect of his
to stop and have our heads pounded on the bricks.

I shudder yet when I think of all the things he
promised to do to us. We went down that street like
a couple of Roman gladiators pacing a hungry bear,
and, by tangling Ole up in the parkings again, managed to get home a few yards ahead.

There was an atmosphere of arnica and dejection
in the house when we got there. Ill-health seemed

to be rampant. "Did you lose him?" asked Bangs
hopefully from behind a big bandage.

"Lose him?" says I with a snort. "Oh, yes, we
lost him all right. He loses just like a foxhound.
That's him, falling over the front steps now. You
can stay and entertain him; I'm going upstairs."

Everybody came along. We piled chairs on the
stairs and listened while Ole felt his way over the
porch. In about a minute he found the door. Then
he·came right in. I had locked the door, but I had
neglected to reënforce it with concrete and boiler
iron. Ole wore part of the frame in with him.

"Come on, yu Baked Pies!" he shouted.

"You're in the wrong house," squeaked that little
fool, Jimmy Skelton.

"Yu kent fule me!" said Ole, crashing around
the loafing-room. "Aye yust can tal das haus by har
skagaroot smell. Come on, yu leetle fallers! Aye
bet aye inittyate yu some, tu!"

By this time he had found the stairs and was plowing through the furniture. We retired to the third
floor. When twenty-seven fellows go up a three-foot
stairway at once it necessarily makes some noise. Ole
heard us and kept right on coming.

We grabbed a bureau and a bed and barricaded
the staircase. There was a ladder to the attic. I
was the last man up and my heart was giving my
ribs all kinds of massage treatment before I got up.
We hauled up the ladder just as Ole kicked the
bureau downstairs, and then we watched him charge

over our beautiful third-floor dormitory, leaving ruin in his wake.

Maybe he would have been satisfied with breaking the furniture. But, of course, a few of us had to sneeze. Ole hunted those sneezes all over the third floor. He could n't reach them, but he sat down on the wreck underneath them.

" Aye ent know vere yu fallers ban," he said, " but Aye kin vait. Aye har yu, yu Baked Pies! Aye gat yu yet, by yimminy! Yust come on down ven yu ban ready."

Oh, yes, we were ready — I don't think. It was a perfectly lovely predicament. Here was the Damma Yappa chapter of Eta Bita Pie penned up in a deucedly-cold attic with one lone initiate guarding the trapdoor. Nice story for the college to tell when the police rescued us! Nice end of our reputation as the best neophyte jugglers in the school! Makes me shiver now to think of it.

We sat around in that garret and listened to the clock strike in the library tower across the campus. At eleven o'clock Ole promised to kill the first man who came down. That bait caught no fish. At twelve he begged for the privilege of kicking us out of our own house, one by one. At one o'clock he remarked that, while it was pretty cold, it was much colder in Norway, where he came from, and that, as we would freeze first, we might as well come down.

At two o'clock we were all stiff. At three we were kicking the plaster off of the joists, trying to keep

from freezing to death. At four a bunch of Sophomores were all for throwing Petey Simmons down as
a sacrifice. Petey talked them out of it. Petey could
talk a stone dog into wagging its tail.

We sat in that garret from ten P. M. until the year
after the great pyramid wore down to the ground. At
least that was the length of time that seemed to pass.
It must have been about five o'clock when Petey
stopped kicking his feet on the chimney and said:

"Well, fellows, I have an idea. It may work or
it may not, but — "

"Shut up, you mental desert!" some one growled.
"Another of your fine ideas will wreck this frat."

"As I was saying," continued Petey cheerfully,
"it may not succeed, but it will not hurt any one
but me if it does n't. I'm going to be the Daniel
in this den. But first I want the officers of the chapter to come up around the scuttle-hole with me."

Five of us crept over to the hole and looked down.
"Aye har yu, yu leetle Baked Pies!" said Ole,
waking in an instant. "Yust come on down. Aye
ban vaiting long enough to smash yu!"

"Mr. Skjarsen," began Petey in the regular dark-
lantern voice that all secret societies use — "Mr.
Skjarsen — for as such we must still call you — the
final test is over. · You have acquitted yourself nobly.
You have been faithful to the end. You have stood
your vigil unflinchingly. You have followed the call
of Eta Bita Pie over every obstacle and through
every suffering."

" Aye ban following him leetle furder, if Aye had ladder," said Ole in a bloodthirsty voice. " Ven Aye ban getting at yu, Aye play hal vid yu Baked Pies! "

" And now," said Petey, ignoring the interruption, " the final ceremony is at hand. Do not fear. Your trials are over. In the dark recesses of this secret chamber above you we have discussed your bearing in the trials that have beset you. It has pleased us. You have been found worthy to continue toward the high goal. Ole Skjarsen, we are now ready to receive you into full membership."

" Come rite on! " snorted Ole. " Aye receeve yu into membership all rite. Yust come on down."

" It won't work, Petey," Bangs groaned. Petey kicked his shins as a sign to shut up.

" Ole Skyjarsen, son of Skjar Oleson, stand up! " he said, sinking his voice another story.

Ole got up. It was plain to be seen that he was getting interested.

" The president of this powerful order will now administer the oath," said Petey, shoving Bangs forward.

So there, at five A. M., with the whole chapter treed in a garret, and the officers, the leading lights of Siwash, crouching around a scuttle and shivering their teeth loose, we initiated Ole Skjarsen. It was impressive, I can tell you. When it came to the part where the neophyte swears to protect a brother, even if he has to wade in blood up to his necktie, Bangs bore down beautifully and added a lot of extra frills.

The last words were spoken. Ole was an Eta Bita Pie. Still, we were n't very sanguine. You might interest a man-eater by initiating him, but would you destroy his appetite? There was no grand rush for the ladder.

As Ole stood waiting, however, Petey swung himself down and landed beside him. He cut the ropes that bound his wrists, jerked off the pillowslip and cut off the blindfold. Then he grabbed Ole's mastodonic paw.

"Shake, brother!" he said.

Nobody breathed for a few seconds. It was darned terrifying, I can tell you. Ole rubbed his eyes with his free hand and looked down at the morsel hanging on to the other.

"Shake, Ole!" insisted Petey. "You went through it better than I did when I got it."

I saw the rudiments of a smile begin to break out on Ole's face. It grew wider. It got to be a grin; then a chasm with a sunrise on either side.

He looked up at us again, then down at Petey. Then he pumped Petey's arm until the latter danced like a cork bobber.

"By ying, Aye du et!" he shouted. "Ve ban gude fallers, ve Baked Pies, if ve did broke my nose."

"What's the matter with Ole?" some one shouted.

"He's all right!" we yelled. Then we came down out of the garret and made a rush for the furnace.

CHAPTER III

IT's a cinch that college life would be a whole lot more congested with pleasure if it was n't for the towns that the colleges are in. I don't mean that a town around a college has n't its uses. Wherever you find a town you can find lunch counters and theaters with galleries from which you can learn the drama at a quarter a throw, and street cars that can be tampered with, and wooden sidewalks that burn well on celebration nights, and nice girls who began being nice four college generations ago and never forgot how. All of these things about a town are mighty handy when it comes to getting a higher education in a good, live college where you don't have to tunnel through three feet of moss to find the college customs. But even all this can't reconcile me to the way a town butts into college affairs. It is something disgusting.

You know it yourself, Bill. Did n't you go to Yellagain where the police arrested the whole Freshman class for painting the Sophomores green? Well, it's the same way all over. No sooner does a college town get big enough to support a rudimentary policeman who peddles vegetables when he is n't putting down anarchy than it gets busy and begins to regulate the college students. And the bigger it gets the more regulating it wants to do. Why, they tell me that at the University of Chicago there has n't been a riot for nine years, and that over in Washington Park, three blocks away, an eleven-ton statue of old Chris. Columbus has lain for ages and no college class has had spirit enough to haul it out on the street-car tracks. That's what regulating a college does for it. There are more policemen in Chicago than there are students in the University. If you give your yell off the campus you have to get a permit from the city council. It's worse than that in Philadelphia, they tell me. Why, there, if a college student comes downtown with a flareback coat and heart-shaped trousers and one of those nifty little pompadour hats that are brushed back from the brow to give the brains a chance to grow, they arrest him for collecting a crowd and disturbing traffic. No, sir, no big-town college for me. Getting college life in those places reminds me of trying to get that world-wide feeling on ice-cream soda. There's as much chance in one as in the other.

Excuse me for getting sore, but that's the way I do when I begin to talk about college towns. They don't know their places. Take Jonesville, where Siwash is, for instance. When Siwash College was founded by " that noble band of Christian truth seekers," as the catalogue puts it, Jonesville was a mud-hole freckled with houses. The railroad trains whistled "get out of my way" to the town when they whooped through it, and when you went into a merchant's store and woke him up he started off home to dinner from force of habit. The only thing they ever regulated there was the clock. They regulated that once a year and usually found that it was two or three days behind time. Had n't noticed it at all.

That's what Jonesville was when Siwash started. You can bet for the first forty years they did n't do much regulating around the college. The students just let the town stay there because it was quiet. The citizens used to elect town marshals over seventy years old, so their gray hairs would protect them from the students, and when the boys had won a debate or a ball game and wanted to burn a barn or two to cheer up the atmosphere at evening, nothing at all was said — at least out loud. Jonesville was meek enough, you bet. Why, back in the seventies the students used to vote at town elections, and once for a joke they all voted for old "Apple Sally" for president of the village board. Made her serve, too. Talk about regulating! Did you ever see a farmer's dog go out and try to regulate a sixty-horse-power automobile? That's about as much as Jonesville would have regulated us thirty years ago.

But, of course, having a real peppery college in its midst, Jonesville could n't help but grow. People came and started boarding-houses. There had to be restaurants and bookstores and necktie emporiums, too, and pretty soon the railroad built a couple of branches into town and started the division shops. Then Jonesville woke up and walked right past old Siwash. In ten years it had street cars, paved streets, water-works, a political machine and a city debt, as large as the law would allow. And worse than that, it had a police force. It had nine officers in uniform, most of whom could read and write and swing big clubs with a strictly American accent. Nice sort of a thing to turn loose in a quiet college town. This was long before my time, but they tell me that the students held indignation meetings for a week after the first arrest was made. You see, the students at Siwash always had their own rules and lived up to them strictly. The Faculty put them on their honor and that honor was never abused. Students were not allowed to burn the college buildings nor kill the professors. These rules were never broken, and naturally the boys felt rather insulted when the city turned loose a horde of blue-coated busybodies to interfere with things that did n't concern them.

Still, Siwash got along very well even after the police force was organized. You see, after a town has had a college in its middle for about fifty years, pretty much everybody in town has attended it at one time or another. None of the police had diplomas, but it was no uncommon thing to see an ex-member of a college debating society delivering groceries, or an ex-president of his class getting up in an engine cab to take the flyer into the city. For years every

police magistrate was an old Siwash man, and, though
plenty of the boys would get arrested, there were
never any thirty-day complications or anything of
the sort. Two classes would meet on the main street
and muss each other up. The police would arrest
nine or ten of the ringleaders. The next morning
the prisoners would appear before Squire Jennings,
who climbed up on the old college building with his
class flag in '54 and kept a rival class away by tearing
down the chimney and throwing the bricks at them.
Naturally, nothing very deadly happened. The good
old fellow would lecture the crowd and let them off
with a stern warning. Maybe two or three Seniors
would come home late at night from their frat hall
and take a wooden Indian cigar sign along with them
just for company. One of those Indians is such a
steady sort of a chap to have along late at night. Of
course, they would be arrested by old Hank Anderson
on the courthouse beat, but it was n't anything serious.
They would telephone Frank Hinckley, who was
editor of the city daily, and just convalescing from
four years of college life himself, and he would come
down and bail them out, and Squire Jennings would
kick them out of court next morning. Frank was
the patron saint of the students for years when it
came to bail. He used to say he had all the fun
of being a doctor and getting called out nights without having to try to collect any fees. Frank was no
Crœsus those days and I've seen him go bail for
fifteen students at one hundred dollars apiece, when

his total assets amounted to a dress suit, three hundred and forty-five photographs and his next week's salary.

By the time I had come to college, getting arrested had gotten to be a regular formality. A Freshman would go up Main Street at night, trying to hide a nine-foot board sign under his spring overcoat. Halvor Skoogerson, a pale-eyed guardian of the peace, who was studying up to be a naturalized, would arrest him for theft, riot, disorderly conduct, suspicious appearance and intoxication, not understanding why any sober man would want to carry a young lumber-yard home under his coat at night. The prisoner would telephone for Hinckley, who would crawl out of bed, come downtown cussing, and bail away in sleepy tones. The next morning the freshie would go up before Squire Jennings, who would ask him in awful accents if he realized that the state penitentiary was only four hours away by fast train, and that many a man was boarding there who would blush to be seen in the company of a man who had stolen a nine-foot sign and carried it down Main Street, interfering with pedestrians, when there was a perfectly good alley which ought to be used for such purposes. Then he would warn the culprit that the next time he was caught lugging off a billboard or a wooden platform or a corncrib he would be compelled to put it back again before he got breakfast; after which he would tell him to go along and try studying for a change, and the Freshman would go back to college and join the hero brigade. It was a mighty meek man in Siwash who could n't get arrested those days. ' Even the hymn singers at the Y. M. C. A. had criminal records. It got so, finally, that whenever we had a nightshirt parade in honor of any little college victory the line of march would lead right through the police station. We knew what was coming and would save the cops the trouble of hauling us over in the hustle wagon.

Take it all in all, it was about as much fun to be regulated as it was to run the town. But one night Squire Jennings put his other foot into the grave and died entirely; and before any of us realized what was happening a special election had been held and Malachi Scroggs had been elected police magistrate.

Malachi Scroggs was a triple extract of grouch who lived on the north side two miles away from college in a big white house with one of those old-fashioned dog-house affairs on top of it. He was an acrimonious quarrel all by himself. Sunlight soured when it struck him. I have seen a fox terrier who had been lying perfectly happy on the sidewalk, get up after Scroggs had passed him and go over and bite an automobile tire. He lived on gloom and lawsuits and the last time he smiled was 1878 — that was when a small boy fell nineteen feet out of a tree while robbing his orchard, and the doctor said he would never be able to rob any more orchards.

This was the kind of mental astringent Malachi

was.   Naturally, he loved the gay and happy little college boys.   Oh, how he loved us!   He had complained to the police regularly during each celebration for twenty years and he had expressed the opinion, publicly, that a college boy was a cross between a hyena and a grasshopper with a fog-horn attachment thrown in free of charge.   He was n't a college man himself, you see — never could find one where the students did n't use slang, probably, and he just naturally did n't understand us at all.   Of course, we did n't mind that.   It 's no credit to carry an interlinear translation of your temperament on your face. So long as he kept in his own yard and quarreled with his own dog for not feeding on Freshmen more enthusiastically, we got along as nicely as the Egyptian Sphinx and John L. Sullivan.   Even when he was elected police magistrate we did n't object.   In fact, we did n't bumpity-bump to the situation until we went up against him in court.

Part of the Senior class had been having a little choir practice in one of the town restaurants.   It was a lovely affair and there was n't a more cheerful crowd of fellows on earth than they were when they marched down the street at one A. M. eighteen abreast and singing one of the dear old songs in a kind of a steam-siren barytone.

Now they had never attempted to regulate mere noise in Jonesville, but that night a brand-new policeman had gone on the courthouse beat, and blamed if he did n't arrest the whole bunch for disturbing the peace — when they had n't broken a single thing, mind you. They were pretty mad about it at first; but after all it was only a joke, and when Hinckley got down to bail them out they were singing with great feeling a song which Jenkins, the class poet, had just composed, and which ran as follows:

"As we walked along the street
Officer Sikes we chanced to meet,
And his shoes were full of feet
As he prowled along his beat.
He took us down and locked us up;
Left us in charge of a Norsky Cop,
And we didn't get home till early in the morning."

Hold that "morning" as long as you can and tonsorialize to beat the band. Even the desk sergeant enjoyed it.

When the bunch lined up the next morning in police court there was Judge Scroggs. They felt as if they ought to treat him nicely, he being a newcomer and all of them being very familiar with the ropes; and Emmons, the class president, started explaining to him that it was all a mistake. Scroggs bit him off with a voice that sounded like a terrier snapping at a fly.

"We're here to correct these mistakes," he said. "You were all singing on the public street at one o'clock in the morning, were n't you?"

"We were trying to," said Emmons, still friendly.

"Ten days apiece," said the magistrate. "Call the next case."

If any one had removed the floor from under these Seniors and let them drop one thousand and one feet into space they could n't have felt more shocked. Even the clerk and the desk sergeant were amazed. They tried to help explain, but the human vinegar-cruet turned around and spat the following through his clenched teeth:

"Gentlemen, I have been appointed to sit on this bench and I don't need any help. Any more objections will be in contempt of court. Sergeant, remove these young thugs and have them sent to the workhouse at once."

Maybe you don't think the college seethed when the news got out. There were the leading lights of the school, including the president of the Senior class, the chairman of the Junior promenade, two halfbacks, the pitcher on the baseball team and the president of the Y. M. C. A., all on the works for ten days, along with as choice an assortment of plain drunks and fancy resters as you could find in ninety miles of mainline railroad. The students fairly went mad and bit at the air. Even the Faculty got busy and Prexy dropped over to the police court to square it. He came out a minute later very white around the mouth. I don't know what Old Maledictions said to him, but it was a great sufficiency, I guess. He seemed as insulted as Lord Tennyson might have been if the milkman had pulled his whiskers.

There was n't a thing to be done. The Faculty appealed to the mayor, but old Scroggs had some regular Spanish-bit hold on him in the way of a short-time note, I guess, and he washed his hands of the whole affair. Our college great men were hauled out to the works and served their time. When they got out they were sights. They were n't strong on sanitation in workhouses in those days. Even their friends shook hands with them with tongs. Think of sixteen proud monarchs of the campus making brick in striped suits, with a cross foreman who used to haul ashes from the college campus lording it over them and tracing their ancestry back through thirty generations of undesirable citizens! Nice, was n't it? Oh, very!

That was the beginning of a sad and serious year for Siwash. For the first time Scroggs enjoyed college boys. Soaking students got to be his specialty. We did our blamedest to behave, but you can't break off the habits of generations in a week or two. Soon after the Seniors got out the Mock Turtles, a Sophomore society, capacity thirty thousand quarts, absentmindedly tipped over a street car on their way home and were jugged for thirty days. They had to enlarge the workhouse to take care of them, and four of our best football players were retired from circulation all through October. Think what that meant! The whole college went up, just before the game with Hambletonian, and knelt on the sidewalk before Judge Scroggs' house. He set the dog on us. Said afterwards he wished the dog had been larger and had n't had his supper. A month later four members of the

glee club tried to do our favorite stunt of putting
the horse in the herdic and hauling him home, and
it cost them twenty-nine days — just enough to break
up the club.   The whole basket-ball team got thirty
days because they took the bronze statue off the
fountain in the public square one night, laid him
on the car tracks in some old clothes, and had the
ambulance force trying to resuscitate him.   Nobody
had ever objected to this little joke before, but it
cost us the state championship and two of the team
left school when they got out.   Said they 'd come to
Siwash for a college education, not for a course of
etymology in a workhouse.

It was terrible.   We scarcely dared to cut out our
mufflers enough to whistle to each other on the street.
By spring we were desperate.   We had lost the
basket-ball championship.   The glee club was ruined.
Muggledorfer had bumped us in football — that was
the year before Ole Skjarsen came to school — and
college spirit at Siwash had been gummed up until
it could have been successfully imitated by a four-
thousand-year-old mummy.   Our college meetings re-
sembled the overflow from a funeral around the front
steps.   We used to shut down all the windows, say
" shsh " nine times, and then write out our college
yell on curl papers and burn the papers.   You could
have swapped Siwash off for a correspondence school
without noticing any difference in the reverberations.

That was Petey Simmons' first year in college — as
a matter of fact, he was a Senior prep.   I 've told

you more or less about Petey before. He was the
only son of one of these country bankers who manage
to get as much fun out of a half million as a New
Yorker could out of a whole railroad. Petey was a
little chap who had always had what he wanted and
would cheerfully sit up all night thinking up new
things to want. He was n't a Freshman yet, but he
could give points to all the college in the matter of
explosive clothes and nifty ways of being expensive
to Dad. He could n't get along without coat-cut
underwear long before we had heard of it, and you
could tell by looking at his shoes just what the rest of
the school would be wearing in two years. That was
Petey all the way through. He was first and Father
Time was nowhere, forty miles back with a busted
tire.

Petey took to college life like a kid to candy and
just soaked himself in college spirit. He proposed
his sixty-five-dollar banjo for membership in the club
and went in with it of course. He was elected yell-
master before he had been in school two weeks, and
if you ever want to know how much noise can come
out of a comparatively small orifice you should have
seen him emitting riot and pandemonium in the
second half of a lively football game. Naturally, it
worried Petey almost to death to see the dear old
Coll. disintegrating under the Scroggs Inquisition,
and he used to sit around the frat house with his
head on his hands for hours, smoking his pipe, which
had the largest bowl in school, and combing his con-

Martha caused some mild sensation

Page 63

volutions for a plan. Then, along in March, he electrified the whole school by taking Martha Scroggs to the college promenade.

Martha was old Malachi's daughter. We had n't known it, but she had been in school all that year. She was a quiet girl who was designed like a tall problem in plane geometry. While it was possible for a clock to run in the same room with her, still she was not what you might call a picnic to look at. She was the kind of girl a man would look at once and then go off and admire the scenery, even if it only consisted of a ninety-acre cornfield and a grain elevator. Martha was only about eighteen, and I never could understand how she got on to the styles of thirty-six years ago and wore them as fluently as she did.

· Naturally, Martha had gotten along in her studies without being pestered by society to any extent. I sometimes think this helped old Scroggs to hate us. She was his only child, and he had taken all the affection and interest that most people distribute over their entire acquaintanceship and concentrated it on her. They had grown up together since she became a motherless baby, and they did say that while you could bombard the old man with gatling guns without jarring his opinions he would lie down, jump through a hoop or play dead whenever Martha wanted him to.

Naturally Martha caused some mild sensation when she appeared at the biggest social spasm of the college year, with her sleeves bulging in the wrong place, and nothing but her own hair on her head. But what caused the real sensation was the fact that Petey had been released from the workhouse the day before. Yes, sir — just turned out with seven more days to serve. He had thrown a brick at a Sophomore who was trying to catch him and dye his hair the Sophomore colors, and the brick had annihilated one of the city's precious thirty-seven-cent street lights. Petey had gone to the works for ten days, leaving a new dress suit that had n't been dedicated and unlimited woe among the girls, for he was a Class A fusser.

Petey was non-committal about his insanity. He had the best eye for beauty in the college, and yet he had been taking Miss Scroggs around to church socials and town affairs for two months. But college boys are n't slow, whatever you want to say about them. We had faith in Petey and we backed up his game. We gave Martha the time of her young life at the Prom. — pulled off three imitation rows over her program — and then we turned in that winter and gave her a good, hot rush — which is a technical college expression for keeping a girl dated up so that she does n't have time to wash the dishes at home once a month.

I must say that it was n't much of a punishment, either, when we got acquainted with Martha. She was a good fellow clear through and had a smile that illuminated her plain face like a torchlight parade.

Of course, after you get out of school you learn that beauty is only skin deep and seldom affects the brain; but this is a wonderful discovery for a college boy to make when there are so many raving beauties about him that he has to take a nap in the afternoon in order to dream about all of them. At any rate, we took Martha to everything that came along, one of us or another, and before a month we didn't have to pretend very much to scrap for her dances, even if you did have to lug her around the room by main strength — she was as heavy on her feet as a motor-bus.

April came and the first baseball game with it, and Saunders, our pitcher, managed to draw a thirty-day sentence for stealing a steam roller one noon and racing off down the avenue with a fat cop in pursuit. We nearly fell dead once more when Saunders came walking into chapel three days later. He had been released by Judge Scroggs with a warning never under any circumstances to do anything of any sort at any time any more, and been assured that he was nothing more than hangman's meat. But he had been released! That night he took Martha Scroggs to the Alfalfa Delt hop. And the next day he held Muggle-dorfer down to two hits and no runs, with Martha waving hurrahs at him from a tally-ho.

We wanted to elect Petey president of the college, for we laid the whole affair to him. But he wouldn't talk at all. If anything, he seemed a little sore about the whole thing. Martha didn't loosen up, either.

She just smiled and told those of us who knew her well enough to ask questions that Saunders was a lovely boy and that she had had that date with him for ages — flies' ages, I guess she meant, for Alice Marsters, one of the beauties of the school, stayed home from the dance after announcing that she was going with Saunders, and never seemed able to remember him by sight after that.

About a week afterward Maxwell, the college orator, a very solemn member of the Siwash brain trust, was arrested for ever so little a thing. I believe he so far forgot himself as to help give the college yell on Main Street the night his literary society won a debate. Anyway, he got ten days, and he was due in three days to orate for Siwash against the whole Northwest. It was the biggest event of the school year — the oratorical contest. We'd won seven of them — more than any other school in the sixteen states — and we stood a good show with Maxwell. We were crazy to win. Of course nobody ever goes to the contests; but we all stay up all night to hear the results, and when we win, which we do once every other college generation, we try to make the celebration bigger than the stories of other celebrations that have been handed down. We'd been planning this celebration all winter and had everything combustible in Jonesville spotted.

Some of us were for going out and burning up the workhouse, but before we got around to it Maxwell appeared. It was the day before the contest. He'd served only two days, but instead of rushing right off to rehearse his oration, which he could n't do in the workhouse, owning to an accountable prejudice the tramps and other prisoners had against oratory, he took the evening off and went driving with Martha Scroggs — about as queer a thing for him to do as it would be for the Pope to take a young lady to the theater. But we did n't ask any questions. We cheered him off on the midnight train, and the next night, when he won and we got the news, we turned out and built a bonfire of everything that was n't nailed down. And when the police got done chasing us they had nineteen of the brightest and best sons of Siwash bottled up in the booby hatch.

We did n't mind that on general principles. The bonfire was worth it, especially since we managed to get a few palings from old Scroggs' fence for it — but, as usual, the wrong men got pinched. There was the intercollegiate track meet due in two weeks, and there, in the list of felons, were Evans, our crack sprinter, Petersen, our hammer heaver, and yours truly, who could pole vault about as high as they run elevators in Europe, even if he was only a sub-Freshman with field mice in his hair.

Now, this was really serious. We could afford to lose an oratorical contest — it just meant no bonfire for another year — but we had our hearts set on that track meet. We were up against our lifelong rivals — Muggledorfer, the State Normal, Kiowa, Hambletonian, and all the rest of them. We had to win — I don't know why. Beats all how many things you have to do in college that don't seem so absolutely necessary a few years afterward. Anyhow, if we three point-gobblers had to spend the next ten days in the works instead of rounding into form, the points Siwash would win in that meet could be added up by a three-year-old boy who was a bad scholar. It was so desperate that we hired a lawyer and laid the case before him that night as we sat in our horrid cells — they would n't take Hinckley for bail any more.

"Get a continuance," said he. And the next morning he appeared with us before the awful presence and demanded the continuance on the score of important evidence, lack of time to perfect a defense, other engagements, poor crops, Presidential election, and goodness knows what — regular lawyer style, you know.

Old Scroggs glared at us the way an unusually hungry tiger might look at a lamb that was being taken away to get a little riper. "I cannot object to a reasonable continuance," he said sourly. "And I don't deny that you will need all the defense you can get. The case is an atrocious one, and I propose to do my small part toward putting down arson and riot in this unhappy town. You will appear two weeks from this morning."

The field meet was two weeks from that afternoon! And we did n't have a ghost of a defense!

We three scraped up the required bail and went back to college feeling cheerful as a man who has been told that his hanging has been postponed until his wedding morning. Of course we sent for Petey Simmons. He arrived dejected. " No use, fellows," he remarked as he came in the door. " I know what you all want. You all want engagements with Martha Scroggs. It's no go. I've been over to see her and she's afraid to tackle it. The old man's told her that if she runs around with any more of this disgraceful, disgusting and nine other epitheted college bunch he'll show her the door. Says he's been worked and he's through. Says he's going to give you the limit and, if possible, he's going to give you enough to keep you in all vacation instead of letting you loose on a defenseless world all summer. That's how strong you are up at the Scroggs house."

There you were! Siwash College, the pride of six decades, mollycoddled by an old parody on a gorilla with a grouch against the solar system! We trained these two weeks in hopes that a chariot of fire would come up and take the old man down, but there was nothing doing. He remained abnormally healthy and supernaturally mad. On the morning before the fatal day we all wrote letters home, explaining that we had secured elegant jobs in various emporiums over the city and wouldn't be home until late in the summer. Then we shivered a shake or two apiece and got ready to retire from this vain world for somewhere between thirty and ninety days. Just about that time Petey Simmons blew down to the college, bursting with information. He demanded a meeting of the Athletic Council at once and of us three sterling athletes as well. We were all in order in ten minutes.

"Fellows, it's this way," said Petey. "Martha Scroggs is very loyal to the college, as you all know. She has done her very best with old Fireworks, but it has n't made a dent in him. No little old party or buggy ride is going to get any one out this time. There's just one chance, she says, and she's taken it. This morning she confessed to her father that she is engaged to one of the men who is to come up for trial to-morrow morning. They think the old man will be well enough to unmuzzle before noon, but he's been acting like a bad case of dog-days all morning. He's given her twenty-four hours to name the man — and Martha thinks that by night he'll be resting comfortably enough to promise to let him off to-morrow. And she has given us the privilege of choosing the man she's engaged to. Now, it's up to this council to pick out the lucky chap. It's our only hope, fellows. We'll have one point-winner anyway — unless the old man eats him alive to-morrow."

Evans and Petersen turned pale — they had real fiancées in college. But each stepped forward nobly and offered himself for the sacrifice. I stepped out, too, though I was so young at that time that I did n't know any more how to go about being engaged to a girl than I did about my Greek lessons. Then the council began to discuss the choice. And just there the trouble began.

It all came about through the frats, of course. Frats are a good thing all right, but they stir up more trouble in a college than a Turk's nine wives can make for him. Ashcroft was president of the council. He was an Alfalfa Delt. So was Evans. Ashcroft hung out for Evans like a bulldog hanging to a tramp. Beeman, a council member, was a Sigh Whoop and so was Petersen. Beeman argued that Petersen could win more points than the rest of the school put together and that it would be unpatriotic, unmanly, disgraceful and un-Siwash-like not to select him. Bailey, the third member, was an Eta Bita Pie, and while sub-Freshmen are not supposed to be anything with Greek letters on, we understood each other, and I was to be initiated the next fall. Bailey pointed out caustically that to imprison a sub-Freshman would be to ruin his reputation, break his spirit and disgrace the school — that one world's record was worth fifty points, and that, if allowed to, I would pole-vault so high the next day that I would have to come down in a parachute. The result was the council broke up in one big row and Martha Scroggs spent the afternoon unengaged.

About five o 'clock Bailey came over to the track, where we were going through the last sad rites, and hauled me aside.

"Take off those togs, kid," he said. "I 've got a stunt. These yaps are going to hold another meeting to-night to decide on Martha Scroggs' fiancée. In the meantime you 're going out to ask the old man for her. Understand? You're going to ask him and take what he gives you like a little man and beg off for to-day, and then you're going to break the pole-vault record. See?"

Unfortunately, I did. I liked the job just as well as I would like getting boiled in oil. But one must stand by one's frat, you know — Gee, how proud I felt when I said that! I did n't have any idea how an engaged man ought to look or act, but I went home, put on the happiest duds I had, and shinned up the street about eight o'clock.

The man-eating dog of the Scroggses was some-where else, gorging himself on another unfortunate, and I got to the front door all right. I rang the bell. Some one opened the door. It was Judge Scroggs. He looked at me as one might look at a bug which had wandered on to the table and was trying to climb over a fork.

" Young man," he said, " what do you want?"

Did you ever have your voice slink around behind your larynx and refuse to come out? Mine did. I only wish I could have slunk with it. I started talk-ing twice. My tongue went all right, but I could n't slip in the clutch and make any sound.

" Well," roared Scroggs, " what is it?"

That jarred me loose. " Mr. Scroggs," I sput-tered, " I am engaged to your daughter. I want to marry her. I want your permission. I — I'll be good to her, sir."

He glared at me for a minute. " Oh! " he said

with a queer look. " Well, come on in with the rest
of them. "

I followed him into the parlor. There sat Evans
and Petersen. They were older than I, but if I
looked as scared as they did I wish somebody had shot
me. In the corner was another student. His name
was Driggs. His specialty was cotillons.

We four sat and looked at each other with awful
suspicions. Something was excessively wrong. I
felt indignant. Can't a fellow go to see his fiancée
without being annoyed by a Roman mob? I noticed
Petersen and Evans looked indignant, too. We took
it out by staring Driggs almost into the collywobbles.
Who was he anyway, and why was he billy-goating
around?

Old Scroggs had called Martha. He sat and looked
at us so peculiarly that I got gooseflesh all over.
Here I was, a Freshman so green that the cows looked
longingly at me, and up against the job of saving the
college, winning out for the frat and becoming engaged to a girl I did n't know before a whole roomful
of rivals. I was n't up to the job. If only I had
gone to the works! They seemed a haven of sweet
peace just then.

Martha Scroggs came into the room. She looked
at the quartet. We looked at her with hunted looks.
Scroggs looked at all of us.

" Martha," he said at last, " each one of these four
young idiots says he is engaged to you. Which of
them shall I throw out? "

The jig was up! The college was ruined! Each one of us had the same bright thought!

For a moment I thought Martha was going to faint. She looked at the mob with a dazed expression. You could almost see her brain grabbing for some explanation. It was just for a moment, though. My, but that girl was a wonder! She gulped once or twice. Then she smiled in an inspired sort of way.

"None of them, Papa," she said ever so sweetly. "I am engaged to all of them."

The eruption of Vesuvius was only a little sputter to what followed. For a moment we had hopes that old Scroggs would explode. I think if he had had us there alone he would have tried to hang us. But every tyrant has his master, so before long we began to see the halter on old Scroggs. And his daughter held the leading rope. She let him rave about so long and then she retired into her pocket-handkerchief and turned on a regular equinoctial. Scroggs looked more uncomfortable than we felt. He took her in his arms and there was a family reconciliation. Every little while Martha would look over his shoulder at us four hopefuls sitting up against the wall as lively as wooden Indians, and then she would bury her face in her handkerchief again and shake her shoulders and writhe with grief — or maybe it was something else. Martha always did have a pretty keen sense of humor.

Suddenly Scroggs remembered us and we went out of the house like projectiles fired from a very loud

My, but that girl was a wonder!

gun. We cussed each other all the way home — we three athletes. We would have cussed Driggs, but he sneaked the other way and we lost him.

The next morning we went up to police court in our old clothes. Judge Scroggs looked at us sourly when our turn came.

"Young men," he said, "my daughter has admitted that she has been foolish enough to engage herself provisionally to all of you, with the idea of choosing the hero in this afternoon's games. I do not admire her taste. I think she is indeed reckless to fall in love with collegians when there are so many honest cab drivers and grocery boys to choose from. But I have, in the interests of peace, consented to allow you to compete this afternoon. You are discharged. I do this the more willingly because I have seen you here before and shall again. You may go."

We did go, and when we got through that afternoon the knobby-legged athletes from our rival schools looked like quarter horses plowing home just ahead of the next race. Siwash won by an enormous lead and we three were the stars of the meet. Why should n't we be when our fiancée sat in a box in the grandstand and cheered us impartially? More than that, old Scroggs sat with her and I have an idea that he got excited, too, in the breath-catching parts.

I think that engagement business must have broken the old man's spirit, or else so much association with college people began to waken dormant brain cells in his head. The rest of the rioters got out of the work-house right away, and that fall he retired from the bench, declaring that if he was to have a college student for a son-in-law, as looked extremely likely, he needed to put in all of his time at home protecting his property. In honor of his retirement we had a pajama parade which was nine blocks long and forty-two blocks loud, and a platoon of six policemen led the way.

Of course that engagement business left all sorts of complications. Scroggs pestered his daughter for about a month to make her decision. He seemed somewhat relieved when she finally announced that she could n't; but it was n't much relief, after all, for by this time he could n't walk around his own house without falling over Petey Simmons. Just two years ago I got cards to Petey's wedding. He and Martha are living in Chicago in one of those flats where you have seven hundred and eighty-nine dollars' worth of bath-room, and eighty-nine cents' worth of living room, and which you have to lease by measure just as you would buy a vest. If Petey hangs on long enough he is going to be a big man in the banking business, too.

I forgot to clear up this Driggs mystery. The evening after the races, Martha called up Petey Simmons. " Petey," said she, " I wish you would tell me who this fourth man is that I 'm engaged to. He does n't seem to be on the track team and I did n't catch his name. I don't mind having to make up an excuse for being engaged to four men right on the spur of the moment if it is necessary, but I'd at least like to know their names."

Petey was as puzzled as she was and lit out to find Driggs. He was gone, but the next day he turned up and confessed all. He had a terrible affair with a girl in the next town, it seems, and had a date to bring her to the games. He was one of the nineteen criminals, and was so terror-stricken at the idea of being compelled to desert his hypnotizer that when the news of the engagement business leaked out he took a long chance and went up and announced himself. It worked, but we caught him two nights later and shaved his hair on one side as a gentle warning not to do it again.

CHAPTER IV

A FUNERAL THAT FLASHED IN THE PAN

HONEST, Bill, sometimes when I sit down in these sober, plug-away days — when we are kind to the poor dumb policemen and don't dare wear straw hats after the first of September — and think about the good old college times, I wonder how we ever had the nerve to imitate insanity the way we did. Here I am, rubbing noses with thirty, outgrowing my belts every year, and sitting eight hours at a desk without exploding. Am I the chap who climbed up sixty feet of waterspout a few short years ago and persuaded the clapper of the college bell to come down with me? Here you are all worn smooth on top and proprietor of an overflow meeting in a nursery. In about ten minutes you'll be tearing your coat-tails out of my hands because you have to go back home before the eldest kid asks for a story. Are you the loafer who spent all one night getting a profane parrot into the cold-air pipes of the college chapel? Maybe you think you are, but I don't believe it. If I were to tip this table over on you now you'd get mad and go home instead of handing me a volume of George Barr McCutcheon in the watch-pocket.

You 're not the good old lunatic you used to be, and neither am I.

Yes, times have changed. I don't feel as unfettered as I used to. There are a few things nowadays that I don't care to do. When I come home at night I take my shoes off and tiptoe to my room instead of standing outside and trying to persuade my landlady that the house is on fire. When I visit a friend in his apartments I do not, as a bit of repartee, throw all of his clothes out of the window while he is out of the room, and it has been a long time since I last hung a basket out of my window on Saturday night, expecting some early-rising friend to put a pocketful of breakfast in it as he came past from boarding-club. I am a slave to conventions and so are you, you slant-shouldered, hollow-chested, four-eyed, flabby-spirited pill-roller, you! The city makes more mummies out of live ones than old Rameses ever did out of his obituary crop.

And yet it 's no time at all since you and I were back at Siwash College, making a dear playmate out of trouble from morning till night. I wonder what it is in college that makes a fellow want to stick his finger into conventions and customs and manners, to say nothing of the revised statutes, and stir the whole mess 'round and 'round! When you 're in college, college life seems big and all the rest of the world so small that what you want to do as a student seems to be the only important thing in life — no matter if what you want to do is only to put a free-lunch sign over the First Methodist Church. What does the college student care for the U. S. A., the planet or the solar system? Why, at Siwash, I remember the biggest man in the world was Ole Skjarsen. Next to him was Coach Bost, then Rogers, captain of the football team, and then Jensen, the quarter. After him came Frankling, of the Alfalfa Delts, whose father picked up bargains in railroads instead of gloves; then came Prexy, and after him the President of the United States and a few scattered celebrities, tailing down to the Mayor of Jonesville and its leading citizens — mere nobodies.

That's how important the outside world seemed to us. Is it any wonder that when we wanted to go downtown in pajamas and plug hats we paddled right along? Or that when we wanted to steal a couple of actors and tie them in a barn, while two of us took their places, we did not hesitate to do so? We felt perfectly free to do just what we pleased. The college understood us, and what the world thought never entered our heads.

Those were certainly nightmarish times for the Faculty of a small but husky college filled with live wires who specialized in applied mischief. It beats all what peculiar things college students can do and not think anything of it at all; and it's funny how closely wisdom and blame foolishness seem to be related. I remember after I had spent two hours putting my Polykon down on a concrete foundation so that I could recite John Stuart Mill by the ream, it

seemed as if I could n't live half an hour longer
without a certain kind of pie that was kept in captivity a mile away downtown at a lunch-counter.
And, moreover, I could n't eat that pie alone. A college student does n't know how to masticate without
an assistant or two. When I think of the hours and
hours I have spent traveling around at midnight and
battering on the doors of perfectly respectable houses,
trying to drag some student out and take him a mile
or two away downtown after pie, I am struck with
awe. When I came to this town I walked two days
for a job and then sat around with my feet on a sofa
cushion for three days. I 'll bet I 've walked twice
as far hunting up some devoted friend to help me
go downtown and eat a piece of pie. And that pie
seemed three times as important as the easy lessons
for beginners in running the earth that I had been
absorbing all the evening.

You need n't grin, Bill. You were just as bad. I
remember you were the biggest math. shark in college.
You could do calculus problems that took all the
English letters from A to Z and then slopped over into
the Greek alphabet; and everybody predicted that you
would be a great man if anybody ever found any use
for calculus. And yet the chief ambition of your life
was to find a way of tampering with the college clock
so that it would run twice as fast as its schedule.
You used to sit around and figure all evening over
it and declare that if you could only do it once and
watch the Profs. letting out classes early and going

home to supper at one P. M. you would consider your life well spent. Sounds fiddling now, does n't it? But I admired you for it then. I really looked up to you, Bill, as a man with a firm, fixed purpose, while I was just a trifler who would be satisfied to steal the hands of the clock or jolly it into striking two hundred times in a row.

There was Rearick, for instance. He was the smartest man in our class. Took scholarship prizes as carelessly as a policeman takes peanuts from a Dago stand. Since then he's gone up so fast that every time I see him I insult him by congratulating him on getting the place he's just been promoted from. But what was Rearick's hobby at Siwash? Stealing hatpins. He had four hundred hatpins when he graduated, and he never could see anything wrong in it. Guess he's got them yet. Perkins is in Congress already. He out-debated the whole Northwest and wrote pieces on subjects so heavy that you could break up coal with them. But I never saw him so earnest in debate as he was the night he talked old Bill Morrison into letting him drive his hack for him all evening. He told me he had driven every hack in town but Bill's, and that Bill had baffled him for two years. It cost him four dollars to turn the trick, but he was happier after it than he was when he won the Siwash-Muggledorfer debate. Said he was ready to graduate now — college held nothing further for him. Perkins' brains were n't addled, because he has been working them double shift ever

since. He just had the college microbe, that's all.
It gets into your gray matter and makes you enjoy
things turned inside out. You remember "Prince"
Hogboom's funeral, don't you?

What year was it? Why, ninety-ump-teen. What?
That's right, you got out the year before. I remember they held your diploma until you paid for
the library cornerstone that your class stole and cut
up into paper-weights. Well, by not staying the
next year you missed the most unsuccessful funeral
that was ever held in the history of Siwash or anywhere else. It was one of the very few funerals
on record in which the corpse succeeded in licking
the mourners. I've got a small scar from it now.
You may think you're going home to that valuable
baby of yours, but you are not. You'll hear me out.
I haven't talked with a Siwash man for a month, and
all of these Hale and Jarhard and Stencilmania fellows give me an ashy taste in my mouth when I talk
with them. It's about as much fun talking college
days with a fellow from another school as it is to
talk ranching with a New England old maid; and
when I get hold of a Siwash man you can bet I
hang on to him as long as my talons will stick.
You just sit right there and start another Wheeling
conflagration while I tell you how we killed Hogboom
to make a Siwash holiday.

· I helped kill him myself. It was my first murder.
It was an awful thing to do, but we were desperate
men. It was spring — in May — and not one of us

had a cut left. You know how unimportant your cuts
are in the fall when you know that you can skip
classes ten times that year without getting called
up on the green carpet and gimleted by the
Faculty. Ten cuts seem an awful lot when you begin.
You throw 'em away for anything. You cut class to
go downtown and buy a cigarette. You cut class to
see a dog fight. I 've even known a fellow to cut a
class in the fall because he had to go back to the
room and put on a clean collar. But, oh, how different
it is in May, when you have n't a cut left to your
name and the Faculty has been holding meetings on
you, anyway; when classroom is a jail and the
campus just outside the window is a paradise, green
and sunshiny and fanned by warm breezes — excuse
these poetries. And you can sit in your class in
Evidences of Christianity — of which you knew as
much as a Chinese laundryman does of force-feed
lubrication — and look out of the window and see
your best girl sitting on the grass with some smug
oyster who has saved up his cuts. How I used to
hate these chaps who saved up their cuts till spring
and then took my girl out walking while I went to
classes! Is there anything more maddening, I 'd like
to know, than to sit before a big, low window trying
to follow a psychology recitation closely enough to
get up when called on, and at the same time watch
five girls, with all of whom you are dead in love,
strolling slowly off into the bright distance with five
job-lot male beings who are dull and uninteresting

and just cold-blooded enough to save their cuts until the springtime? If there is I've never had it.

In this spring of umpty-steen it seemed as if only one ambition in the world was worth achieving — that was to get out of classes. Most of us had used up our cuts long ago. The Faculty is never any too patient in the spring, anyhow, and a lot of us were on the ragged edge. I remember feeling very confidently that if I went up before that brain trust in the Faculty room once more and tried to explain how it was that I was giving absent treatment to my beloved studies, said Faculty would take the college away from me and wouldn't let me play with it never no more. And that's an awful distressing fear to hang over a man who loves and enjoys everything connected with a college except the few trifling recitations which take up his time and interfere with his plans. It hung over five of us who were trying to plan some way of going over to Hambletonian College to see our baseball team wear deep paths around their diamond. We were certain to win, and as the Hambletonians hadn't found this out there was a legitimate profit to be made from our knowledge — profit we yearned for and needed frightfully. I wonder if these Wall Street financiers and Western railroad men really think they know anything about hard ·times? Why, I've known times to be so hard in May that three men would pool all their available funds and then toss up to see which one of them would eat the piece of pie the total sum bought. I 've known Seniors to begin selling their personal effects in April — a pair of shoes for a dime, a dress suit for five dollars — and to go home in June with a trunk full of flags and dance programs and nothing else. I 've known students to buy velveteen pants in the spring and go around with big slouch hats and very long hair — not because they were really artistic and Bohemian, but because it was easier to buy the trousers and have them charged than it was to find a quarter for a haircut.

That 's how busted live college students with unappreciative dads can get in the spring. That 's how busted we were; and there was Hambletonian, twenty miles away, full of money and misguided faith in their team. If we could scrape up a little cash we could ride over on our bicycles and transfer the financial stringency to the other college with no trouble at all. But it was a midweek game and not one of us had a cut left. That was why we murdered Hogboom.

It happened one evening when we were sitting on the front porch of the Eta Bita Pie house. That was the least expensive thing we could do. We had been discussing girls and baseball and spring suits, and the comparative excellence of the wheat cakes at the Union Lunch Counter and Jim's place. But whatever we talked about ran into money in the end and we had to change the subject. There 's mighty little a poor man can talk about in spring in college, I can tell you. We discussed around for an hour or two, bumping into the dollar mark in every direction, and finally got so depressed that we shut up and sat around with our heads in our hands. That seemed to be about the only thing to do that did n't require money.

"We 'll have to do something desperate to get to that game," said Hogboom at last. Hogboom was a Senior. He ranked "sublime" in football, "excellent" in baseball, "good" in mandolin, "fair" in dancing, and from there down in Greek, Latin and Mathematics.

"Intelligent boy," said Bunk Bailey pleasantly; "tell us what it must be. Desperate things done to order, day or night, with care and thoroughness. Trot out your desperate thing and get me an axe. I 'll do it."

"Well," said Hogboom, "I don't know, but it seems to me that if one of us was to die maybe the Faculty would take a day off and we could go over to Hambletonian without getting cuts."

"Fine scheme; get me a gun, Hogboom." "Do you prefer drowning or lynching?" "Kill him quick, somebody." "Look pleasant, please, while the operator is working." "What do you charge for dying?" Oh, we guyed him good and plenty, which is a way they have at old Harvard and middle-aged Siwash and Infant South Dakota University and wherever two students are gathered together anywhere in the U. S. A.

Hogboom only grinned. "Prattle away all you please," he said, "but I mean it. I've got magnificent facilities for dying just now. I'll consider a proposition to die for the benefit of the cause if you fellows will agree to keep me in cigarettes and pie while I'm dead."

"Done," says I, "and in embalming fluid, too. But just demonstrate this theorem, Hoggy, old boy. How extensively are you going to die?"

"Just enough to get a holiday," said Hogboom. "You see, I happen to have a chum in the telegraph office in Weeping Water, where I live. Now if I were to go home to spend Sunday and you fellows were to receive a telegram that I had been kicked to death by an automobile, would you have sense enough to show it to Prexy?"

"We would," we remarked, beginning to get intelligent.

"And, after he had confirmed the sad news by telegram, would you have sense enough left to suggest that college dismiss on Tuesday and hold a memorial meeting?"

"We would," we chuckled.

"And would you have foresight enough to suggest that it be held in the morning so that you could rush away to Weeping Water in the afternoon to attend the funeral?"

"Yes, indeed," we said, so mildly that the cop two blocks away strolled down to see what was up.

"And then would you be diplomatic enough to pro-

duce a telegram saying that the report was false, just
too late to start the afternoon classes?"

"You bet!" we whooped, pounding Hogboom with
great joy. Then we sat down as unconcernedly as if
we were planning to go to the vaudeville the next
afternoon and arranged the details of Hogboom's
assassination. As I was remarking, positively nothing looks serious to a college boy until after he has
done it.

That was on Friday night. On Saturday we killed
Hogboom. That is, he killed himself. He got permission to go home over Sunday and retired to an
upper back room in our house, very unostentatiously.
He had already written to his operator chum, who
had attended college just long enough to take away
his respect for death, the integrity of the telegraph
service and practically everything else. The result
was that at nine o'clock that evening a messenger boy
rang our bell and handed in a telegram. It was
brief and terrible. Wilbur Hogboom had been submerged in the Weeping Water River while trying to
abduct a catfish from his happy home and had only
just been hauled out entirely extinct.

It was an awful shock to us. We had expected him
to be shot. We read it solemnly and then tiptoed up
to Hogboom with it. He turned pale when he saw
the yellow slip.

' "What is it?" he asked hurriedly. "How did it
happen?"

"You were drowned, Hoggy, old boy," Wilkins

said. "Drowned in your little old Weeping Water River. They have got you now and you're all damp and drippy, and your best girl is having one hysteric after another. Don't you think you ought to throw that cigarette away and show some respect to yourself? We've all quit playing cards and are going to bed early in your honor."

"Well, I'm not," said Hogboom. "It's the first time I have ever been dead, and I'm going to stay up all night and see how I feel. Another thing, I'm going down and telephone the news to Prexy myself. I've had nothing but hard words out of him all my college course, and if he can't think up something nice to say on an occasion like this I'm going to give him up."

Hogboom called up Prexy and in a shaking voice read him the telegram. We sat around, choking each other to preserve the peace, and listened to the following cross section of a dialogue — telephone talk is so interesting when you just get one hemisphere of it.

"Hello! That you, Doctor? This is the Eta Bita Pie House. I've some very sad news to tell you. Hogboom was drowned to-day in the Weeping Water River. We've just had a telegram — Yes, quite dead — No chance of a mistake, I'm afraid — Yes, they recovered him — We're all broken up — Oh, yes, he was a fine fellow — We loved him deeply — I'm glad you thought so much of him — He was always so frank in his admiration of you — Yes, he was honorable — Yes, and brilliant, too — Of course, we valued him for his good fellowship, but, as you say, he was also an earnest boy — It's awful — Yes, a fine athlete — I wish he could hear you say that, Doctor — No, I'm afraid we can't fill his place — Yes, it is a loss to the college — I guess you just address telegram to his folks at Weeping Water — That's how we're sending ours — Good-night — Yes, a fine fellow — Good-night.''

Hogboom hung up the 'phone and went upstairs, where he lay for an hour or two with his face full of pillows. The rest of us weren't so gay. We could see the humor of the thing all right, but the awful fact that we were murderers was beginning to hang over our heads. It was easy enough to kill Hogboom, but now that he was dead the future looked tolerably complicated. Suppose something happened? Suppose he didn't stay dead? There's no peace for a murderer, anyway. We didn't sleep much that night.

The next day it was worse. We sat around and entertained callers all day. Half a hundred students called and brought enough woe to fit out a Democratic headquarters on Presidential election night. They all had something nice to say of Hoggy. We sat around and mourned and gloomed and agreed with them until we were ready to yell with disgust.

Hogboom was the most disgracefully lively corpse I ever saw. He insisted on sitting at the head of the stairs where he could hear every good word that was said of him, and the things he demanded of us during the day would have driven a stone saint to crime. Four times we went downtown for pie; three times for cigarettes; once for all the Sunday newspapers, and once for ice cream. As I told you, it was May, the time of the year when street-car fare is a problem of financial magnitude. We had to borrow money from the cook before night. Hoggy had us helpless, and he was taking a mean and contemptible advantage of the fact that he was a corpse. Half a dozen times we were on the verge of letting him come to life. It would have served him right.

Old Siwash was just naturally submerged in sorrow when Monday morning came. The campus dripped with sadness. The Faculty oozed regret at every pore. We loyal friends of Hogboom were looked on as the chief mourners and it was up to us to fill the part. We did our best. We talked with the soft pedal on. We went without cigarettes. We wiped our eyes whenever we got an audience. Time after time we told the sad story and exhibited the telegram. By noon more particulars began to come in. Prexy got an answer to his telegram of condolence. The funeral, the telegram said, would be on Tuesday afternoon. There was great and universal grief in Weeping Water, where Hogboom had been held in reverent esteem. Hoggy's chum in the telegraph office simply laid himself out on that telegram. Prexy read it to me himself and wiped his eyes while he did it. He was a nice, sympathetic man, Prexy was, when he wasn't discussing cuts or scholarship.

Getting the memorial meeting was so easy we hated to take it. The Faculty met to pass resolutions Monday afternoon, and when our delegation arrived they treated us like brothers. It was just like entering the camp of the enemy under a flag of truce. Many a time I've gone in on that same carpet, but never with such a feeling of holy calm. "They would, of course, hold the memorial meeting," said Prexy. They had in fact decided on this already. They would, of course, dismiss college all day. It was, perhaps, best to hold the memorial in the morning if so many of us were going out to Weeping Water. It was nice so many of us could go. Prexy was going. So was the mathematics professor, old "Ichthyosaurus" James, a very fine old ruin, whom Hogboom hated with a frenzy worthy of a better cause, but who, it seemed, had worked up a great regard for Hogboom through having him for three years in the same trigonometry class.

We went out of Faculty meeting men and equals with the professors. They walked down to the corner with us, I remember, and I talked with Cander, the Polykon professor, who had always seemed to me to be the embodiment of Comanche cruelty and cunning. We talked of Hogboom all the way to the corner. Wonderful how deeply the Faculty loved the boy; and with what Spartan firmness they had concealed all indications of it through his career!

When Monday night came we began to breathe more easily. Of course there was some kind of a deluge coming when Hogboom appeared, but that was his affair. We did n't propose to monkey with the resurrection at all. He could do his own explaining. To tell the truth, we were pretty sore at Hogboom. He was making a regular Roman holiday out of his demise. It kept four men busy running errands for him. We had to retail him every compliment that we had heard during the day, especially if it came from the Faculty. We had to describe in detail the effect of the news upon six or seven girls, for all of whom Hogboom had a tender regard. He insisted upon arranging the funeral and vetoed our plans as fast as we made them. He was as domineering and ugly as if he was the only man who had ever met a tragic end. He acted as if he had a monopoly. We hated him cordially by Monday night, but we were helpless. Hoggy claimed that being dead was a nerve-wearing and exhausting business, and that if he did n't get the respect due to him as a corpse he would put on his plug hat and a plush curtain and walk up the main street of Jonesville. And as he was a foot-ball man and a blamed fool combined we did n't see any way of preventing him.

However, everything looked promising. We had made all the necessary arrangements. The students were to meet in chapel at nine o'clock in the morning and eulogize Hogboom for an hour, after which college was to be dismissed for the day in order that unlimited mourning could be indulged in. There were to be speeches by the Faculty and by students.

Maxfield, the human textbook, was to make the address for the Senior class. We chuckled when we thought how he was toiling over it. Noddy Pierce, of our crowd, was to talk about Hogboom as a brother; Rogers, of the football team, was to make a few grief-saturated remarks. So was Perkins. Every one was confidently expecting Perkins to make the effort of his life and swamp the chapel in sorrow. He was in the secret and he afterward said that he would rather try to write a Shakespearean tragedy offhand than to write another funeral oration about a man who he knew was at that moment sitting in a pair of pajamas in an upper room half a mile away and yelling for pie.

As a matter of fact, there were so many in the secret that we were dead afraid that it would explode. We had to put the baseball team on so that they would be prepared to go over to Hambletonian at noon. The game had been called off, of course, and Hambletonian had been telegraphed. But I was secretary of the Athletic Club and had done the telegraphing. So I addressed the telegram to my aunt in New Jersey. It puzzled the dear old lady for months, I guess, because she kept writing to me about it. We had to tell all the fellows in the frat house and every one of the conspirators let in a friend or two. There were about fifty students who were n't as soggy with grief as they should have been by Monday night.

I blame Hogboom entirely for what happened. He

started it when he insisted that he be smuggled into
the chapel to hear his own funeral orations. We
argued half the Monday night with him, but it was
no use. He simply demanded it. If all dead men are
as disagreeable as Hogboom was, no undertaker's job
for me. He was the limit. He put on a blue bath-
robe and got as far as the door on his promenade
downtown before we gave in and promised to do anything he wanted. We had to break into the chapel
and stow him away in a little grilled alcove in the
attic on the side of the auditorium where he could
hear everything. Sounds uncomfortable, but don't
imagine it was. That nervy slavedriver made us lug
over two dozen sofa pillows, a rug or two, a bottle
of moisture and three pies to while away the time
with. That was where we first began to think of
revenge. We got it, too — only we got it the way
Samson did when he jerked the columns out from
under the roof and furnished the material for a general funeral, with himself in the leading rôle.

By the time we got Hogboom planted in his lux-
urious nest, about three A. M., we were ready to do
anything. Some of us were for giving the whole snap
away, but Pierce and Perkins and Rogers objected.
They wanted to deliver their speeches at the meeting.
If we would leave it to them, they said, they would
see that justice was ladled out.

The whole college and most of the town were at
the memorial meeting. It was a grand and tear-
spangled occasion. There were three grades of emo-

tion plainly visible. There was the resigned and almost pleased expression of the students who were n't in on the deal and who saw a vacation looming up for that afternoon; the grieved and sympathetic sorrow of the Faculty who were attempting to mourn for what they had always called a general school nuisance; and there was the phenomenally solemn woe of the conspirators, who were spreading it on good and thick.

The Faculty spoke first. Beats all how much of a hypocrite a good man can be when he feels it to be his duty. There was Bates, the Latin prof. He had struggled with Hogboom three years and had often expressed the firm opinion that, if Hoggy were removed from this world by a masterpiece of justice of some sort, the general tone of civilization would go up fifty per cent. Yet Bates got up that morning and cried — yes, sir, actually cried. Cried into a large pocket handkerchief that was n't water-tight, either. That's more than Hoggy would ever have done for him. And Prexy was so sympathetic and spoke so beautifully of young soldiers getting drawn aside by Fate on their way to the battle, and all that sort of thing, that you would have thought he had spent the last three years loving Hogboom — whereas he had spent most of the time trying to get some good excuse for rooting him out of school. You know how Faculties always dislike a good football player. I think, myself, they are jealous of his fame.

Maxfield made a telling address for the Senior

class. He and Hoggy had always disagreed, but it was all over now; and the way he laid it on was simply wonderful. I thought of Hoggy up there behind the grilling, swelling with pride and satisfaction as Maxfield told how brave, how tender, how affectionate and how honorable he was, and I wished I was dead, too. Being dead with a string to it is one of the finest things that can happen to a man if he can just hang around and listen to people.

Pierce got up. He was the college silver-tongue, and we settled back to listen to him. Previous speakers had made Hoggy out about as fine as Sir Philip Sidney, but they were amateurs. Here was where Hoggy went up beside A. Lincoln and Alexander if Pierce was anywhere near himself.

There is no denying that Pierce started out magnificently. But pretty soon I began to have an uneasy feeling that something was wrong. He was eloquent enough, but it seemed to me that he was handling the deceased a little too strenuously. You know how you can damn a man in nine ways and then pull all the stingers out with a "but" at the end of it. That was what Pierce was doing. "What if Hogboom was, in a way, fond of his ease?" he thundered. "What if the spirit of good fellowship linked arms with him when lessons were waiting, and led him to the pool hall? He may have been dilatory in his college duties; he may have wasted his allowance on billiards instead of in missionary contributions. He may have owed money — yes, a lot of money.

He may, indeed, have been a little selfish — which one of us is n't? He may have frittered away time for which his parents were spending the fruit of their early toil — but youth, friends, is a golden age when life runs riot, and he is only half a man who stops to think of petty prudence."

That was all very well to say about Rameses or Julius Cæsar or some other deceased who is pretty well seasoned, but I 'll tell you it made the college gasp, coming when it did. It sounded sacrilegious and to me it sounded as if some one who was noted as an orator was going to get thumped by the late Mr. Hogboom about the next day. I perspired a lot from nervousness as Pierce rumbled on, first praising the departed and then landing on him with both oratorical feet. When he finally sat down and mopped his forehead the whole school gave one of those long breaths that you let go of when you have just come up from a dive under cold water.

Rogers followed Pierce. Rogers was n't much of a talker, but he surpassed even his own record that day in falling over himself. When he tried to illustrate how thoughtful and generous Hogboom was he blundered into the story of the time Hoggy bet all of his money on a baseball game at Muggledorfer, and of how he walked home with his chum and carried the latter's coat and grip all the way. That made the Faculty wriggle, I can tell you. He illustrated the pluck of the deceased by telling how Hogboom, as a Freshman, dug all night alone to rescue

a man imprisoned in a sewer, spurred on by his cries
— though Rogers explained in his halting way, it
afterward turned out that this was only the famous
" sewer racket " which is worked on every green
Freshman, and that the cries for help came from a
Sophomore who was alternately smoking a pipe and
yelling into a drain across the road.   Still, Rogers
said, it illustrated Hogboom's nobility of spirit.   In
his blundering fashion he went on to explain some
more of Hoggy's good points, and by the time he sat
down there was n't a shred of the latter's reputation
left intact.   The whole school was grinning uncom-
fortably, and the Faculty was acting as if it was
sitting, individually and collectively, on seventeen
great gross of red-hot pins.

By this time we conspirators were divided between
holy joy and a fear that the thing was going to be
overdone.   It was plain to be seen that the Faculty
was n't going to stand for much more loving frank-
ness.   Pierce whispered to Tad Perkins, Hogboom's
chum, and the worst victim of his posthumous whims,
to draw it mild and go slow.   Perkins was to make
the last talk, and we trembled in our shoes when he
got up.

We need n't have feared for Perkins.   He was
as smooth as a Tammany orator.   He praised Hogboom so pathetically that the chapel began to show
acres of white handkerchiefs again.   Very gently he
talked over his career, his bravery and his achievements.   Then just as poetically and gently he glided

on into the biggest lie that has been told since Ananias short-circuited retribution with his unholy tale.

"What fills up the heart and the throat, fellows," he swung along, "is not the loss we have sustained; not the irreparable injury to all our college activities; not even the vacant chair that must sit mutely eloquent beside us this year. It's something worse than that. Perhaps I should not be telling this. It's known to but a few of his most intimate friends. The saddest thing of all is the fact that back in Weeping Water there is a girl — a lovely girl — who will never smile again."

Phew! You could just feel the feminine side of the chapel stiffen — Hogboom was the worst fusser in college. He was chronically in love with no less than four girls and was devoted to dozens at a time. We had reason to believe that he was at that time engaged to two, and spring was only half over at that. This was the best of all; our revenge was complete.

"A girl," Perkins purred on, "who has grown up with him from childhood; who whispered her promise to him while yet in short dresses; who sat at home and waited and dreamed while her knight fought his way to glory in college; who treasured his vows and wore his ring and — "

"'T ain't so, you blamed idiot!" came a hoarse voice from above. If the chapel had been stormed by Comanches there could n't have been more of a commotion. A thousand pairs of eyes focused themselves

on the grill. It sagged in and then disappeared with
a crash. The towsled head of Hogboom came out of
the opening.

"I'll fix you for that, Tad Perkins!" he yelled.
"I'll get even with you if it takes me the rest of my
life. I ain't engaged to any Weeping Water girl.
You know it, you liar! I've had enough of this—"
You couldn't hear any more for the shrieks. When
a supposedly dead man sticks his head out of a jog
in the ceiling and offers to fight his Mark Antony it
is bound to create some commotion. Even the professors turned white. As for the girls — great smell-
ing salts, what a cinch! They fainted in windrows.
Some of us carried out as many as six, and you had
better believe we were fastidious in our choice, too.

There had never been such a sensation since Siwash
was invented. Between the panic-stricken, the dazed,
the hilarious, the indignant and the guilty wretches
like myself, who were wondering how in thunder there
was going to be any explaining done, that chapel was
just as coherent as a madhouse. And then Hogboom
himself burst in a side door, and it took seven of us
to prevent him from reducing Perkins to a paste and
frescoing him all over the chapel walls. Everybody
was rattled but Prexy. I think Prexy's circulation
was principally ice water. When the row was over
he got up and blandly announced that classes would
take up immediately and that the Faculty would meet
in extraordinary session that noon.

How did we get out of it? Well, if you want to

catch the last car, old man, I'll have to hit the high
spots on the sequel. Of course, it was a tremendous
scandal — a memorial meeting breaking up in a fight.
We all stood to be expelled, and some of the Faculty
were sorry they could n't hang us, I guess, from the
way they talked. But in the end it blew over because there was n't much of anything to hang on any
one. The telegrams were all traced to the agent at
Weeping Water, and he identified the sender as a
long, short, thick, stout, agricultural-looking man in a
plug hat, or words to that effect. What's more, he
declared it was n't his duty to chase around town con-
firming messages — he was paid to send them. Hogboom had a harder time, but he, too, explained that
he had come home from Weeping Water a day late,
owing to a slight attack of appendicitis, and that
when he found himself late for chapel he had climbed
up into the balcony through a side door to hear the
chapel talk, of which he was very fond, and had
found, to his amazement, that he was being reviled
by his friends under the supposition that he was
dead and unable to defend himself. Nobody believed
Hogboom, but nobody could suggest any proof of his
villainy — so the Faculty gave him an extra five-
thousand-word oration by way of punishment, and
Hogboom made Perkins write it in two nights by
threats of making a clean breast. Poor Hoggy came
out of it pretty badly. I think it broke both of his
engagements, and what between explaining to the
Faculty and studying to make a good showing and

redeem himself, he did n't have time to work up another before Commencement — while the rest of us lived in mortal terror of exposure and did n't enjoy ourselves a bit all through May, though it was some comfort to reflect on what would have happened if the scheme had worked — for Hambletonian beat us to a frazzle that afternoon.

That 's what we got for monkeying with a solemn subject. But, pshaw! Who cares in college? What a student can do is limited only by what he can think up. Did I ever tell you what we did to the English Explorer? Take another cigar. It is n't late yet.

CHAPTER V

MIND you, old head, I'm not saying that a little education is n't a good thing in a college course. I learned a lot of real knowledge in school myself that I would n't have missed for anything, though I have forgotten it now. But what irritate me are the people who think that the education you get in a modern American super-heated, cross-compound college comes to you already canned in neat little textbooks sold by the trust at one hundred per cent profit, and that all you have to do is to go to your room with them, fill up a student lamp with essence of General Education and take the lid off.

Honest, lots of them think that. It might have been so, too, in the good old days when there was only one college graduate for each town and he had to do the heavy thinking for the whole community. But, pshaw! the easiest job in the world nowadays is to stuff your storage battery full of Greek verbs and obituaries in English literature, and the hardest job is to get it hitched up to something that will bring in the yellowbacks, the chopped-wood furniture, the automobile tires and the large majorities in the fall

elections. I've seen brilliant boys at old Siwash go
out of college knowing everything that had ever happened in the world up to one hundred years ago, and
try to peddle hexameters in the wholesale district in
Chicago. And I've seen boys who slid through the
course just half a hair's breadth ahead of the Faculty
boot, go out and do the bossing for a whole Congressional district in five years. They had n't learned
the exact chemical formula of the universe, but they
had learned how to run the blamed thing from prac-
ticing on the college during study hours.

Not that I'm knocking on knowledge, you understand. Knowledge is, of course, a grand thing to
have around the house. But nowadays knowledge
alone is n't worth as much as it used to be, seems
to me. A man has to mix it up with imagination,
and ingenuity, and hustle, and nerve, and the science
of getting mad at the right time, and a fourteen-year
course of study in understanding the other fellow.
The college professors lump all this in one course
and call it applied deviltry. They don't put it down
in the catalogue and they encourage you to cut classes
in it. But, honestly, I would n't trade what I learned
under Professor Petey Simmons, warm boy and
official gadfly to the Faculty, for all the Lat. and
Greek and Analit. and Diffy. Cal., and the other
studies — whatever they were — that I took in good
old Siwash.

You remember Petey, of course. He went through
Siwash in four years and eight suspensions, and

came out fresh — as fresh as when he went in, which is saying a good deal. Every summer during his career the Faculty went to a rest cure and tried to forget him. He was as handy to have around school as a fox terrier in a cat show. There are two varieties of college students — the midnight-oil and the natural-gas kind; and Petey was a whole gas well in himself. Not that he did n't study. He was the hardest student in the college, but he did n't recite much in classes. Sometimes he recited in the police court, sometimes to his Pa back home, and sometimes the whole college took a hand in looking over his examination papers. He used to pass medium fair in Horace; sub-passable in Trig., and extraordinary mediocre in Polikon. But his marks in Imagination, the Psychological Moment and Dodging Consequences were plus perfect, extra magnificent, and superlatively some, respectively.

I saw Petey last year. He is in Chicago now. You have to bribe a doorkeeper and bluff a secretary to get to him — that is, you do if you are an ordinary mortal. But if you give the Siwash yell or the Eta Bita Pie whistle in the outside office he will emerge from his office out over the railing in one joyous jump. He came to Chicago ten years ago equipped with a diploma and a two-year tailor-bill back at Jonesville that he had been afraid to tell his folks about. If he had been a midnight-oil graduate he would have worn out three pairs of shoes hunting for a business house which was willing to let an earnest young scholar enter its employ at the bottom and rise gradually to the top as the century went by. But Petey was n't that kind. He had been used to running the whole college and messing up the universe as far as one could see from the Siwash belfry if things did n't suit him. So he picked out the likeliest-looking institution on Dearborn Street and offered it a position as his employer. He was on the pay-roll before the president got over his daze. Two weeks later he promoted the firm to a more responsible job — that of paying him a bigger salary — and a year ago the general manager gave up and went to Europe for two years; said he would take a positive pleasure in coming back and looking at the map of Chicago after Petey had done it over to suit himself.

Imagination was what did it. You can't take Imagination in any college classroom, but you can get more of it on the campus in four years than you can anywhere else in the world. You 've got to have a mighty good imagination to get into any real warm trouble — and by the time you have gotten out of it again you have had to double its horse-power. That was Petey's daily recreation. In the morning he would think up an absolutely air-tight reason for being expelled from Siwash as a disturber, an anarchist, a superfluosity and a malefactor of great stealth. That night he would go to his room and figure out an equally good proof that nothing had happened or that whatever had happened was an act of Providence and not traceable to any student. Figuring out ways for selling bonds in carload lots was just recreation to him after a four-year course of this sort.

But to back in on the main track. I whistled outside of Petey's office the other day and went in with him past two magnates, three salesmen and a bank president. I sat with my feet on a mahogany table — I wanted to put them on an oak desk, but Petey declared mahogany was none too good for a Siwash man — and we spent an hour talking over the time when Petey manufactured excitement in wholesale lots at Siwash, with me for his first assistant and favorite apprentice. Those are my proudest memories. I won my track S. and got honorably mentioned in three Commencement exercises; but when I want to brag of my college career do I mention these things? Not unless I have a lot of time. When I want to paralyze an alumnus of some rival college with admiration and envy, I tell him how Petey and I manufactured a real Wild West college — buildings, Faculty, bad men and all — for one day only, for the benefit of an Englishman who had gotten fifteen hundred miles inland without noticing the generol color scheme of the inhabitants.

We met this chap accidentally — a little favor of Providence, which had a special pigeonhole for us in those days. Our team had been using the Kiowa football team as a running track on their own field that afternoon, and the score was about 105 to 0 when the

timekeeper turned off the massacre. Naturally all Siwash was happy. I will admit we were too happy to be
careful. About two hundred of us made the hundred-
mile trip home by local train that night, and I remember wondering, when the boys dumped the stove off the
rear platform and tied up the conductor in his own
bell-rope, if we were n't getting just a little bit indiscreet; and when a college boy really wonders if he
is getting indiscreet he is generally doing something
that will keep the grand jury busy for the next few
months.

I was in the last car, and had just finished telling
" Prince " Hogboom that if he poked any more window-lights out with his cane he would have to finish
the year under an assumed name, when Petey crawled
over two mobs of rough-housers and came up to me.
He was seething with indignation. It was breaking
out all over him like a rash. Petey was excitable
anyway.

" What do you suppose I 've found in the next
car ? " he said, fizzing like an escape valve.

" Prof ? " said I, getting alarmed.

" Naw," said Petey; " worse than that. A chap
that has never heard of Siwash. Asked me if it was
a breakfast food. He 's an Englishman. I 'm ag'in'
the English." He stopped and began kicking a water-
tank around to relieve himself.

" How did he get this far away from home ? " I
asked.

" He 's traveling," snorted Petey; " traveling to

improve his mind. Hopeless job. He's one of those quarter-sawed old beef-eaters who stop thinking as soon as they've got their education. He's the editor of a missionary publication, he told me, and he is writing some articles on Heathen America. Honest, it almost made me boil over when he asked me if anything was being done to educate the aborigines out here."

"What did you do?" I asked.

"Do?" said Petey. "Why, I answered his question, of course. I told him he was n't fifty miles from a college this minute, and he said, 'Oh, I say now! Are you spoofing me?' What's 'spoofing'?"

"Kidding, stringing, stuffing, jollying along, blowing east wind, turning on the gas," says I. "'Spoofing' is University English. They don't use slang over there, you know."

"Well, then, I spoofed him," said Petey, grinning. "He said it was remarkable how very few revolvers he had seen, and then he wanted to know why there was no shooting on the train with so much disorder. He's pretty well posted now. I'd go a mile out of my way to help a poor dumb chap like him. I told him this was the Y. M. C. A. section of Siwash and that the real rough students were coming along on horseback. I said they were n't allowed on the trains because they were so fatal to passengers. I informed him that all the profs at Siwash went armed, and that the course of study consisted of mining, draw poker, shooting from the hip, broncho-busting, sheep-shearing, History of Art, bread-making and Evidences of Christianity."

"Did he admit by that time that you were a good, free-handed liar?" I asked.

"Admit nothing," said Petey; "he took it all down in his notebook and remarked that in a wild country like this, remote from civilization, a knowledge of bread-making would undoubtedly be invaluable to a man."

"He was spoofing you," says I.

"He wasn't," said Petey; "he thinks he's a thousand miles from a plug hat this minute. He's so interested he is going to stop over for a day or two and write up the college for his magazine. I've invited him to stay at the Eta Bita Pie House with us, and we're going to show him a real Wild West school if we have to shoot blank cartridges at the cook to do it."

"Petey," said I solemnly, "some day you'll bump an asteroid when you go up in the air like this. This friend of yours will take one look at Siwash and ask you if Sapphira is feeling well these days."

"Bet you five, my opera hat, a good mandolin and a meal ticket on Jim's place against your dress suit," said Petey promptly. "And you better not take it, either."

"Done!" says I. "I bet you my hunting-case suit against your earthly possessions that you can't tow old Britannia-rules-the-waves around Siwash for a day without disclosing the fact that you are the best catch-as-catch-can liar in this section of the solar system."

"All right," said Petey. "But you 've got to help me win the stuff. This is a great big contract. It 's going to be my masterpiece, and I need help."

"I 'm with you clear to Faculty meeting, as usual," says I. "But what 's the use? He 'll catch on."

"Leave that to me," said Petey. "Anyway, he won't catch on. When I told him we had a check-room for pappooses in the Siwash chapel he wrote it down and asked if the Indians ever massacred the professors. He would n't catch on if we fed him dog for dinner. Just come and see for yourself."

I agreed with Petey when I took a good look at the victim a minute later. We found him in the car ahead, sitting on the edge of the seat and looking as if he expected to be eaten alive, without salt, any minute. You could have told that he was from ex-tremely elsewhere at first glance. He was as different as if he had worn tattoo-marks for trousers. He was a stout party with black-rimmed eyeglasses, side whis-kers that you would n't have believed even if you had seen them, and slabs of iron-gray hair with a pepper-and-salt traveling cap stuck on top of his head like a cupola. He was beautifully curved and his black preacher uniform looked as if it had been put on him by a paperhanger. I forgot to tell you that his name was the Reverend Ponsonby Diggs. He had to tell it to me four times and then write it down, for the way he handled his words was positively heartless. He clipped them, beheaded them, disemboweled them and warped them all out of shape. Have you ever heard a real ingrowing Englishman start a word in the roof of his mouth and then back away from it as if it was red-hot and had prickles on it? It's interesting. They seem to think it is indecent to come brazenly out and sound a vowel.

The Reverend Ponsonby Diggs — as near as I could get it he called himself "Pubby Daggs" — greeted Petey with great relief. He seemed to regard us as a rescue brigade. "Reahly, you know, this is extraordinary," he sputtered. "I have never seen such disorder. What will the authorities do?"

That touched my pride. "Pshaw, man!" I says; "we're only warming up. Pretty soon we'll take this train out in the woods and lose it."

I meant it for a joke. But the Reverend Mr. Diggs hadn't specialized in American jokes. "You don't mean to say they will derail the train!" he said anxiously. Then I knew that Petey was going to win my dress suit.

I assured the Reverend — pshaw, I'm tired of saying all that! I'm going to save breath. I assured Diggsey that derailing was the kindest thing ever done to trains by Siwash students, but that as his hosts we would stand by him, whatever happened. Then Petey slipped away to arrange the cast and I kept on answering questions. Say! that man was a regular magazine gun, loaded with interrogation points. Was there any danger to life on these trains?

Would it be possible for him to take a ride in a stage-coach? Were train robbers still plentiful? Had gold ever been found around Siwash? Were the Indians troublesome? Did we have regular school buildings or did we live in tents? Had not the railroad had a distinctly — er — civilizing influence in this region? Was it not, after all, remarkable that the thirst for learning could be found even in this wild and desolate country?

And Siwash is only half a day from Chicago by parlor car!

I answered his questions as well as I could. I told him how hard it was to find professors who would n't get drunk, and how we had to let the men and women recite on alternate days after a few of the hen students had been winged by stray bullets. I had never heard of Greek, I said, but I assured him that we studied Latin and that we had a professor to whom Cæsar was as easy as print. I told him how hard we worked to get a little culture and how many of the boys gave up their ponies altogether, wore store clothes and took 'em off when they went to bed all the time they were in college; but, try as I would, I could n't make the answers as ridiculous as his questions. He had me on the mat, two points down and fighting for wind all the time. His thirst for knowledge was wonderful and his objection to believing what his eyes must have told him was still more wonderful. There he was, half-way across the country from New York, and he must have looked out

of the car windows on the way; but he had n't seen
a thing. I suppose it was because he was n't looking
for anything but Indians.

All this time Petey was circulating about the car,
taking aside members of the Rep Rho Betas and
talking to them earnestly. The Rep Rho Betas were
the Sophomore fraternity and were the real demons
of the college. Each year the outgoing Sophomore
class initiated the twenty Freshmen who were most
likely to meet the hangman on professional business
and passed on the duties of the fraternity to them.
The fraternity spent its time in pleasure and was
suspected of anything violent which happened in the
county. Petey was highbinder of the gang that year
and was very far gone in crime.

We were due home about ten P. M., and just before
they untied the conductor Petey hauled me off to
one side.

"It's all fixed," he said; "it's glorious. We'll
just make Siwash into a Wild West show for his
benefit. The Rep Rho Betas will entertain him days
and he'll stay at the Eta Pie House nights.
I'm putting the Eta Bites on now. You've got to
get him off this train before we get to the station
and keep him busy while I arrange the program.
Just give me an hour before you get him there.
That's all I ask."

Now I never was a diplomat, and the job of lugging
a fat old foreigner around a dead college town at
night and trying to make him think he was in peril

of his life every minute was about three numbers larger than my size. I could n't think of anything else, so I slipped the word to Ole Skjarsen that Diggs was a Kiowa professor who was coming over to get notes on our team and tip them off to Muggledorfer College. I judged this would create some hostility and I was n't mistaken. Ole began to climb over his fellow-students and I was just able to beat him to his prey.

"Come on," I whispered. "Skjarsen's on the warpath. He says he wants to bite up a stranger and he thinks you'll do."

"Oh, my dear sir," said the Reverend Ponsonby, jumping up and grabbing a hatbox, "you don't mean to tell me that he will use violence?"

"Violence nothing!" I yelled, picking up four pieces of baggage. "He won't use violence. He'll just eat you alive, that's all. He's awful that way. Come, quick!"

"Oh, my word!" said Diggsey, grabbing his other five bundles and piling out of the car after me.

The train was slowing down for the crossing west of Jonesville, and I judged it would n't hurt the great collector of Western local color to roll a little. So I yelled, "Jump for your life!" He jumped. I swung off and went back till I met him coming along on his shoulder-blades, with a procession of baggage following him. He was n't hurt a bit, but he looked interesting. I brushed him off, cached the baggage — all but a suitcase and the hatbox which he had n't dropped for a minute — and we began to edge unostentatiously into Jonesville.

For an hour or more we dodged around in alleys and behind barns, while up on the campus the boys burned a woodshed, an old fruit-stand, half a hundred drygoods boxes and half a mile of wooden sidewalk by way of celebration. The glare in the sky was wild enough to satisfy any one, and when some of the boys got the old army muskets that the cadets drilled with out of the armory and banged away, I was happy. But how I did long to be close up to that fire! It was a cold night in early November, and as I lay behind woodsheds, with my teeth wearing themselves out on each other, I felt like an early Christian martyr — though it was n't cold they suffered from as a rule. As for the Reverend Pubby, he wanted to creep away to the next town and then start for England disguised as a chorus girl, or anything; but I would n't let him. We sneaked around till nearly midnight and then crept up the alley to the Eta Bita Pie House, wondering if we would ever get warm again.

I 've seen some grand transformation scenes, but I never saw anything more impressive than the way the Eta Bita Pie House had been done over in two hours. We always prided ourselves on our house. It cost fifteen thousand dollars, exclusive of the plumber's little hold-up and the Oriental rugs, and it was full of polished floors and monogram silverware and fancy pottery and framed prints, and other bang-up-to-date incumbrances. But in two hours thirty boys can change a whole lot of scenery. They had spread dirt and sand over the floor, had ripped out the curtains and chased the pictures. They had poked out a window-light or two, had unhung a few doors, and had filled the corners with saddles, old clothes, flour barrels and dogs. You never saw so many dogs. The whole neighborhood had been raided. They were hanging round everywhere, homesick and miserable; and one of the Freshmen had been given the job of cruising around and kicking them just to keep them tuned up.

A dozen of the fellows were playing poker on an old board table in the middle of the big living-hall when we came in. Their clothes were hand-me-downs from Noah's time, and every one of them was outraging some convention or other. Our boys always did go in for amateur theatricals pretty strongly, and the way our most talented members abused the English language that night when they welcomed the Reverend Pubby was as good as a book.

"Proud ter meet you," roared Allie Bangs, our president, taking off his hat and making a low bow. "Set right in and enjoy yourself. White chips is a dime, limit is a dollar and no gunplay goes."

When Pubby had explained for the third time that he had never had the pleasure of playing the game, Bangs finally got on to the curves in his pronunciation and understood him.

"What! Never played poker!" he whooped.

" Hell a humpin', where was you raised? You sure
ain't a college man? Any lop-eared galoot that
did n't play poker in Siwash would get run out by
the Faculty. You ought to see our president put up
his pile and draw to a pair of deuces. What! — a
Reverend! I beg your pardon, friend. 'S all right.
Jest name the game you 're strong at and we 'll try
to accommodate you later on. Here, you fellows,
watch my chips while I show the Reverend around
our diggin's. You nip one like you did last time,
Turk Bowman, and there 'll be the all-firedest row
that this shack has ever seed. Come right along,
Reverend."

That tour was a great triumph for Bangs. We
always did admire his acting, but he outdid himself that night. The rest of us just kept quiet and
let him handle the conversation, and I must say it
sounded desperate enough to be convincing. Of
course he slipped up occasionally and stuck in words
that would have choked an ordinary cow-gentleman,
but Diggsey was that dazed he would n't have suspected if they had been Latin. I thought it would
be more or less of a job to explain how we were
living in a fifteen-thousand-dollar house instead of
dugouts, but Bangs never hesitated a minute. He
explained that the house belonged to a millionaire
cattle-owner who had built it from reading a society
novel, and that he let us live in it because he preferred to live in the barn with the horses. The boys
had filled their rooms full of junk and one of them

"Har's das spy!" he yelled. "Kill
him, fallers; he ban a spy!"

See *page 132*

had even tied a pig to his bed — while the way
Bangs cleared rubbish out of the bathtub and promised to have some water heated in the morning was
convincingly artless. He had just finished explaining that, owing to the boiler-plate in the walls, the
house was practically Indian proof, when an awful
fusillade of shots broke out from the kitchen. Bangs
disappeared for a moment, gun in hand, and I
watched our guest trying to make himself six inches
narrower and three feet shorter. I don't know when
I ever saw a chap so anxious to melt right down into
a corner and be mistaken for a carpet tack.

"'S all right," said Bangs, clumping in cheerfully.
" Jest the cook having another fit. We've got a cook,"
he explained, "who gets loaded up 'bout oncet a
month so full that he cries pure alcohol, and when
he gits that way he insists on trying to shoot cock-
roaches with his gun. He ain't never killed one, but
he's gotten two Chinamen and a mule, and we've
got to put a stop to it. He's tied up in the cellar
a-swearin' that if he gits loose he'll come upstairs
and furnish material for nineteen fancy funerals
with silver name-plates. But, don't you worry,
Reverend. He can't hurt a fly 'less he gits loose.
Here's your room. That hoss blanket on the cot's
brand new; towel's in the hall and you'll find a
comb somewheres round. Just you turn in if you
feel like it, and when you hear Wall-Eye Denton and
Pete Pearsall trying to massacre each other in the
next room it's time to git up."

Pubby said he would retire at once, and we left him looking scared but relieved. I'll bet he sat up all night taking notes and expecting things to happen. We sat up, too, but for a different reason. You can't imagine how much work it took to get that house running backward. And it was an awful job to do the Wild West stunt, too. We sat and criticised each other's dialect and actions until there were as many as three free fights going on at once. One man favored the Bret Harte style of bad man; another adhered to the Henry Wallace Phillips brand; while still another insisted on following the Remington school. We compromised on a mixture and then spent the rest of the night learning how to forget our table manners.

The result was magnificent. I shall never forget the Reverend Pubby's pained but fascinated expression as he sat at breakfast the next morning and watched thirty hungry savages shoveling plain, unvarnished grub into their faces. The breakfast couldn't have gone better if we had had a dress rehearsal. Our guest couldn't eat. He was afraid to talk. He just held on to his chair, and we could see him stiffen with horror every time some eater would rise up so as to increase his reach and spear a piece of bread six feet away with his fork. The breakfast was a disgusting display of Poland-China manners and was successful in every particular.

We confidently expected Petey Simmons to turn up during the meal and tell us what to do next.

He had spent the night with his odoriferous Rep Rho Beta brothers cooking up the rest of the plot and had promised to run up at breakfast. But no Petey appeared. We strung the meal along as far as we could toward dinner and then took up the job of keeping the Reverend Pubby contented and in the house until the life-saving crew arrived. Did you ever try to lie all morning with a slow-speed imagination? That's what we had to do. We explained to Pubby that the students caroused all night and never came to college in the morning; we told him it was against the rules for strangers to go on the campus in the morning; we told him it was dangerous to go out-of-doors because of the Alfalfa Delts, who were suspected of being cannibals; we told him forty thousand things, most of which contradicted each other. If it hadn't been for the boys who kindly started a fight whenever his reverence had tangled Bangs and me up hopelessly on some question we couldn't have survived the inquisition. As it was, I perspired about a barrel and my brain ached for a week.

We went to lunch and put on another exhibition of free-hand feeding, getting more grumpy and disgusted every minute. We were all ready to yell for mercy and put on our civilized clothes when we heard a terrific riot from outside. Then Petey came in.

If there ever was a sure-enough Wild Westerner it was Petey that afternoon. He had on the whole works — two-acre hat, red woolen shirt, spurs, and

even chaps — nice hairy ones. I discovered next day
that he had swiped my fine bearskin rug and cut
it up to make them. In his belt he had a revolver
which could n't have been less than two feet long.
Petey was a little fellow, with one of those nineteen-
sizes-too-large voices, and when he turned the full
organ on you would have thought old Mount Vesuvius
had wakened up and rumbled into the room.

"Howdy, Reverend," he thundered. "We jest
come along to take you on a little ride over to
college. Got a nice gentle cow-pony out here. She
bucks as easy as a rockin'-horse. Don't mind about
your clothes. Just hop right on. The boys is some
anxious to get along, it being most classtime."

We followed the two of them out to the back yard.
There were seven Rep Rho Betas on seven moth-
eaten ponies which they had dug up from goodness
knows where. The rigs they had on represented
each fellow's idea of what a cowboy looked like,
and would have made a real cowpuncher hang himself for shame. Petey confessed afterward that, of
all the Rep Rho Betas, only seven had ever been on
a horse, and, of these, three kept him in agony for
fear they would fall off and compel him to explain
that they were on the verge of delirium tremens.
They were a weird-looking bunch, but, gee! they were
fierce. Pirates would have been kittens beside them.

I guess the Reverend Pubby had never done much
in the Centaur line, for he came very near balking
entirely right there. It took us five minutes to

We spent another five minutes hoisting him aboard a prehistoric plug

Page 125

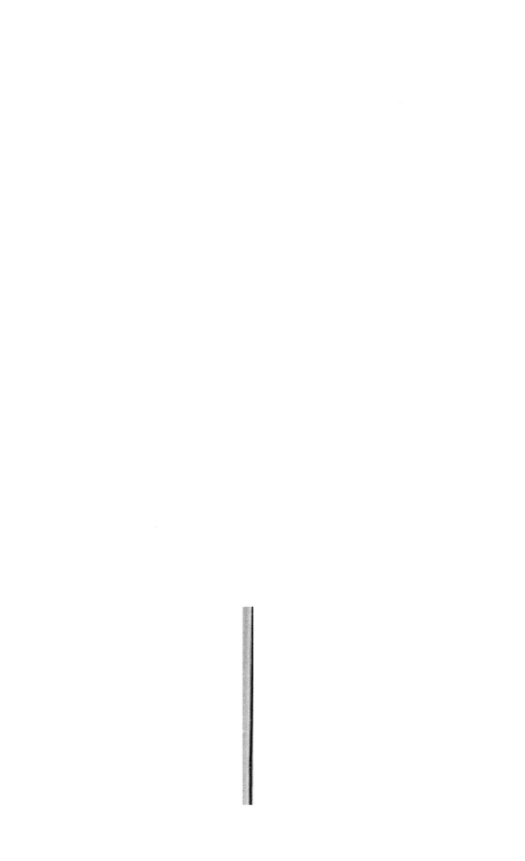

explain that there was no other way of getting out to Siwash and that the Faculty would take it as a personal insult if he did n't come. We also had to explain how disagreeable the Faculty was when it was insulted. And then after he had consented we spent another five minutes hoisting him aboard a prehistoric plug and telling him how to stick on. Then the line filed out through the alley with a regular ghost-dance yell, while we detained Petey. We were about to massacre him for leaving us to sweat all morning, but we forgot all about it when Petey told us what he had been doing. He admitted that, in order not to annoy the profs and cause unnecessary questions, he had taken the liberty to build a temporary Siwash College for this special occasion.

Yes, sir; nothing less than that. You remember Dillpickle Academy, the extinct college in the west part of town? It had been closed for years because the only remaining student had gotten lonesome. But most of the equipment was still there, and Petey had borrowed it of the caretaker for one day only, promising to give it back as good as new in the morning. Petey could have borrowed the great seal away from the Department of State. He and his Rep Rho Betas had let a lot of students into the deal, had been working all morning, and Siwash was ready for business at the new stand.

We wanted to measure Petey for a medal then and there, but he refused, being needed on the firing-line. He rode off and we made a grand rush for

the new Siwash College — special one-day stand,
benefit performance. We got there before the es-
corting committee and had a fine view of the grand
entry. The Reverend Pubby had fallen off four
times, and the last mile he had led his horse. It was
a sagacious scheme bringing him along, as none of the
others had a chance to exhibit their extremely sketchy
horsemanship in anything better than a mile-an-
hour gait.

Old Dillpickle Academy was busier than it had
ever been in real life when we got there. Fully fifty
students were on the scene. They were decked out
in cowboy clothes, hand-me-downs, big straw hats,
blankets — any old thing. One thing that impressed
me was the number of books they were carrying.
At Siwash we always refused to carry books except
when absolutely necessary. It seemed too affected
— as if you were trying to learn something. But
out there at near-Siwash every man had at least
six books. I saw geographies, spellers, Ella Wheeler
Wilcox's poems, Science and Health, and the Congressional Record. Learning was just naturally rampant out there. Students were studying on the fence.
They were walking up and down the campus
" boning " furiously. They were even studying in
the trees. You get fifty college boys to turn actors
for a day and you will see some mighty mixed
results. There was " Bay " Sanderson, for instance.
" Bay's " idea of being a wild and Western student
was to sit on the front gate with a long knife stuck

in his belt and read detective stories. He did it all through the performance, and whenever the guest was led past him he would turn the book down carefully, pull the knife out of his belt and whoop three times as solemn as a judge.

You never saw any one so interested as the Reverend Ponsonby Diggs. His eyes stuck out like incandescent globes. He had been pretty well jolted up, and he yelled in a low, polite way every time he made a quick movement, but his thirst for information was still vigorous. As head host Petey was pumpee, and he was always four laps ahead of the job.

"Eh, I say," said Pubby, after surveying the scene for a few minutes. "This is all very interesting, you know. But what a little place!"

"Hell, Reverend," said Petey emphatically. "she's the biggest school in the world."

The Reverend was a man of guile. He didn't bat an eye.

"How many students has the college?" he inquired.

"We've got a hundred, all studying books and learning things," said Petey proudly.

"Reahly, now?" said the Reverend; "I say, reahly? And these cows! Might I ask if these cows are a part of the college?"

"Sure thing," said Petey. "Sophomore roping class uses 'em. Great class to watch."

"I say now, this is extraordinary," said the Reverend. "You don't mean to tell me you tie up cows?"

"Rope 'em and tie 'em and brand 'em," said Petey. "What's college for if it ain't to learn you things?"

"I say now, this is extraordinary," said the Reverend. I gave him four more "extraordinaries" before I did something violent. He'd used two hundred that morning. "Might I see the class at work?" he inquired.

Petey did n't even hesitate. "Sorry, Reverend," says he. "But the Professor of Roping and Branding has been drunk for a week. Class ain't working now."

The college bell tapped three times. "That's cleaning-up bell," said Petey.

"Oh, I say now," said the Reverend, hauling out his notebook. "What's cleaning-up bell?"

"Why, to clean up the college," said Petey. "We clean it up once a week. With the fellows riding their horses into class and tracking mud and clay in, and eating lunches and stuff around, it gets pretty messy before the end of the week. We make the Freshmen clean it out. There they go now."

A dozen "supes" filed slowly into the building with brooms and shovels. Pubby could n't have looked more interested if they had been crowned heads of Europe.

Just then a fine assortment of sounds broke out in the old building. The doors burst open and a young

red-headed Mick from the seventh ward near by rode
a pony down the steps and away for dear life. Behind him came a double-sized gent with yard-wide
mustaches. He was dressed in a red shirt, overalls
and firearms. He was a walking museum of weap-
ons. Petey told me afterward that he had borrowed
him from the roundhouse near by, and that for a
box of cigars he had kindly consented to play the
part of an irritable arsenal for one afternoon only.

"That's the janitor," said Petey in an awestruck
whisper. "Get behind a tree, quick. He's sure
some vexed. He hates to have the boys ride their
ponies into classroom."

We got a fine view of the janitor as he swept past.
He was a regular volcano in pants. Never have I
heard the English language more richly embossed
with profanity. Firing a fat locomotive up the grades
around Siwash with bad coal gives a man great
talent in expression. We listened to him with awe.
Pubby was entranced. He asked me if it would be
safe to take anything down in his notebook, and when
I promised to protect him he wrote three pages.

By this time the campus was filling up. Word
had gotten around the real college that the big show
of the season was being pulled off up at Dillpickle,
and the students were arriving by the dozen. We
were getting pretty nervous. The new arrivals
were n't coached, and sooner or later they were bound
to give the snap away. We decided to introduce our
guest to the president. If we could keep things

quiet another half hour all would be safe, Petey assured us.

We took the Reverend up to the main entrance, Petey's thinker working like a well-oiled machine all the way. He pointed out the tree where they hanged a horse thief, and Pubby made us wait till he had gotten a leaf from it. The Senior classes at Dillpickle had had the custom of hauling boulders on to the campus as graduation presents. Petey explained that each boulder marked the resting place of some student whose career had been foreshortened accidentally, and he described several of the tragedies — invented them right off the reel. Pubby was so interested he did n't care who saw his notebook. When Petey told him how a pack of timber wolves had besieged the school for nine days and nights, four years before, he almost cried because there was no photograph of the scene handy. We had to promise him a wolf skin to comfort him.

Dillpickle Academy was a plain old brick building, with one of those cupolas which were so popular among schools and colleges forty years ago. I don't know just what mysterious effect a cupola has on education, but it was considered necessary at that time. In front of the building was a wide stone porch. Inside we could see half a dozen dogs and a horse. Pubby looked a bushel of exclamation points when Petey explained that they belonged to the president. He looked a lot more when he saw a counter with a fine assortment of chewing tobacco and pipes on it. That, Petey whispered to me, was his masterpiece. He had borrowed the whole thing from a corner grocery store.

Petey had just put his eye to the window of the president's room, ostensibly to find out whether Prexy was in a good humor and in reality to find out whether Kennedy, an old grad who had consented to play the part, was on duty, when one of the boys hurried up and grabbed me.

" Just evaporate as fast as you can," he whispered; " there are six cops on the way out. They 're going to pinch the whole bunch of us."

Now this was a fine predicament for a young and promising college — to be arrested by six lowly cops on its own campus, in the act of showing a distinguished visitor how it ran the earth, and was particular Hades with the trigger-finger! Bangs was showing Pubby the window through which the Professor of Arithmetic had thrown him the term before, and I told Petey. He sat down and cried.

"After all this work and just as we had it cinched!" he moaned. "I 'll quit school to-morrow and devote my life to poisoning policemen. This has made an anarchist of me."

There was nothing to do. We could n't very well explain that the college would now have to run away and hide because some enthusiastic Freshman had fired a horse-pistol on the streets of Jonesville. I looked at the crowd of fantastic students getting ready to bolt for the fence. I looked at our victim, fairly punching words into his notebook. It was the brightest young dream that was ever busted by a fat loafer in brass buttons. Then I saw Ole Skjarsen and had my one big inspiration.

"Excuse me," I said, rushing over to Pubby, "but you'll have to mosey right out of here. There's Ole Skjarsen, and he looks ugly."

"Oh, my word!" said Pubby; he remembered Ole from the night before.

"Right around the building!" yelled Petey, grabbing the cue. Naturally Ole heard him and saw those whiskers. "Har's das spy!" he yelled. "Kill him, fallers; he ban a spy!" We dashed around the building, Ole following us. And then, because the cops had arrived at the front gate, the whole mob thundered after us.

Well, sir, you never saw a more successful race in your life. There were no less than a hundred Siwash students behind us, and, though no one but Ole Skjarsen had any interest in us, they were all trying to break the sprint record in our direction, it being the line of least resistance. And, say! We certainly had misjudged the Reverend Ponsonby Diggs. He may have been fat, but how he could run! His work was phenomenal. I think he must have been on a track team himself at some earlier part of his career, for the way he steamed away from the gang would have reminded you of the *Lusitania* racing the Statue of Liberty. He lost his cap. He shed his long black coat. He rolled over the fence

He may have been fat, but how he could run!

Page 132

at the rear of the campus without even hesitating, and the last we saw of him he was going down the road out of Jonesville into the west, his legs revolving in a blue haze. Even if we had wanted to stop him, we could n't have caught him. And besides, Ole caught Petey and me just outside of the campus and we had to do some twenty-nine-story-tall explaining to keep from getting punched for harboring spies. No one had thought to put him next to the game.

That all? Goodness, no! We cleaned up for a week and had been so good that the Faculty had about decided that nothing had happened when the Reverend Ponsonby Diggs appeared in Jonesville again. He came with a United States marshal for a bodyguard, too. He had footed it to the next town, it seems, and had wired the nearest British consul that he had been attacked by savages at Siwash College and robbed of all his baggage. They say he demanded battleships or a Hague conference, or something of the sort, and that the consul's office asked a Government officer to go out and pacify him. They stepped off the train at the Union Station and went right up to college — only four blocks away.

Petey and I remained considerably invisible, but the boys tell me that the look on the Reverend's face when he arrived at the real Siwash was worth perpetuating in bronze. He went up the fine old avenue, past the fine new buildings, in a daze; and when our good old Prexy, who had him skinned forty ways for dignity, shook hands with him and handed him a little talk that was a saturated solution of Latin, he could n't even say " most extraordinary." You can realize how far gone he was.

Some of the boys got hold of the marshal that day and told him the story. He laughed from four p. m. until midnight, with only three stops for refreshments. The Reverend Pubby Diggs stayed three days as the guest of the Faculty and he did n't get up nerve enough in all that time to talk business. We saw him at chapel where he could n't see us, and he looked like a man who had suddenly discovered, while falling out of his aeroplane, that somebody had removed the earth and had left no address behind. His baggage mysteriously appeared at his room in the hotel on the first night, and when he left he had n't recovered consciousness sufficiently to inquire where it came from. I think he went right back to England when he left Siwash, and I 'll bet that by now he has almost concluded that some one had been playing a joke on him. You give those Englishmen time and they will catch on to almost anything.

CHAPTER VI

THE GREEK DOUBLE CROSS

SUFFERING bear-cats! Say! excuse me while I take a long rest, Jim. I need it. I've just read a piece of information in this letter that makes me tired all over.

What is it? Oh, just another variety of competition smothered with a gentlemanly agreement — that's all; another bright-eyed little trust formed and another readjustment of affairs on a business basis. We old fellows need n't break our necks to get back to Siwash and the frat this fall, they write me. Of course they'll be delighted to see us and all that; but there's no burning need for us and we need n't jump any jobs to report in time to put the brands on the Freshmen and rescue them from the noisome Alfalfa Delts and Sigh Whoops — because there is n't going to be any rescuing this fall.

They've had an agreement at Siwash. They're going to approach the Freshies under strict rules. No parties. No dinners at the houses. No abductions. No big, tall talk about pledging to-night or staggering through a twilight life to a frowzy-headed and unimportant old age in some bum bunch. All

done away with. Everything nice and orderly.
Freshman arrives. You take his name and address.
Call on him, attended by referees. Maintain a general temperature of not more than sixty-five when
you meet him on the campus. Buy him one ten-cent
cigar during the fall and introduce him to one girl
— age, complexion and hypnotic power to be carefully regulated by the rushing committee. Then
you send him a little engraved invitation to amalga-
mate with you; and when he answers, per the self-
addressed envelope inclosed, you are to love him like
a brother for the next three and a half years. Gee!
how that makes me ache!

Think of it! And at old Siwash, too! — Siwash,
where we never considered a pledge safe until we
had him tied up in a back room, with our colors
on him and a guard around the house! That settles
me. I've always yearned to go back and cavort over
the campus in the fall when college opened; but
not for me no more! Why, if I went back there
and got into the rushing game, first thing I knew
they'd have me run up before a pan-Hellenic council, charged with giving an eligible Freshman more
than two fingers when I shook hands with him;
and I'd be ridden out of town on a rail for rushing in an undignified manner.

Rushing? What's rushing? Oh, yes; I forgot
that you never participated in that delicious form
of insanity known as a fall term in college. Rushing is a cross between proposing to a girl and abduct-

ing a coyote. Rushing a man for a frat is trying
to make him believe that to belong to it is joy and
inspiration, and to belong to any other means misery
and an early tomb; that all the best men in college
either belong to your frat or could n't get in; that
you 're the best fellows on earth, and that you 're
crazy to have him, and that he is a coming Senator;
that you can't live without him; that the other gang
can't appreciate him; that you never ask men twice;
that you don't care much for him anyway, and that
you are just as likely as not to withdraw the spike
any minute if you should happen to get tired of the
cut of his trousers; that your crowd can make him
class president and the other crowds can make him
fine mausoleums; that you love him like real brothers
and that he has already bound himself in honor to
pledge — and that if he does n't he will regret it all
his life; and, besides, you will punch his head if
he does n't put on the colors. That 's rushing for
you.

What 's my crowd? Why, the Eta Bita Pie, of
course. Could n't you tell that from my skyscraper
brow? We Eta Bites are so much better than any
other frat that we break down and cry now and
then when we think of the poor chaps who can't belong to us. We 're bigger, grander, nobler and
tighter about the chest than any other gang. We 've
turned out more Senators, Congressmen, Supreme
Justices, near-Presidents, captains of industry, for-
eign ambassadors and football captains than any two

of them. We own more frat houses, win more college elections, know more about neckties and girls, wear louder vests and put more cross-hatch effects on our neophytes than any three of them. We're so immeasurably ahead of everything with a Greek-letter name that every Freshman of taste and discrimination turns down everything else and waits until we crook our little finger at him. Of course, sometimes we make a mistake and ask some fellow that is n't a man of taste and discrimination; he proves it by going into some other frat; and that, of course, keeps all the men of poor judgment out of our gang and puts them in the others. Regular automatic dispensation of Providence, is n't it?

It 's been a long time since I had a chance to gather with the brethren back at Siwash and agree with them how glorious we are, but this note brings it all back. My! how I 'd like this minute to go back about ten years and cluster around our big grate fire, which used to make the Delta Kaps so crazy with envy. Those were the good old days when we came back to college in the fall, looked over the haycrop in the Freshman class, picked out the likeliest seed repositories, and then proceeded to carve them out from the clutches of a round dozen rival frats, each one crazy to get a spike into every new student who looked as if he might be president of the Senior class and an authority on cotillons some day. No namby-pamby, drop-three-and-carry-one crochet effects about our rushing those days!

We just stood up on our hind legs and scrapped it out. For concentrated, triple-distilled, double-X excitement, the first three weeks of college, with every frat breaking its collective neck to get a habeas corpus on the same six or eight men, had a suffragette riot in the House of Parliament beaten down to a dove-coo.

There was nothing that made us love a Freshman so hard as to have about six other frats after him. I've seen women buy hats the same way. They've got to beat some other woman to a hat before they can really appreciate it. And when we could swat half a dozen rival frats over the heart by waltzing a good-looking young chap down the walk to chapel with our colors on his coat, and could watch them turning green and purple and clawing for air — well, I guess it beat getting elected to Congress or marrying an heiress-apparent for pure, unadulterated, unspeckled joy!

Competition was getting mighty scarce in the country even then. There were understandings between railroad magnates and beef kings and biscuit makers — and even the ministers had a scale of wedding fees. But competition had a happy home on our campus. About the best we had been able to do had been to agree not to burn down each other's frat houses while we were haltering the Freshmen. I've seen nine frats, with a total of one hundred and fifty members, sitting up nights for a week at a time working out plans to despoil each other of a runty little fellow in a pancake hat, whose only accomplishment was playing the piano with his feet. One frat wanted him and that started the others.

Of course we'd have got along better if we'd put the whole Freshman class in cold storage until we could have found out who the good men were and who the spoiled fruit might be. We were just as likely to fall in love with a suit of clothes as with a future class orator. We took in one man once because he bought a pair of patent-leather tan shoes in his Junior year. We argued that, if he had the nerve to wear the things to his Y. M. C. A. meetings, there must be some originality in him after all — and we took a chance. We won. But it's a risky business. Once five frats rushed a fellow for a month because of the beautiful clothes he wore — and just after the victorious bunch had initiated him a clothing house came down on the young man and took the whole outfit. You can't always tell at first sight. But then, I don't know but that college fraternities exercise as much care and judgment in picking brothers as women do in picking husbands. Many a woman has married a fine mustache or a bunch of noble clothes and has taken the thing that wore them on spec. That's one more than we ever did. You could fool us with clothes; but the man who came to Siwash with a mustache had to flock by himself. He and his whiskers were considered to be enough company for each other.

There were plenty of frats in Siwash to make

things interesting in the fall. There were the Alfalfa
Delts, who had a house in the same block with us
and were snobbish just because they had initiated
a locomotive works, two railroads and a pickle factory. Then there were the Sigh Whoopsilons, who
got to Siwash first and who regarded the rest of us
with the same kindly tolerance with which the
Indians regarded Daniel Boone. And there were
the Chi Yis, who fought society hard and always
had their picture taken for the college annual in
dress suits. Many 's the time I 've loaned my dress
suit to drape over some green young Chi Yi, so
that the annual picture could show an unbroken row
of open-faced vests. And there were the Shi Delts,
who were a bold, bad bunch; and the Fli Gammas,
who were good, pious boys, about as exciting as a
smooth-running prayer-meeting; and the Delta
Kappa Sonofaguns, who got every political office
either by electing a member or initiating one; and
the Delta Flushes; and the Mu Kow Moos; the
Sigma Numerous; and two or three others that we
did n't lie awake nights worrying about. Every one
of these bunches had one burning ambition — that
was to initiate the very best men in the Freshman
class every fall. That made it necessary for us, in
order to maintain our proud position, to disappoint
each one of them every year and to make ourselves
about as popular as the directors of a fresh-air. and
drinking-water trust.

Of course we always disappointed them. Would n't

admit it if we did n't. But, holy mackerel! what a
job it was! Herding a bunch of green and timid
and nervous and contrary youngsters past all the
temptations and pitfalls and confidence games and
blarneyfests put up by a dozen frats, and landing
the bunch in a crowd that it had never heard of two
weeks before, is as bad as trying to herd a bunch
of whales into a fishpond with nothing but hot air
for gads. It took diplomacy, pugnacity and psychological moments, I tell you; and it took more: it·
took ingenuity and inventiveness and cheek and
second sight and cool heads in time of trouble and
long heads on the job, from daybreak to daybreak.
I 'd rather go out and sell battleships to farmers, so
far as the toughness of the job is concerned, than
to tackle the job of persuading a wise young high-
school product with two chums in another frat that
my bunch and he were made for each other. What
did he care for our glorious history? We had to
use other means of getting him. We had to hypno-
tize him, daze him, waft him off his feet; and if
necessary we had to get the other frats to help us.
How? Oh, you never know just how until you have
to; and then you slip your scheme wheels into gear
and do it. You just have to; that 's all. It 's like
running away from a bear. You know you can't,
but you 've got to; and so you do.

Makes me smile now when I think of some of the
desperate crises that used to roll up around old Eta
Bita Pie like a tornado convention and threaten to

engulf the bright, beautiful world and turn it into
a howling desert, peopled only by Delta Kappa
Whoops and other undesirables. I'm far enough
away, now, to forget the heart-bursting suspense and
to see only the humor of it. Once I remember the
Shi Delts, in spite of everything we could do, managed so to befog the brain of the Freshman class
president that he cut a date with us and sequestered
himself in the Shi Delt house in an upper back
room, with the horrible intention of pledging himself
the next morning. Four of the largest Shi Delts
sat on the front porch that evening and the telephone
got paralysis right after supper. They had told the
boy that if he joined them he would probably have
to leave school in his Junior year to become governor;
and he did n't want to see any of us for fear we
would wake him up. I chuckle yet when I think
of those four big bruisers sitting on the front porch
and guarding their property while I was shinning up
the corner post of the back porch, leaving a part of
my trousers fluttering on a nail and ordering the
youngster in a blood-curdling whisper to hand down
his coat, unless he wanted to lose forever his chance
of being captain of the football team in his Sophomore year. He weighed the governorship against the
captaincy for a minute, but the right triumphed and
he handed down his coat. I sewed a big bunch of
our colors on it, discoursed with him fraternally
while balancing on the slanting roof, shook hands
with him in a solemn, ritualistic way and bade him

be firm the next morning. When the Shi Delts came in and found that Freshman pledged to another gang they had a convulsion that lasted a week; and to this day they don't know how the crime was committed.

There was another Freshman, I remember, who was led violently astray by the Chi Yis and was about to pledge to them under the belief that their gang contained every man of note in the United States. We had to get him over to the house and palm off a lot of our alumni as leading actors and authors, who had dropped in to dinner, before he was sufficiently impressed to reason with us. Of course this is not what the English would call " rully sporting, don't you know! " but in our consciences it was all classified as revenge. We got the same doses. Pillings, of the Mu Kow Moos, pulled one of our spikes out in beautiful fashion once by impersonating our landlord. He rushed up the steps just as a Freshman rushee was starting down all alone and demanded the rent for six months on the spot, threatening to throw us out into the street that minute. The Freshman hesitated just long enough to get his clothes out of the house, and we did n't know for a month what had frozen his feet.

The Fli Gams were n't so slow, either. They found out once that one of the men we were just about to land had a great disgust for two of our men. What did one of their alumni do but happen craftily over our way and mention in the most

casual manner the undying admiration that the boy
had for those two? Of course we sandwiched him
between them for a week — and of course we were
pained and grieved when he tossed us into the discard; but we got even with them the next year. We
picked up an eminent young pugilist, who made his
headquarters in the next town, and for a little con-
sideration and a suit of clothes that was a regular
college yell we got him to hang around the campus for
a week. We rushed him terrifically for a day and
then managed to let the Fli Gams get him. They
rushed him for a week in spite of our carefully
regulated indignation and then proposed to him.
When he told them that he might consider coming
to school — as soon as he had gone South and had
cleaned up a couple of good scraps — they let out
an awful shriek and fumigated the house. They
were nice young chaps, but no judge of a pugilist.
They expected to be able to see his hoofs.

Well, it was this way every year all fall. Ding-
dong, bing-bang, give and take, no quarter and pretty
nearly everything fair. As I said, it was n't considered exactly proper to burn a rival frat house
in order to distract the attention of the occupants
while they were entertaining a Freshman, but otherwise we did pretty nearly what we pleased to each
other — only being careful to do it first. Of course
a lot of things are fair in love and war that would
not be considered strictly ethical in a game of croquet. And rushing a Freshman is as near like love

as anything I know of. It is n't that we love the
Freshman so much. When I think of some of the
trash we fought over and lost I have to laugh. But
we could n't bear the idea of losing him. To sit by
and watch another gang win the affections of a young
fellow who you know is designed by Nature for your
frat and the football team; to note him gradually
breaking off the desperate chumminess that has
grown up between you in the last forty-eight hours;
to think that in another day he will have on the
pledge colors of another fraternity and will be lost
to you forever and ever and ever, and then some —
what is losing a mere girl to some other fellow compared with that? Of course I realize now that, even
if a Freshman does join another frat, you can eventually get chummy with him again after college days
are over if you find him worth crossing the street to
see; and I find myself lending money to Shi Delts
and borrowing it from Delta Whoops just as freely
as if they were Eta Bites. But somehow you don't
learn these things in time to save your poor old
nerves in college.

When I was in school the Alfalfa Delts, the Sigh
Whoopsilons and the Chi Yis were giving us a horrible race. I 'm willing to admit it now, though I 'd
have fought Jeffries before doing it ten years ago.
Each fall was one long whirlwind. The President
of the United States in an office-seekers' convention
would have had a placid time compared with the
Freshmen. We did n't exactly use real axes on each

Naturally I was somewhat dazzled

Page 147

other and we didn't actually tear any Freshman in
two pieces, but we came as near the limit as was
comfortable. No frat was safe for a minute with
its guests. If you tried to feed 'em there was kerosene in the ice cream. If you entertained them some
frat with a better quartet worked outside the house.
If you took them out to call the parlor would fill up
with riffraff in no time; and if you took your eye
off your victim for a minute he was gone — some
other gang had got him. I sometimes think some
of the crowds knew how to palm Freshmen the way
magicians do, from the way they disappeared.

Even the girls took a hand in it. When I was a
Sophomore I was intrusted with the task of leading
a Freshman three blocks down to Browning Hall to
call on one of our solid girls, and before I had gone
a block two Senior girls met us. They were bare
acquaintances of mine, being strong Delta Kap.
allies, and they usually managed to see me only after
a severe effort; but this time you'd have thought
I was a whole regiment of fiancés. They literally
fell on my neck. It was cruel of me, they declared,
to be so unsociable. There I was, a football hero —
I'd just broken my rib on the scrub team — and
every girl in school was dying to tell me how grand
it was to suffer for one's college; and yet I wouldn't
so much as hint that I wanted to come to the sorority
parties — and lots more talk of the same kind.
Naturally I was somewhat dazzled and I'd walked
about half a block with the prettiest one before I

noticed that the other one was steering Freshie the other way. I turned around and never even said "Good day" to that girl; but it was too late. About a dozen Delta Kaps appeared out of the ground and tried to look surprised as they gathered around that scared little Freshman and engulfed him. We never saw him again — that is, in his innocent condition — and the boys would n't even trust me with the pledges we were rushing around for bait the rest of the fall term. Bait? Oh, yes. Sometimes we 'd pledge a man on the quiet and leave him out a week or two, so that plenty of frats could bid him — made them appreciate his worth, you know, and got every one well acquainted.

By the time I was a Senior the competition was desperate. We spent the summers scouring the country for prospects and we spent the first week of school smuggling our trophies into our houses and pledging them, without giving the other fellow a look in — that is, we tried to. We came back fairly strong in my Senior year, with a good bunch of prospects; but the one that excited us most was a telegram from Snooty Vincent in Chicago. It was brief and erratic, like Snooty himself, and read as follows:

Freshman named Smith will register from Chicago. Son of old .man Smith, multimillionaire. Kid 's a comer. Get him sure! SNOOTY.

That was all. One of the half million Smiths of
Chicago was coming to college — age, weight, complexion, habits and time of arrival unknown. That
telegram qualified Snooty for the paresis ward. We
did n't even know what Smith his millionaire father
was. The world is full of Smiths who are pestered
by automobile agents. All we knew was the fact
that we had to find him, grab him, sequester him
where no meddling Alfalfa Delt or Chi Yi could
find him, and make him fall in love with us inside
of forty-eight hours. Then we could lead him forth,
with the colors and his *art-nouveau* clothes on, spread
the glad news — and there would n't have to be any
more rushing that fall. ,We 'd just sit back and take
our pick.

We sat back and built brains full of air-castles
for about three minutes — and then got busy. It
was matriculation day. There were half a dozen
trains to come yet from Chicago on various roads.
We had to meet them all, pick out the right man by
his aura or by the way the porter looked when he
tipped him, and grab him out from under the rave-
nous foe. The next train was due in ten minutes and
the depot was a mile away. We sent Crawford down.
He was trying for the distance runs anyway.

The rest of us went out to show a couple of classy
boys from a big prep school how to register and find
a room, and pick out textbooks; and incidentally
how to distinguish a crowd of magnificent young
student leaders from eleven wrangling bunches of

Petey grabbed his hat and discharged himself toward the depot. We brought in those big prep school boys and tried to give them the time of their lives, but our hearts were n't in it. We were thinking of those Mu Kow Moos — that frat of all others — blissfully towing home a prize they'd stumbled onto and did n't know anything about! We thought of those beautifully designed air-castles we were hoping to move into and we got pumpkins in our throats. Stung on the first day of school by a bunch that had to wear their pins on their neckties to keep from being mistaken for a literary society! Oh, thunder! We went in to dinner all smeared up with gloom. Then the door opened and Petey came in. He was five feet five, Petey was, but he stooped when he came under the chandelier. He had a suitcase in one hand and a stranger in the other.

"Boys," he said, "I want you to meet Mr. Smith, of Chicago."

* * *

At first glance you would n't have taken Smith for a perambulating national bank, with a wheelbarrow of spending-money every month. He was well-enough dressed and all that, but he did n't loom up in any mountainous fashion as to looks. He was runty and his hair was a kind of discouraged red. He had freckles, too, and he was so bashful that his voice blushed when he used it. He did n't have a word to say until dinner, when he said "thank you" to Sam, the waiter. Altogether he was so meek that he had us worried; but then, as Allie Bangs said, you can't always tell about these multimillionaires. Some of them did n't have the nerve of a mouse. He 'd seen millionaires in New York, he said, who were afraid of cab drivers.

"And besides," said Petey, when a few of us were talking it over after dinner, "I 'd never have got him if he had n't been so meek. I was determined that no Mu Kow Moo was going to hang anything on us; and when I saw the three of them coming I waded right in. Allison and Briggs, those two dumb Juniors, were doing the steering. It was like taking candy from the baby. I just fell right into them and took about five minutes to tell those two how glad I was to see them back. I introduced myself to Smith; and — would you believe it ? — he was still carrying his suitcase! I grabbed it and apologized for not having carried it all the way up from the station. You should have seen those yaps scowl. They wanted to shred me up, but I never noticed them again. I pointed out all the sights to Smith and told him his friends had written me about him. There was so little room on the sidewalk that I suggested we two walk ahead; and I shoved him right into the middle of the walk and made Allison and Briggs fall behind. I had a piece of luck just then. Old Pete and his sawed-off cab came by and I flagged him in a minute. I shoved Smith in and got in after him. Then I told the two babes that I could take care of Smith all right and that

there was no need of their walking clear up to the
house. After that I shut the door and we came
away. If looks could kill I'd be tuning up my
harp this minute. Say, if I didn't have any more
nerve than those two I'd get a permit from the
city to live. And all the time Smith never made a
kick. I had him hypnotized. Now I'm going in
and make him jump through a hoop."

We should have been very happy — and we would
have been, but just then Symington came in with
some astounding news. The Alfalfa Delts had a
man named Smith, of Chicago, over at their house.
He was on the front porch, with the whole gang
around him; and from the looks of things they'd
have him benevolently assimilated before twenty-
four hours. Naturally this created a tremendous lot
of emotion around our house. It was a serious situation. We might have the right Smith and then
again we might have a Smith who would be borrowing money for car fare inside of ten minutes. We
had to find out which Smith it was before we tampered with his young affections.

Did you ever snuggle up to a young captain of
industry and ask him who his father was and whether
he was important enough in the business world to
be indicted by the Government for anything? That
was the job we tackled that night. Smith was meek
enough, but somehow even Petey's nerve had its
limits. We approached the subject from every corner of the compass. We led up to it, we beat around

it — and finally we got desperate and led the boy
up to it. But he was too shy to come down with
the information. Yes, he lived in Chicago. Oh, on
the North Side. Yes, he guessed the stock market
was stronger. Yes, the Annex was a great hotel.
No, he did n't know whether they were going to
put a tower on the Board of Trade or not. Yes,
the Lake Shore Drive was dusty in summer. —
[Good!] — He would n't care to live on it. —
[Bah!] — Altogether he was as unsatisfactory to
pump as a well full of dusty old brickbats. Just
then Rawlins, who had been scouting around seeing
what he could run against in the dark of the moon,
arrived with the stunning information that the Chi
Yis had a man named Smith, of Oak Park, at their
house and that every corner of the lawn was guarded
by picked men!

When we got this news most of us went upstairs
and bathed our heads in cold water. Oak Park
sounded even more suspicious than Chicago. It 's
a solid mahogany suburb and everybody there is
somebody or other. You have to get initiated into
the place just as if it were a secret society, it 's so
exclusive. That meant there were three Smiths from
Chicago in school. We had only one Smith. We
had a one-in-three shot.

We stuck the colors on the boys from the big prep
school just to keep our hands in and went to bed
so nervous that we only slept in patches. Still, two
Chicago Smiths in other frat houses were better than

one. It meant that at least one frat was n't sure of
its man. Maybe neither one was. Our scouts had
reported that, from what they could pick up, neither
Smith had it on our Smith much in looks. That
could only mean one thing: there had been a leak
in the telegraph office again. What show has a guileless sixty-five-dollar-a-month operator against a
bunch of crafty young diplomatists? They had read
our telegram and were after the same Smith that
we were.

By morning the suspense around the house could
have been shoveled out with a pitchfork. If one
of the other frats had the right Smith and knew
it, and had pledged him during the night, there was
positively no use in living any longer. Petey, who
had shared his room with our Smith, reported that
he was now like wax in our hands. But that did n't
comfort us much. It was too confoundedly puzzling.
Maybe we had the heir to a subtreasury panting to
join us and maybe his freckles were his fortune. All
Petey had gouged out of him during the night was
the fact that his father wanted him to come to
Siwash because it was a nice, quiet place. Oh, yes;
it was deadly calm!

It could n't have been more than seven o'clock
when the telephone rang. Petey answered it. A
relative of Smith's was at the hotel and had heard
the boy was at our house. Would we please tell
him to come right down? Petey said he would and
then rang off. Then he grabbed the 'phone again

and asked Central excitedly why she had cut him off. Central said she had n't, but of course she rang the other line again.

"Hello!" said Petey blandly. "This is the Alfalfa Delt house?"

"No; it's the Chi Yi house," was the answer. Petey put the receiver up contentedly and we all turned handsprings over the library table. Fifty per cent safe, anyway. The Chi Yis were trying to sort out the Smiths, too.

It was an hour before anything else happened. Then Matheson of the Alfalfa Delts, a ponderous personage, who wore a silk hat on Sunday and did instructing, came over and asked if we had a man named Smith with us. He was to be a pupil of his, he said, and he wanted to arrange his work. Of course Matheson was hoping to get a green man at the door, but he did n't have any luck. Bangs himself let him in and let him read two or three magazines through in the library while we turned some more handsprings — in the dining room this time. The Alfalfa Delts were fishing, too. It was a fair field and no favors.

After a while Bangs told Matheson that the man named Smith presented his compliments and said it was all a mistake. His tutor's name was not Matheson, but Muttonhead. That sent Matheson away as pleasant as you please.

All that day we sat around and beat off the enemy and got beaten off ourselves. Our Smith got a

Faculty notice to appear at once and register —
that is, it got as far as the door. We sent it back
to the Chi Yi house. We sent the Alfalfa Delt
Smith a telegram from Chicago, reading: "Father
ill. Come at once." That only got as far as a door,
too. Some Alfalfa Delt got it and sent the boy back
with the answer: "So careless of father!" Blanchard called up the fire department and sent it over
to the Chi Yi house, hoping to be able to slip over
and cut out Smith in the confusion that followed;
but the game was too old. The Chi Yis had played
it themselves the year before and refused to bite.
Meantime we had found a Chi Yi alumnus in the
kitchen trying to sell a book to the cook; and in the
proceedings that followed we discovered that the
book had a ten-dollar bill in it. All around, it was
an entertaining but profitless day. By night, there
was n't another idea left in the three camps. We
sat exhausted, each clutching its Smith and glaring
at the other two.

As far as our Smith was concerned we almost
wished some one would steal him. He was about
as interesting as a pound of baking powder. What
with fishing for his Bradstreet rating, and inventing
lies to keep him from going out and seeing the town,
and watching the horizon for predatory Alfalfa
Delts and Chi Yis, we were plumb worn out. We
were so skittish that, when the bell rang about eight
o'clock, we let it ring four times more before we
answered it; and when the ringer claimed to be an

Eta Bita Pie from Muggledorfer who had come over to attend Siwash, we made him repeat pretty nearly the whole ritual before we would consider his credentials good.

He got in at last, slightly peevish at our unbrotherly welcome, and took his place in the library circle. We were explaining the whole situation to him, when Allie Bangs gave an earnest yell and stood on his head in the corner.

"What did you say your name was?" he asked the visitor after he had been set right side up again.

"Maxwell, of Fella Kappa chapter," said the latter.

"No, it is n't," said Bangs earnestly. "You ought to know your own name!" he went on severely. "It's Smith — and you 're a barb from the cornfield! You 've come to Siwash to forget how to plow and to-morrow you 're going to organize a Smith Club. Do you hear? Don't let me catch you forgetting your name now — and listen closely."

It was all as simple as beating a standpat Congressman. Maxwell was a stranger, of course. He was to pin his Eta Bita Pie pin on his undershirt and go forth in the morning a brand-new Smith, green and guileless. It was to occur to him just before chapel that a Smith Club ought to be formed and he was to post a notice to that effect. He would get a couple of well-known non-fraternity Smiths interested and have them visit the houses and see the Chicago Smiths. With all the Smiths in session

that night he ought to have no difficulty in finding
out which was the son of old man Smith. He could
be lowdown and vulgar enough to ask right out if
he wished. If he found out he was to cut out that
Smith and bring him to our house — if he had to
bind and gag him. If he did n't he was to bring
all three — if he could.

There was a quiet and most reassuring tone in
Maxwell's voice as he said: "I can." They evidently had their little troubles at Muggledorfer, too.

"After we get them here," said Bangs earnestly,
"we 'll just pledge all three. We 'll surely get the
right one that way and perhaps the other two will
not be so bad."

Upstairs, Petey Simmons was wearily explaining
.to our Smith for the ninth time that Freshmen were
not allowed to appear on the campus for the first
three days; and that it was considered good form
to keep indoors until the Sophomore rush; and that
there was n't a room left in town anyway, and he
might as well stay with us a while; and that the
police were looking for college students downtown
and locking them up, as they did each fall, to show
their authority. Blanchard relieved him of his task
and he came downstairs mopping his brow. Then
we went to work and planned details until midnight.
It was to be the plot of the century and every wheel
had to mesh.

We spent the next day in a cold perspiration.
Neither Alfalfa Delt nor Chi Yi paraded any

pledged Freshmen. They were still hunting for the right Smith, too — evidently. They fell for the Smith Club plan with such suspicious eagerness that it was plain each bunch had some nasty, low-lived scheme up its sleeves. We were righteously indignant. It was our game and they ought not to butt in. But Maxwell only smiled. He was a Napoleon, that boy was. He just waved us aside. " I 'll run this little thing the way we do at Muggledorfer," he explained. " You fellows can play a few lines of football pretty well, but when it comes to surrounding a Freshman and making a Greek out of him, I would n't take lessons from old Ulysses himself." And so we left him alone and held each other's hands and smoked and cussed — and hoped and hoped and hoped.

Maxwell went after the three Smiths himself that night. He had taken a room in an out-of-the-way part of town and his plan was to take them over there after the meeting to discuss the future good of the Smith Club. Then about a dozen of us would slide gently over there — and a curtain would have to be drawn over the woe that would ensue for the other gangs. Meanwhile, all we had to do was to sit around the house and gnaw our fingers. Maxwell called for our Smith last and he had the other two in tow. Oh, no; we did n't invite them in. Two Alfalfa Delts and three Chi Yis were sitting on our porch, visiting us. Three Chi Yis and two Eta Bita Pies were sitting on the Alfalfa Delt porch.

Four Eta Bites and two Alfalfa Delts were calling on the Chi Yi house. It was a critical moment and none of us was taking chances. We could n't keep our Smiths from wandering, but we could make sure they did n't wander into the wrong place.

Maxwell led his flock of Smiths away and we all sat and talked to each other in little short bites. The Chi Yis were nervous as rabbits. They looked at their watches every five minutes. The Alfalfa Delts listened to us with one ear and swept the other around the gloom. The night was charged with plots. Innumerable things seemed trembling in the immediate future. When the visitors excused themselves a little later, and went away very hurriedly, we learned with pleasure from one of our boys, who had been wandering around to break in a new pair of shoes or something, that the Smith meeting, which had been called for the Erosophian Hall, had been attended by four nondescript and unknown Smiths and fourteen Chi Yis, who had dropped in casually. First blood for us! Maxwell had evidently succeeded in segregating his Smiths. We expected a telephone call from his room at any minute.

We kept on expecting it until midnight and then strolled down that way. The house was dark. A very mad landlady came down in response to our earnest request and informed us that the young carouser who had rented her room had not been there that evening; and that if we were his rowdy

friends we could tell him that he would find his
trunk in the alley.   Then we went home and our
brains throbbed and gummed up all night long.

We went to chapel the next morning to keep from
going insane outright.   The Chi Yis were there looking perfectly sour.   The Alfalfa Delts on the other
hand were riotous.   Every one of them had a pleasant
greeting for us.   They slapped us on the back and
asked us how we were coming on in our rushing.
Matheson was particularly vicious.   He came over to
Bangs and put his arm around him in a friendly way.
" I am going to have dinner with my pupil to-night,"
he said triumphantly.   " He wants me to come over
and get his trunk.   Says he 's got a good room now
and he 's much obliged to you fellows for your
trouble.   Have you heard that there 's another
Smith in school — son of a big Chicago man?
There 's some great material here this fall, don't you
think ? "

Bangs tripped on Matheson's pet toe and went
away.   Something horrible had happened.   How we
hated those Alfalfa Delts!   They had stung us before, but this was a triple-expansion, double-back-
action, high-explosive sting, with a dum dum point.
We hurt all over; and the worst of it was, we had n't
really been stung yet and did n't know where it was
going to hit us.   Did you ever wait perfectly helpless while a large, taciturn wasp with a red-hot tail
was looking you over?

The Alfalfa Delts frolicked up and down college

that day, Smithless but blissful. We consoled ourselves with a couple of corking chaps whom the Delta
Flushes had been cultivating, and put the ribbons on
them in record time. Ordinarily we would have
been perfectly happy about this, but instead we were
perfectly miserable. We detailed four men at a time
to be gay and carefree with our pledges; and the
rest of us sat around and listened to our bursting
hearts. Of all the all-gone and utterly hopeless feelings, there is nothing to compare with the one you
have when your frat — the pride of the nation —
has just been tossed into the discard by some hollow-
headed Freshman.

I took my head out of my hands just before dinner and went down the street to keep a rushing
engagement. I had to pass the Alfalfa Delt house.
It hurt like barbed wire, but I had to look. I was
that miserable that it could n't have bothered me
much more, anyway, to see that wildly happy bunch.
But I did n't see it. I saw instead a crowd of fellows on the porch who made our dejection look like
disorderly conduct. There was enough gloom there
to fit out a dozen funerals, and then there would
have been enough left for a book of German phi-
losophy. The crowd looked at me and I fancied I
heard a slight gnashing of teeth. I did n't hesitate.
I just walked right up to the porch and said:
" Howdedo? Lovely evening! " says I. " How
many Smiths have you pledged to-day? "

The gang turned a dark crimson. Then Matheson

got up and came down to me. He was as safe-looking
as somebody else's bull terrier.

"We don't care to hear any more from you," he
said, clenching his words; "and it would be safer
for you to get out of here. We're done with your
whole crowd. You're lowdown skates — that's what
you are. You're dishonorable and sneaky. You're
cads! We'll get even. I give you warning. We'll
get even if it takes a hundred years."

"Thanks!" says I. "Hope it takes twice as
long." Then I went back home and let my date
take care of itself.

We went through dinner in a daze and sat around,
that night, like a bunch of vacant grins on legs.
Our grins were vacant because we didn't know why
we were grinning. We'd stung the Alfalfa Delts.
We didn't know why or how or when. But we'd
stung them! We had their word for it. Sooner or
later something would turn up in the shape of particulars; only we wished it would hurry. If it
didn't turn up sooner we were extremely likely to
burst at the seams.

It turned up about nine o'clock. There was a
commotion at the front door and Maxwell came in.
He was followed by an avalanche of Smiths. There
was our Smith, and a tall, lean Smith, and a Smith
who waddled when he walked. They were all dirty
and dusty; they all wore our pink-and-blue pledge

ribbons on their coat lapels and when they got in
the house they gave the Eta Bita Pie yell and sang
about half of the songbook. Maxwell had not only
pledged them, but he had educated them.

After we had stopped carrying the bunch about
on our shoulders, and had put the roof of the house
back, and had righted the billiard table, and persuaded the cook to come down out of a tree in the
back yard, we allowed Maxwell to tell his story.

"It was perfectly simple," he said. "Did n't
expect to be kidnapped, of course; but it's all in the
day's work. You 've no idea what a job I had
getting colors to pin on these chumps. If it had n't
been for my pink garters and a blue union suit I 'd
put on yesterday — "

We stopped Maxwell and backed him up to the
starting pole again. But he was no story-teller.
He skipped like a cheap gas engine. We had to take
the story away from him piece by piece. He 'd
dodged his Smiths down a side street, it seems, on
the plea that there were n't any more Smiths coming
— and they might as well go over to his room. All
would have been well if one Smith had n't got an
awful thirst. There was a corner drug store on the
way to the room and while the quartet were insulting
their digestions with raspberry ice-cream soda a
college man with a wicked eye came by. A few
minutes later, just as they were crossing the railroad
viaduct near Smith's home, two closed carriages
drove up and six husky villains fell upon them,

shouting: " Chi Yi forever! " And after dumping them in the carriages, they sat on them while the teams went off.

"After I 'd got my man's knee out of my neck," said Maxwell, " I did n't seem to care much whether I was kidnapped or not. It would bind us four closer together after we escaped; and, besides, I have never found kidnapping to pay — too much risk. Anyway, they drove us nothing less than twenty miles and bundled us into an old deserted house. The leader told us, with a whole lot of unnecessary embroidery, that we were to stay there until we pledged to Chi Yi if we rotted in our shoes. Then, of course, I saw through the whole thing. It was an Alfalfa Delt gang disguised as Chi Yis. The Alfalfa Delts would send another gang out the next day, rout the bogus Chi Yis and allow the poor Freshies to fall on their necks and pledge up. That used to be popular at Muggledorfer.

" I did the talking and let my knees knock together considerably. I told them that we 'd been too badly shaken up to think, but if they would let us alone that night we 'd try to learn to love them by morning. So they put us upstairs and warned us that every window was guarded; then we lay down together and I began at the first chapter and pumped those chaps full of Eta Bita Pie all night.

" It was six o'clock when they finally pledged. When the gang came up they found us adamant. ' Never! ' said I. ' We 'll pledge Alfalfa Delt or

With our colors on and four particularly wicked-looking chair legs in our hands

die martyrs to a holy cause!' Of course they did n't dare give themselves away. They could n't even shout for joy. All they could do was to wait for the rescuing party. I spent the day teaching the boys the songs and the yell in whispers; and about three o'clock I got my grand inspiration about the colors and rigged them out. Then I dug my own pin out and put on my vest and about four o'clock the rescuing party drove up. Say, you'd have laughed to see that fight! Ham-actors in Richard the Third would have made it look tame. The Chi Yis put up a fist or two, threw a brick and then cut for the timber; and the noble Alfalfa Delts burst open the door just as I got the chorus going on that grand old song:

> "'Oh, you've got to 'be an Eta Bita Pie
> Or you won't get a scarehead when you die !'

"When they saw us there, with our colors on and four particularly wicked-looking chair legs in our hands, they gave one simultaneous gasp — and say, boys, I don't believe in ghosts, but I don't see yet how they disappeared so instantaneously! And anyway, for Heaven's sake, bring out the prog. We drilled eight miles to a railroad station and my vest buttons are tickling my backbone."

Just then a telegram arrived.

"Don't look for Smith. Changed his mind and went to Jarhard!

"SNOOTY."

No wonder we could n't blast any information out of our Smiths! Oh, they were our Smiths all right — and they were n't such a bad bunch at that. The fat one turned out to be the champion mandolin teaser in school and the lean one made the debating team; while our own particular first-edition Smith won the catch-as-catch-can chess championship of the college three years later.

Just the same, I 'd like to get one fair crack at that Smith who went to Jarhard. I 'd get even for those three days, I 'll bet a few!

CHAPTER VII

HONESTLY, Bill it's so hard to keep up to date these days, that sometimes I'm afraid to go to sleep at night for fear I'll find myself in an ethnological museum when I wake up the next morning, with people making funny cracks about the strange clothes I was wearing when they caught me.

I'm not constitutionally a back number myself either. I come as near wearing next year's styles as most fellows, and I had my wrist broken cranking an automobile before most Americans believed the things would go. I was tired of this hand-chopped furniture fad years ago, and if you hand me any slang that I can't catch on the fly you'll have to make it up right now. But there's no use talking. No one man can keep up with this world all by himself. Sometimes I get to thinking I'm so far ahead that I can afford to sit down and get a breath or two, and when I get up I have to eat dust for the next year trying to catch up.

Take colleges, for instance. I've been conceited enough to think that these flappy little college boys, with their front hair brushed back down on their

necks, could n't show me anything that I was n't
tired of. I 've kept up to date on college things,
I 've always flattered myself. You might lose me
now and then on some new way of abusing lettuce
during a salad course, perhaps, but as far as looking
startled at anything that might be said or done
around a college campus goes, I 've had a notion
that I was n't in the learning class — which shows
how much I knew about it. This morning a gosling
from the old school — a Sophomore — came in and
visited with me for a few minutes, on the strength
of the fact that he knew my baby brother in high
school. We had n't talked a minute before he handed
me "pragmatism" and "zing-slingers." While I
was rolling my eyes and clawing for a foothold he
confessed that he was the best glider in college.
When I remarked that I had been somewhat of a
glider myself, but that I had preferred the twostep,
he laughed and explained that he was captain of the
aviation team — that they had three gliders and were
finishing a monoplane that had a home-made engine
with concentric cylinders.

Can you beat it? There I was, Petey Simmons'
best friend, and personally acquainted with eleven
thousand forms of college excitement, listening to
an infant with my mouth open and stopping him
every few words to say "land sakes," "dew tell"
and "what d' ye mean by that?" I never was so
humiliated in my life, but there 's no getting around
the truth. I 've been ten years out of college, and

when I go back they 'll pull the grandfather clause
on me and wheel me in early nights. I 'm a back
number and I know the symptoms. When that young
Sophomore told me the boys of Eta Bita Pie had just
spent twenty dollars apiece on a formal dance and
house party, I put up the same kind of a lecture
to him that my father gave me when I explained that
we simply had to spend five dollars apiece on our
party, or belong in the fag end of things. And I
suppose when my father's crowd blew in a couple
of dollars for a load of wood, his father reminded
him that when HE went to college they did n't coddle
themselves with fires in their dormitories. And I
suppose that some day this Sophomore will be telling
his son that when he was in college a simple little
home-made aeroplane furnished amusement for
twenty fellows, and that they never dreamed of
dropping over to the coast on Saturdays for a dip
in the surf in their private monoplanes. Oh, well,
it 's human nature and natural law, I suppose. No
use trying to put a rock on the wheels of progress
— and there 's no use trying to ride the darned
thing either. It 'll throw you every time.

When I went to college, Billy — loud pedal on that
" I " — things were different. We did n't spend our
time fooling with gliders or blow ourselves up monkeying with pragmatism. We attended strictly to
business. We were there for educational purposes
and we had no time to chase humming birds and
chicken hawks. Why, the gasoline money of a young

collegian to-day would have paid my board bills then! We did n't go to Japan on baseball tours, or lug telescopes around South America when we ought to have been studying ethics. We lived simply and plainly. There was n't an automatic piano in a single frat house when I was in college, and as for wasting our money on motion-picture shows and taxicabs — nonsense. We 'd have died first.

You see I 'm getting into practice. Some day I 'll have a son, I hope, and he 'll go back to Siwash. Just wait till he comes home at the end of the first semester and tries to put across any bills for radium stickpins and lookophonic conversations with the co-eds at Kiowa. I 'll pull a When-I-was-at-Siwash lecture on him that will make him feel like a spider on a hot stove. If I 've got to be a back number I want to romp right back far enough to have some fun out of it. I 'll make him sweat as much lugging me up to date as I had to perspire in the old days to illuminate things for Pa.

After all, there is no question at college more serious than the Pa question, anyway, Bill. It was always butting into our youthful ambitions and tying pig iron to our coat-tails when we wanted to soar. It 's simply marvelous how hard it is to educate a Pa a hundred miles or more away into the supreme importance of certain college necessities. It is n't because they forget, either. It 's because they don't realize that the world is roaring along.

I can see it all since this morning. Take my

father, for instance. There was no more generous
or liberal a Pa up to a certain point. He wanted me
to have a comfortable room and vast quantities of
good food, and he was glad to pay literary society
dues, and he would stand for frat dues; but when
it came to paying cab hire, you could jam an appro-
priation for a post-office in an enemy's district past
Joe Cannon in Congress more easily than you could
put a carriage bill through him. He just said "no"
in nine languages; said that when he went to
Siwash — "and it turned out good men then, too,
young fellow" — the girls were glad to walk to enter-
tainments through the mud; and when it was unusually muddy they were n't averse to being carried
a short distance. I believe I would have had to
lead disgusted co-eds to parties on foot through my
whole college course if I had n't happened across an
old college picture of father in a two-gallon plug
hat. That gave me an idea. I put in a bill for a
plug hat twice a year and he paid it without a murmur. Then I paid my carriage bills with the money.
Plug hats had been the peculiar form of insanity
prevalent at Siwash in his day and he thought they
were still part of the course of study.

I got along much easier than many of the boys,
too. Allie Bangs' Pa made him buy all his clothes
at home, for fear he 'd get to looking like some of the
cartoons he 'd seen in the funny papers. "Prince"
Hogboom was a wonder of a fullback, and his favorite amusement was to get out at night and try to pull

gas lamps up by the roots. He was a natural born
holy terror, but his father thought he was fitted by
nature to be a missionary, and so Hoggie had to
harness himself up in meek and long-suffering clothes
and attend Bible-study class twice a week. The
' crimes he committed by way of relieving himself after
each class were shocking. Then there was Petey Simmons, who was a perpetual sunbeam and greatly beloved because it was so easy to catch happiness from
him. And yet Petey went through school with a cloud
over his young life, in the shape of a Pa who gave him
a thousand dollars a year for expenses and would n't
allow a single cent of it to be spent for frivolity.
And he had a blanket definition for frivolity that
covered everything from dancing parties to pie at
an all-night lunch counter. By hard work Petey
could spend about four hundred dollars on necessary
expenses, and that left him six hundred dollars a year
to blow in on illuminated manuscripts, student lamps,
debating club dues and prints of the old masters.
He had to borrow money from us all through the
year, and then hold a great auction of his art trophies
and student lamps, before vacation came, in order to
pay us back.

But all of these troubles were n't even annoyances
beside what Keg Rearick had to endure. Keg was
an affectionate contraction of his real nickname —
" Keghead." He had the worst case of " Pa " I ever
heard of. He was a regular high explosive — one of
these fine, old, hair-triggered gentlemen, who consider

that they have done all the thinking that the world
needs and refuse to have any of their ideas altered
or edited in any particular. Keg had had his life
laid out for him since the day of his birth, and when
he left for Siwash — on the precise day announced
by his father eighteen years before — the old man
stood him up and discoursed with him as follows:

" My son, I am about to give you the finest education obtainable. You are to go down to Siwash and
learn how to be a credit to me. Let me impress it
on you that that is your only duty. You will meet
there companions who will try to persuade you that
there are other things to be done in college besides
becoming a scholar. You will pay no attention to
them. You are to spend your time at your books.
You are to lead your class in Latin and Greek.
Mathematics I am not so particular about. You
are to waste no time on athletics and other modern
curses of college. I shall pay your expenses and
I shall come down occasionally to see how you are
progressing. And you know me well enough to know
that if I find you deviating from the course I have
laid out in any particular, you will return home and
go into the store at six dollars a week."

That's the way Keg always repeated it to us.
With that affectionate farewell ringing in his ears
he came on down to Jonesville; and when the Eta
Bita Pies saw his honest features and his particularly
likable smile, they surrounded and assimilated him
in something less than fifteen minutes by the clock.

And then his troubles began. Keg's father had come
down the week before school and had selected a quiet
place about three miles from the college — out beyond
the cemetery in a nice lonely neighborhood, where
there was just about enough company to keep the telephone poles from getting despondent. Moreover, he
had n't given Keg any spending money.

"Education is the cheapest thing in the world,"
he roared. "You don't have to keep your pockets
full of dollars to live in the times of Homer and
Horace. I 've told them to let you have what you
need at the bookstore. For the rest, the college
library should be your haunt and the debating society
your recreation." If ever any one was getting
knowledge put down his throat with a hydraulic ram,
it certainly was Keg Rearick.

It is n't hard to imagine the result. Keg toiled
away three miles from anything interesting and got
bluer and gloomier and more anarchistic every day.
Would n't have been so bad if nobody had loved him.
Lots of fellows go through college with no particular
friends and emerge in good health and spirits. But
we had courted Keg and had tried to make it impossible for him to live without us. We liked him
and we hankered for his company. We wanted to
parade him around the campus and confer him upon
the prettiest co-ed in his boarding hall, and teach
him to sing a great variety of interesting songs, with
no particular sense to them, and snatch off two or
three important offices around school. Instead of that

he only got to say "howdy" to us between classes, and the rest of his time he spent Edward Payson Westoning back and forth from his suburban lair, without a cent in his pockets and the street-car motormen giving him the bell to get off of the track into the mud every other block.

We very soon found this wasn't going to do. Keg's spirits were down about two notches below the absolute zero. If this was college life, he said, would somebody kindly take a pair of forceps and remove it. It ached. The upshot was we made Keg steward of the frat-house table, which paid his board and room and moved him into the chapter house. He objected at first, because of what his father would say when he heard of it. But he finally concluded that anything he might say would be pleasanter than going all day without hearing anything, so he surrendered and came along.

The first night at dinner, when we pushed back our chairs and sang a few lines by way of getting ready to go upstairs and chink a little assorted learning into our headpieces, Keg cried for pure joy. He buckled down to work the way a dog takes hold of a root, and inside of a week he couldn't remember a time in his young existence when he had been unhappy. He was tossing out Greek declensions to the prof. like a geyser, and Conny Matthews, our champion Livy unraveler, had shown him how to hold a Latin verb in his teeth while he broke open the rest of the sentence. And, besides that, we had introduced

him to all the nicest girls in the college and had
assisted the glee club coach to discover that he had
a fine tenor voice. He was a sure-enough find, and
fitted into college life as if it had been made to
measure for him.

Of course all this pleasantness had to have a gloom
spot in it somewhere. Rearick's father furnished the
gloom. He was certainly the most rambunctious, most
unreconstructed and most egregious Pa that ever
tried to turn the sunshine off of a bright young
college career. Regularly once a week a letter would
come to Keg from him. It always began " When
I was in college," and it always wound up by ordering Keg to eat a few assorted lemons for the good
of his future. He was to go to morning prayer,
regularly — there had n't been any for twenty years.
He was to become as well acquainted as possible with
his professors, because of the inspiration it would give
him — fancy snuggling up to old Grubb. He was to
take a Sunday-school class at once. He was to remember above all things that though it was a disgrace to waste a minute of the precious college years
it was equally a disgrace to go through college without being self-supporting. He should by all means
learn to milk at once. He, Keg's father, had been
valet to a couple of very fine Holstein cows while he
was in college, and he attributed much of his success
to this fact. He would of course pay Keg's expenses
while he had to, but he would hold it to his discredit.
He must at once begin to find work.

This last command impressed Keg deeply, for he had been sailing along with us without a cent. He'd been earning his board and room, of course, but that was already paid for for a month out on the edge of the planet; and as it was the first time the family that owned the house had ever got a student boarder they firmly declined to rebate. It's pretty hard to butterfly joyously along with the fancy-vest gang without any other assets than unlimited credit at the bookstore, so Keg began to prowl for a job. Presently he picked up a laundry route. The laundry wagon was a favorite vehicle on which to ride to fame and knowledge in those days. By getting up early two mornings a week and working late nights, Keg managed to put away about six dollars and forty-five cents a week, providing every one paid his laundry bill. He was so pleased and tickled over the idea that he wrote to his father at once explaining that he now had plenty of work, but had had to move downtown in order to do it.

Did this please old pain-in-the-face? Not noticeably. There had been no such things as laundry wagons in his day. Students were lucky if they had a shirt to wear and one to have washed at the same time. He wrote a letter back to Keg that bit him in every paragraph. He was to give up the frivolous laundry job and get some wood to saw. That and tending cows were the only real methods of toiling through college. He, Keg's father, had received his board and room for milking cows and doing chores, and he had sometimes earned as much as three dollars a week after school hours and before breakfast sawing cord-wood at seventy-five cents a cord. It was healthful and classic. He would send his old saw by express. And he was further to remember — there were about four more pages to memorize, a headache in every page.

Good old Keg did his best to be obedient, but he had no chance. In the first place, cord-wood was phenomenally scarce in Jonesville, and anyway, people had a vicious habit of hindering the cause of education by sawing it at the wood-yards with a steam saw. There were plenty of cows in the outskirts, but they were either well provided with companions for their leisure hours, or their owners declined to allow Keg to practice on them — he knowing about as much about a cow as he did about a locomotive. And so he dawdled on with us at the chapter house, gulping down Livy, getting a strangle hold on Homer, and pulling in six or seven dollars a week at his frivolous laundry job, some of which cash he was saving up for a dress suit. And then, one day, Pa Rearick blew in for another visit and caught his son playing a mandolin in our lounging room — far, far from the nearest cyclone cellar.

To judge from the conversation that followed — we could n't help hearing it, although we went out-of-doors at once — one might have thought that Keg had been caught in a gilded den of sin, playing poker with body-snatchers. Pa Rearick simply cut loose and bombarded the neighborhood with red-hot adjectives. That he should have brought up a son to do him honor and should have found him dawdling his college moments away with loafers; fawning on the idle sons of the rich; tinkling a mandolin instead of walking with Homer; wasting time and money instead of trying to earn his way to success — " Bah," likewise " Faugh," to say nothing of other picturesque expressions of entire disgust — from all of which one would judge almost without effort that Keg was in bad, and in all over.

I suppose Keg attempted to explain. Possibly some people try to argue with a funnel-shaped cloud while it is juggling the house and the barn and the piano. Anyway the explanations were n't audible. Presently Pa Rearick announced, for most of the world to hear, that he was going to take his idle, worthless, disgraced and unspeakable nincompoop of a son back to his home and set him to weighing out dried apples for the rest of his life. Then up rose Keg and spoke quite clearly and distinctly as follows:

" No, you 're not, Dad."

" Wh-wh-wh-whowhowwy not ! " said Pa Rearick, with perfect self-possession but some difficulty.

" Because I like this college and I 'm going to stay here," said Keg. " I 'm standing well in my studies and I 'm learning a lot all around."

" All I have to say is this," said Pa Rearick. I really have n't time to repeat all of those few words, but the ukase, when it was completely out, was the

following: Keg was to have a chance to ride home
in the cars if he packed up within ten minutes.
After that he could walk home or dance home or play
his way home with his mandolin. And he was given
to understand that, when he finally arrived, the nearest substitute to a fatted calf that would be prepared
for dinner would be a plate of cold beans in the
kitchen with the hired man.

"You may stay here and dawdle with your worthless companions if you desire," shouted Pa Rearick
to a man in an adjoining county. "The lesson may
be a good one for you. I wash my hands of the
whole matter. But understand. Don't write to me
for a cent. Not one cent. You've made your bed.
Now lie on it."

With which he went away, and we tiptoed carefully
in to rearrange the shattered atmosphere and comfort
Keg. We found him looking thoughtfully at nothing,
with his hands deep in his pockets, from which about
six dollars and seventy-five cents' worth of jingle
sounded now and then. We waited patiently for
him to speak. At last he turned on us and grinned
pensively.

"Do you know, boys," he said, "as a bed-maker
I can beat the owner of that prehistoric old corn-husk
mattress out in the suburbs with one hand tied
behind me."

.   .   .   .

Of course it is a sad thing to be regarded with
indignation and disgust by one's only paternal parent,

but Keg bore up under it pretty manfully. He dug
into his work harder than ever — and he was a good
student. Latin words stuck to him like sandburrs.
That was n't his fault, of course. Some men are
born with a natural magnetism for Latin words;
and others, like myself, have to look up *quoque* as
many as nine times in a page of Mr. Horace's celebrated metrical salve-slinging. Keg went into a
literary society, too, and developed such an unholy
genius at wadding up the other fellow's words and
feeding them back to him that he made the Kiowa
debate in his Freshman year. He also chased locals
for the college paper, made his class football team,
got on the track squad and won the Freshman essay
prize. In fact, he killed it all year long and likewise
he trained all year long with his idle and vicious
companions — meaning us.

It beats all how much benefit you can get from
training with idle and vicious companions, if you
are built that way. Of course we taught him how
to play a mandolin, and how to twostep on his own
feet exclusively, and how to roll a cigarette without
carpeting the floor with tobacco, and how to make a
pretty girl wonder if she is as beautiful as all that,
without really saying it himself, and dozens of other
pretty and harmless little tricks. But that was n't
half he picked up while he was loafing away the golden
hours of his college course in our chapter house.
Conny Matthews, whose hobby was Latin verse,
plugged him up to sending in translated sonnets from

Horace for Freshman themes. Noddy Pierce showed
him how to grab the weak point in the other fellow's
debate and hang on to it through the rebuttal, while
the enemy floundered and struggled and splattered
disjointed premises all over the hall. Allie Bangs
had a bug on fencing, and because he and Keg used
to tip over everything in the basement trying to
skewer each other, they got to reading up on old
French customs of producing artistic conversations
and deaths and other things, and eventually they
wrote one of those " Ha " and " Zounds " plays for
the Dramatic Club. In fact, there 's no limit to what
you can absorb from idle and vicious companions. In
one term alone I myself picked up banjo playing,
pole vaulting, a little Spanish, a bad case of mumps,
and two flunks, simply by associating with the Eta
Bita Pie gang twenty-seven hours a day.

But nobody had to show Keg how to get jobs after
his first experience. He had a knack of scenting a
soft financial snap a mile away to leeward, and working his way through college was the least of his
troubles. It used to make me tired to see the non-
chalance with which he would sleuth up to a nice fat
thing like a baseball season program, and put away
a couple of hundred with a single turn of the wrist
and about four days' hard soliciting among the long-
suffering Jonesville merchants. I never could do it
myself. I had the popular desire to work my way
through school when I entered Siwash, and I pic-
tured myself at the end of my college career receiving

my diploma in my toil-scarred fist, without having
had a cent from home. But pshaw! I was a joke. I
mowed one lawn in my Freshman year, after hunting
for work for three weeks; and I lost that engagement
because the family decided the hired girl could do it
better. After that I gave up and took my checks
from home like a little man. In Siwash it is all
right to get sent through school, and nobody looks
down on you for it. The boys who make their own
way are very kind and never taunt you if you have
to lean on Pa. But all the same, you feel a little bit
disgraced. Why, I've seen a cotillon leader run all
the way home from a downtown store where he clerked
after school hours, in order to get into his society
harness on time; and when the winner of the Inter-
state Oratorical in my Freshman year had received
his laurel wreath and three times three times three
times three from the crazy student body, he excused
himself and went off to the house where he lived, to
fill up the hard-coal heater and pump the water for
the next day's washing.

As I started to say, some time ago, Keg proved to
be a positive genius in nailing down jobs. He had n't
been with us three months until he had presented
his laundry route to one of the boys. He did n't have
time to attend to it. He had hauled down a chapel
monitorship that paid his tuition. He got his board
and room from us for being steward, and how he
ever got the fancy eats he gave us out of four dollars
per week per appetite is an unsolved wonder. He

made twenty-five dollars in one week by introducing
a new brand of canned beans among the hash clubs.
He took orders for bookbinding on Saturdays, and
sold advertising programs for the college functions
after school hours.   More than once I borrowed ten
dollars from him that year, while I was living on
hope and meeting the mailman half-way down the
block each morning just before the first of the month.
And I was n't the only man who did it, either.

Perhaps you wonder how he had time to do all
this and to mix up in all the various departments of
student bumptiousness, besides absorbing enough information laid down and prescribed by the curriculum
to batter an " A " out of old Grubb, who hated to give
a top mark worse than most men hate to take quinine.
That 's one of the mysteries of college life.   No one
has time to do anything but the busy man.   In every
school there are a few hundred joyous loafers who
hold down an office or two, and make one team, and
then have only time to take a few hasty peeps at a
book while running for chapel; and there are a dozen
men who do the debating and the heavy thinking for
half a dozen societies, and make some athletic team,
and get their lessons and make their own living on
the side — and who always have time, somehow, to
pick up some new and pleasant pastime, like reading
up for an oration on John Randolph, of Roanoke, or
some other eminent has-been.   When I think of my
wasted years in college and of how I was always going to take hold of Psych. and Polykon and Advanced

German, and shake them as a terrier does a rat, just as soon as I had finished about three more hands of whist — oh, well, there's no use of crying about it now. What makes me the maddest is that my wife says I'm an imposingly poor whist player at that.

Keg went home with one of us for the semester holidays. And at commencement time he wrote an affectionate letter home to his volcanic old sire, and told him that he was going to stride forth into the unappreciative world and yank a living away from it that summer. That was the great ambition of almost every Siwash boy. When we were n't thinking of girls and exams in the blissful spring days, we were stalking some summer job to its lair and sitting down to wait for it. There was n't anything that a Siwash boy would n't tackle in the summer vacation. The farmer boys had a cinch, of course. They were skilled laborers; and, besides, they came back in the fall in perfect condition for the football squad. Some of the town boys became street-car conductors. The new railroad that was built into Jonesville about that time was a bonanza for us. It was no uncommon thing, the summer of my Sophomore year, to find a dozen muddy society leaders shoveling dirt in a construction crew and singing that grand old hymn composed by Petey Simmons, which ran as follows:

> *I've a blister on me heel, and me beak's begun to peel;*
> *I've an ache for every bone that's in me back.*
> *I've a feeling I could eat rubber hose and call it sweet,*
> *And me hands is warped from lugging bits of track.*

Oh, me closes they are tore, and me shoulders they are
  sore,
 And I sometimes wish that I had died a ' borning ';
And me eye is full of dirt, and there's gravel in me shirt,
  But I'm going back to Siwash in the mor-r-r-r-r-r-rning.

One of our own boys is a division superintendent
on one of the big western roads to-day, and he caught
the railroad microbe in the shovel gang.

The boys got newspaper positions and clerked in
the stores, and one or two of them tooted cornets or
other disturbances at summer-resort hotels.   One
junior, during my time, aroused the envy of the whole
college by painting the steeple of the First Baptist
Church during vacation; and when he finished the
job his class numerals were painted in big letters on
top of the ornamental knob that tipped the spire.   At
least, so he announced, and no rival class had the
nerve to investigate.

But the most popular road to prosperity during the
summer was the canvassing route.   About the last of
April various smooth young college chaps from other
schools would drift into Siwash and begin to sign
up agents for the summer.   There were three favorite
lines — books, stereopticon slides and a patent combination desk, blackboard, sewing-table, snow-shovel,
trundle-bed and ironing-board — which was sold in
vast numbers at that time by students all over the
country.   All though May the agents fished for victims.   They signed them up with contracts guaran-
teeing them back-breaking profits, and then instructed

them with great care in a variety of speeches. Speech
No. 1, introductory. Speech No. 2, to women.
Speech No. 3, clinching talk for waverers. Speech
No. 4, to parents. Speech No. 5, rebuttal to argument
that victim already has enough reading matter.
Speech No. 6, general appeal to patriotism and love
of progress. Then on Commencement day the hopeful young collegians would go forth to argue with the
calm and unresponsive farmer's wife and sell her
something that she had never needed and had never
wanted, until hypnotized by the classic eloquence of
a bright-eyed young man with his foot in the crack
of the half-opened door.

I chose the book game one summer, and went out
with about thirty others. Twenty-five of them quit at
the end of the first week. That was about the usual
proportion — but the rest of us stuck. I devastated
a swath of territory fifty miles wide and a hundred
miles long. I talked, argued, persuaded, plead,
threatened and mesmerized. I sold books to men on
twine binders, to women with their hands in the
bread dough, and once, after a farmer had come
grudgingly out to rescue me from his dog, I sold a
book to him from a tree. I worked two months,
tramped four hundred miles, told the same story of
impassioned praise for and confidence in my book
eleven hundred times, and sold sixty-five volumes at a
gross profit of seventy-nine dollars — my expenses
being eighty dollars even. But it was worth the
effort. I was a shy young thing at the beginning

of the summer, who believed that strangers would invariably bite when spoken to. When school began I was a tanned pirate who believed the world belonged to him who could grab it, and who would have walked up to a duke and sold him a book on practical farming with as much assurance as if it were a subpœna I was serving.

Keg went out with the desk crowd, and it was evident from the first minute that he was going to return a plutocrat. He sold a desk to the train brakeman on his way to his field, and another to a kind old gentleman who incautiously got into conversation with him. He raged through four counties like a plague, selling desks in farmhouses, public libraries, harness stores, banks and old folks' homes. He was the season's sensation and won a prize every month from the proud and happy company. When he had finished collecting he took a hasty run to Denver on a sight-seeing trip, and came back to Siwash that fall in a parlor car, with something over four hundred dollars in his jeans.

Naturally we would have ceased worrying about the probability of keeping Keg with us then if we had not done so long before. As a matter of fact, he was more prosperous than any of us. He had made his own money and he drew his own checks when he pleased, instead of taking them the first of the month wrapped up in a cayenne coating composed of parental remarks on extravagance and laziness. He gave away all of his little jobs to the rest of us first thing, and said he was content with what he had; but, pshaw! — when a man has the gift he can't dodge prosperity. Keg had to manage the college paper that year because no one else could do it quite so well; and it netted him about fifty dollars a month. When the glee-club manager got cold feet over the poor prospects, Keg backed a trip himself — and I hate to say how much he cleared from it. That was the first year we swept the West with our famous football team of trained mastodons; and at the earnest solicitation of about a dozen daily papers here and there, Keg dashed off something like one hundred yards of football dope at five dollars a column — sort of a literary hundred-yard dash. He used to write it between bites at the dinner table. And then to top off everything, his precious desk company came along and stole him from us early in April. It considered him too valuable a man to tramp the country selling desks, while there were other young collegians who only needed the touch of a magic tongue to get them into the great calling. So Keg made a tour of Kiowa and Muggledorfer and Hambletonian and Ogallala colleges, lining up canvassers at a net profit of something like fifty dollars per head — full or empty. When he blew in at the end of the year to spend Commencement week with us he was nothing short of an amateur Crœsus. He bulged with wealth. I remember yet the awe with which the rest of us, hoarding our last nickels at the end of the long and billful year, took a peep at the balance in his checkbook and touched him humbly for advances, great and small.

Keg had gone out the second evening of Commencement week to bring a little pleasure into the barren life of a girl who had n't been shown any attention by any one for upward of four hours. The rest of the boys were also away scattering seeds of kindness in a similar manner, and so I was alone when Pa Rearwick stumped up the walk to the chapter-house ˙ porch and glared at me.

" I want to see my boy," he said, out of the corner of his beard. He seemed to suspect that I had made him into a meat pie or otherwise done away with him.

" He 's out," I said, not very scared; " but if you want to wait for him, won't you make yourself quite at home ? "

He took a seat on the porch without a word. I went on smoking a cigarette in my most abandoned style and saying all I had to say, which was nothing. After a while Pa Rearick glared over at me again in a most belligerent manner.

" Is he well ? " he asked.

" Finer 'n silk," I answered, most disrespectfully.

" Humph ! " said he; which, being freely translated, seemed to mean: " If I had an impudent, lazy, immoral, shiftless, unlicked cub like you, I 'd grind him up for hen feed."

Much more silence. I lit another cigarette.

" Does he get enough to eat ? "

"When he has time," I said. "He's generally pretty busy."

"Playing the mandolin, I suppose."

"Most of the time," said I. "He runs the college in his odd moments."

"He wouldn't have run the Siwash I went to," said Pa Rearick grimly.

"No," said I, "you egregious timber-head, he'd have spent his time limping after Homer." But as I said it only to myself, no one was insulted.

"Has he learned anything?" said old Hostilities, after some more silence.

"Took the Sophomore Greek prize this year," I said, blowing one of the most perfect smoke rings I had ever achieved.

"I don't believe it," said Pa Rearick deliberately.

I blew another ring that was very fair, but it lacked the perfect double whirl of the first one. And presently the neatest spider phaeton that was owned by a Jonesville livery stable drew up before the house and Keg jumped out, telling a delicious chiffon vision to hold old Bucephalus until he got his topcoat. Keg was a good dresser, but I never saw him quite as letter-perfect and wholly immaculate as he was just then. He hurried up the steps, took one look, and yelled "Dad," then made a rush; and I went inside to see if I couldn't beat that smoke ring where there was not so much atmospheric disturbance.

.   .   .   .

Pa Rearick stayed the rest of the week, and after
he had interviewed certain professors the next day
he moved over to the house and stayed with us. Mrs.
Rearick came down, too, and on this account we
did n't see quite as much of Keg as we had hoped to.
The girl in chiffon did n't, either, but that 's neither
here nor there. She was only a passing fancy, anyway. By successive degrees Keg's father viewed the
rest of us with disapproval, suspicion, tolerance, be-
nevolence, interest and friendliness. But I am convinced that it was only on Keg's account. He gave us
credit for exercising unexpected good taste in liking
him. And maybe it was n't interesting to see him
thaw and melt and struggle with a stiff, wintry smile,
as a young man does with his first mustache, and
finally give himself up unreservedly to fatherly pride.
When a father has religiously put away these things
all his life for fear of spoiling a son, and finally finds
that that son is unspoilable, even by friendliness and
parental tenderness, he has a lot of pleasure to indulge
himself in during his remaining years.

It was like the old fire-eater to call us together
before he went and punished himself. I suppose it was
his sense of justice which was too keen for any good
use. " I 've misjudged my son," he said to us; " and
I want to make public admission of it. I am perhaps
a little out of date — a little old-fashioned. The
world did n't move so fast when I was a boy here.
When I was in school we saved our money and
studied. My son tells me he can't afford to save

money — that time is too precious. I don't pretend to understand all your ways, but he seems to think you have been good to him and I want to thank you for it. My son has made his way alone these two years. I threw him out to support himself. When I casually mentioned yesterday that times were very hard in the business just now, he wanted to put five hundred dollars into it. I want you to know I 'm proud of him. I hope you young gentlemen will feel free to stop and visit us when you come through our town. I must say, times seem to have changed."

Right he was. Times have changed. And here I have been dunderheading along in just his way, imagining that I was pacing them, instead of sitting on the fence and watching them go by. If I can find that little Sophomore who insulted me this morning, I 'm going to make him come to dinner and tell me some more about the way they do things this afternoon. As for to-morrow — what does he or any one else know about it?

CHAPTER VIII

FRAPPÉD FOOTBALL

AS a rule there is only about one thing to mar the joy of college days and nights and early mornings. That is the Faculty. Honestly, I used to sit up until long after bedtime every little while trying to figure out some real reason for a college Faculty. They interfere so. They are so inappropriate. Moreover, they are so confoundedly ignorant of college life.

How a professor can go through an assorted collection of brain stufferies, get so many college degrees that his name looks like Halley's Comet with an alphabet tail, and then teach college students for forty years without even taking one of them apart to find out what he is made of, beats my time! That's a college professor for you, right through. He thinks of a college student only as something to teach — whereas, of all the nineteen hundred and eighty-seven things a college student is, that is about the least important to his notion. A boy might be a cipher message on an early Assyrian brick and stand a far better chance of being understood by his professor.

A college Faculty is a collection of brains tied

together by a firm resolve — said resolve being to
find out what miscreant put plaster of Paris in the
keyhole of the president's door. It is a wet blanket
on a joyous life; it is a sort of penance provided
by Providence to make a college boy forget that he's
glad he's alive. It's a hypodermic syringe through
which the student is supposed to get wisdom. It
takes the place of conscience after you've been de-
stroying college property. When I sum it all up it
seems to me that a college Faculty is a dark, rainy
cloud in the middle of a beautiful May morning —
at least that's the way the Faculty looked to me
when I was a humble seeker after the truth in Siwash
College.

The Faculty was to boys in Siwash what indigestion
is to a jolly good fellow in the restaurant district.
It was always either among us or getting ready to land
on us. Our Faculty had thirty-two profs and thirty-
three pairs of spectacles. It also had two good average
heads of hair and considerable whiskers. It could
figure out a perihelion or a Latin bill-of-fare in a
minute, but you ought to hear it stutter when it tried
to map out the daily relaxations of a college full of
husky young hurricanes, who had come to school to
learn what life looks like from the inside. Fairy
tales in the German and tea and wafers with quo-
tations looked like a jolly good time to the Faculty;
and it couldn't understand why some of us liked
to put gunpowder in the tea.

Now don't understand me to say that there isn't

anything good about a college professor. Bless you, no! There's a lot of it. A Faculty is a lot of college profs in a state of inflammation, but individually most of the Siwash profs were nearly human at times. I look back at some of them now with awe. They really knew a lot. They knew so much that most of them are there yet; and I go back and look at them with a good deal more respect than I used to have. I'll tell you it fills a chap with awe to see a man teaching along for twenty years at eighteen hundred dollars per, and raising children, and buying books, and going off to Europe now and then on that princely sum — and coming through it all happy and content with life. I go around them nowadays with my hat off and try to persuade them that if it was n't for my sprained arm I could quote Latin almost as well as the stone dog in front of Prexy's house.

And some of them are bully good fellows, too. Nowadays they take me into their studies at Commencement and give me good cigars, making sure first that there are no undergraduates around. Why, one of the profs I worried the most, when I was a cross between a Sophomore and a spotted hyena, is as glad to see me nowadays as though I owed him money. He runs a little automobile, and I hope I may get laid out in the subway if I have n't heard him cuss in real United States when the clutch slipped. And he was the chap who used to pick out the passages in Livy that had inflammatory rheumatism and make me recite on them, and who always told

me that a student who smoked cigarettes would be
making a wise business move if he brought his hat to
recitation and left the less important part of his
head at home.

But, as I was saying, the Faculty at Siwash, like
all other Faculties, did n't know its place. It was n't
satisfied with teaching us Greek and Latin and Evidences of Christianity and tall-brow twaddle of all
sorts. It had to butt into our athletics and regulate
them. Did you ever see a farmer regulate a weed
patch with a hoe? You know how unhealthy it is
for the weeds. Well, that was the way the Faculty
regulated our athletics. It did n't believe in athletics
anyway. They were too interesting. They might
not have been sinful, but they were not literary and
they were uneconomic. Of course all the professors
admitted that good outdoor exercise was healthy
for college boys, but most of them believed that you
ought to get it in the college library out of Nature
books. And so the way they went at the real athletics,
to keep them pure and healthful, almost drove us
into the violent ward.

Those were the days at Siwash when our football
team could start out for a pleasant stroll through
any teams in our section and wonder after it had
passed the goal line, why those undersized fellows
had been jogging their elbows all the way down the
field. That was the kind of a team we built up
every fall; and it was n't half so much trouble to
keep other teams from beating it as it was to keep

the Faculty from blowing it to pieces with non-eligibility notices. There was something diabolical about that Faculty when it was wrestling with the athletic problem. It was n't human. It was like Mount Etna. You never could tell just when it would stop being lovely and quiet, and scatter ruin all over the vicinity.

Its idea of regulating athletics at Siwash was to think up excuses for flunking every man who weighed over one hundred and fifty-five and could have his toes stepped on without saying " Ouch! " And it never got the excuses thought up until the night before the most important games. The Faculty pretended to be as bland and innocent as Mary's lamb, but no one can ever tell me it did n't know what it was about. Men have to have real genius to think up the things it did. You could n't do it accidentally. When a Siwash Faculty could moon along happily all fall until twenty-four hours before the Kiowa game and then discover with regret that our two-hundred-and-twenty-pound center had mis-spelled three words in an examination paper the year before; that our two-hundred-pound backs did n't put enough rear-end collisions into their words when they read French; and that Ole Skjarsen read Latin with a Norwegian accent and was therefore too big an ignoramus to play football, I decline to be fooled. I never was fooled. Neither was Keg Rearick. But that is hurdling about three chapters.

Honestly, we used to spend one day out of six

building up our football team and the other five defending it from the Faculty. It positively hungered for a bite out of the line-up. It had us helpless. If we did n't like the way it ran things we could take our happy young college life up by the roots and transplant it to some other school, where the football team moved around the field like a parade. Theoretically, the Faculty could sit around and take our best players off the team, as fast as we developed them, for non-attention to studies. But, as a matter of fact, it was n't an easy matter. It beats all how early in the morning you have to get up to get ahead of college lads who have got it into their heads that the world will gum up on its axle and stop dead still if their innocent little pleasures are interfered with.

·I remember the fall that the Faculty decided Miller could n't play because he had n't attended chapel quite persistently enough the spring before. Miller was our center and as important to the team that year as the mainspring of a watch. The ponderous brain trust that sat on this case did n't decide it until the day before the big game with Muggledorfer; then they practically ruled that he would have to go back to last spring and take his chapel all over again. It took us all night to sidestep that outrage, but we did it. The next morning an indignation committee of fifty students met the Faculty and presented alibis that were invincible. It was demonstrated by a cloud of witnesses that Miller had been absent nine times hand-running because he

had been sitting up nights with a sick chum. The
Faculty was inexperienced that year and let him
play; but, when it found out the next day by con-
sulting the records that the chum had attended chapel
every one of those nine mornings, it got more particular than ever and its heart seemed to harden.

On the day before the Thanksgiving game that year
the Faculty held a long meeting and decided that
our two guards were ineligible. There was n't a
word of truth in it. They weighed two hundred
and twenty pounds apiece and were eligible to the
All-American team, but you could n't make the human
lexicons look at it that way. They found them de-
ficient in trigonometry and canned them off the team.
It was an outrage, because the two chaps did n't know
what trigonometry meant even and could n't take an
examination. We had to call the trig. professor out
of town by a telegram that morning and then have
the suspended men demand an immediate examination. That worked, too; but every time we managed
to preserve a glory of old Siwash, the Faculty seemed
to get a little more crabby and unreasonable and
diabolically persisted in its determination to regulate
athletics.

The next fall it was well understood when football
practice began that there was going to be war to
the knife between the Faculty and the football team.
We were meek and resigned to trouble, but you can
bet we were not going to sit around and embrace it.
The longest heads in the school made themselves into

a sort of an unofficial sidestepping committee; and we decided that if the Faculty succeeded in massacring our football team they would have to outpoint, out-foot, outflank and outscheme the whole school. Just to draw their fire, we advertised the first practice game as a deadly combat, in which the honor of Old Siwash was at stake. It was just a little romp with the State Normal, which had a team that would have had to use aeroplanes to get past our ends; but the Faculty bit. It held a special session that night and declared the center, the two backs and the captain ineligible because they had not prepared orations the spring before at the request of the rhetoric professor. That was first blood for us. We chased the Normalites all over the lot with a scrub team and Keg Rearick sat up nights the next week writing the orations. The result was we got four fine new dry-cleaned records for our four star players and the Faculty was so pleased with their fine work on those orations that we could scarcely live with it for a week.

That was only a skirmish, however. We knew very well that the sacred cause of education would come right back at us and we decided to be else-where when it struck its next blow for progress. We talked it all over with Bost, the coach, and the result was that a week before the Muggledorfer game, the last week in September, Bost gave out his line-up for the season in chapel. There were a good many surprises in the line-up to some of us. It seemed

funny that Miller should n't make the team out and
that Ole Skjarsen should have been left off; but
the best of men will slump, as Bost explained, and he
had picked the team that he thought would do the
most good for Siwash. It was a team that I would n't
have hired to chase a Shanghai rooster out of a garden patch, but the blind and happy Faculty did n't
stop to reason about its excellence. It held a meeting the night before the Muggledorfer game and
suspended nine of the men for inattention to chapel,
smoking cigarettes during vacation and other high
crimes. The whole school roared with indignation.
Bost appeared before the Faculty meeting and almost
shook his fist in Prexy's face. He told the Faculty
that it was the greatest crime of the nineteenth century; and the Faculty told him in very high-class
language to go chase himself. So Bost went sorrow-
fully out and put in the regular team as substitutes.
The next day we whipped Muggledorfer 80 to 0.

I think that would have discouraged the Faculty
if it had n't been for Professor Sillcocks. Did I
ever tell you about Professor Sillcocks? It 's a shame
if I have n't, because every one is the better and
nobler for hearing about him. He was about a
nickel's worth of near-man with Persian-lamb whiskers and the disposition of a pint of modified milk.
Crickets were bold and quarrelsome beside him. He
knew more musty history than any one in the state
and he could without flinching tell how Alexander
waded over his knees in blood; but rather than take

Our peculiar style of pushing a football right through
the thorax of the whole middle west

off his coat where the world would have seen him he would have died. He was just that modest and conventional. He had to come to his classes through the back of the campus up the hill; and they do say that one day, when half a dozen of the Kappa Kap Pajama girls were sitting on the low stone wall at the foot of the hill swinging their feet, he cruised about the horizon for a quarter of an hour waiting for them to go away in order that he might go up the hill without scorching his collar with blushes. That was the kind of a roaring lion Professor Sillcocks was.

Well, to get back from behind Robin Hood's barn, Professor Sillcocks had a great hobby. He believed that college boys should indulge in athletics, but that they should do it with their fingers crossed. Those were n't his exact words, but that was what he meant. It was noble to play games, but wicked to want to win. In his eyes a true sport was a man who would start in a foot race and come in half a mile behind carrying the other fellow's coat. Our peculiar style of pushing a football right through the thorax of the whole Middle West nearly made him shudder his shoes off and every fall in chapel he delivered a talk against the reprehensible state of mind that finds pleasure in the defeat of others. We always cheered those talks, which pleased him; but he never could understand why we did n't go out afterward and offer ourselves up to some high-school team as victims. It pained him greatly.

Naturally Professor Sillcocks participated with great enthusiasm in the work of pruning our line-up, and after the Faculty had thrown up its hands he climbed right in and led a new campaign. We had to admire the scientific way in which he went about it, too. For a man whose most violent exercise consisted of lugging books off a top shelf, and who had learned all he knew about football from the Literary Pepsin or the Bi-Weekly Review, he got onto the game in wonderful style. Somehow he managed to learn just who were our star players — what they played and how badly they were needed — and then he went to work to quarantine these players.

First thing we knew the Millersburg game, which was always a fierce affair, arrived; and on the morning of the game Bumpus and Van Eiswaggon, our two star halfbacks, got notices to forget there was such a game as football until they had taken Freshman Greek over again — they being Seniors and remembering about as much Greek as their hats would hold on a windy day. I'll tell you that mighty near floored us; but virtue will pretty nearly always triumph, and when you mix a little luck into it, it is as slippery to corner as a corporation lawyer. We had the luck. There were two big boners, Pacey and Driggs, in college who wore whiskers. There always are one or two landscape artists in college who use their faces as alfalfa farms. We took Bumpus and Van Eiswaggon and the leading man of a company that was playing at the opera house that night over to these two Napoleons of mattress stuffing and they kindly consented to be imitated for one day only. Old Booth and Barrett had a tremendous layout of whiskers in his valise and before he got through he had produced a couple of mighty close copies of Pacey and Driggs. That afternoon the two real whisker kings went out in football suits and ran signals with the team until their wind was gone. Then they went back into the gym and their improved editions came out. Most of the college cried when they found that the two eminent authorities on tonsorial art were going to try to interfere with Millersburg's ambition, but those of us who were on to the deal simply prayed. We prayed that the whiskers would n't come off. They did n't, either. It was a grand game. We won, 20 to 0; and the school went wild over Pacey and Driggs. Even Prexy came out of it for a little while and went into the gym to shake hands with them. It took lively work to detain him until we could get them stripped and laid out on the rubbing boards. They were the heroes of the school for the rest of the year and, being honest chaps, they naturally objected. But we persuaded them that they had saved the college with their whiskers; and before they graduated we begged a bunch from each of them to frame and hang up in the gym some day when the incident was n't quite so fresh.

Naturally, by this time, we believed that the Faculty ought to consider itself lucky to be allowed to hang around the college. Professor Sillcocks looked rather depressed for a day or two, but he soon cheered up and seemed to forget the team's existence. We swam right along, beating Pottawattamie, scoring sixty points on Ogallala and getting into magnificent condition for the Kiowa game on Thanksgiving. That was the game of the year for us. Time was when Kiowa used to beat us and look bored about it, but that was all in the misty past. For two years we had tramped all the lime off her goal lines; and maybe we were n't crazy to do it again! As early as October we used to sit up nights talking over our chances, and as November wore along the suspense got as painful as a good lively case of too much pie. We watched the team practise all day and dreamed of it all night. And then the blow fell.

It was n't exactly a blow. It was more like a dynamite explosion. School let out the day before Thanksgiving, and when announcement time came in chapel Professor Sillcocks got up and begged permission to make a few remarks. Then this little ninety-eight-pound thinking machine, who could n't have wrestled a kitten successfully, paralyzed half a thousand husky young students and a whole team of gladiators with the following remarks:

" I have long held, young gentlemen, that the pursuit of athletic exercises for the mere lust of winning is one of the evils of college life. It does not strengthen the mind or build up one's manhood. It does not encourage that sporting spirit which leads a man to smile in defeat or to give up his chances of winning rather than take an undue advantage. It does not make for gentleness, mildness or generosity. I have, young gentlemen, endeavored to make you see this in the past year by all the poor means at my disposal. I have not succeeded. But this morning I propose to bring it to you in a new way. As chairman of the credentials committee which passes upon the eligibility of your football players I have decided that the entire team is ineligible. If you ask for reasons, I have them. They may not, perhaps, suit you, but they suit me. These players are ineligible because they play too well. With them you cannot hope to be defeated and I am determined that the Siwash football team shall be defeated to-morrow. Your college experience must be broadened. Your football team, I understand, has not been defeated in three years. This is monstrous. All of you, except the Seniors, are totally uneducated in the art of taking defeat. This education I propose to open to you to-morrow. I have made it more certain by suspending all of what you call your second team and your scrubs — I believe that is correct. And the Faculty joins me, young gentlemen, in assuring you that if the game with Kiowa College is abandoned — abrogated — called off, I believe you express it — football will cease permanently at Siwash. Young gentlemen, accept defeat to-morrow as an opportunity and try to appreciate its great benefits. That is all."

That last was pure sarcasm. Imagine an executioner carving off his victim's head and murmuring politely, "That is all," to the said victim when he had finished! There we were, wiped out, utterly extinguished — legislated into disgrace and defeat — and all by a smiling villain who said "That is all" when he had read the death sentence!

There was n't a loophole in the decree. Sillcocks had carved the entire football talent of the school right out of it with that little list of his. We would have to play Kiowa with a bunch of rah-rah boys who had never done anything more violent than break a cane on a grandstand seat over a touchdown. The chaps who were butchered to make a Roman holiday did n't have anything at all on us. We were going to be tramped all over by our deadly rival in order to afford pleasure to a fuzzy-faced old fossil who had peculiar ideas and had us to try them out on.

I guess, if the students had had a vote on it that day, Professor Sillcocks would have been elected resident governor of Vesuvius. We seethed all day and all that night. The board of strategy met, of course, but it threw up its hands. It did n't have any first aid to the annihilated in its chest. Besides, Professor Sillcocks had n't played the game. He had just grabbed the cards. It was about to pass resolutions hailing Sillcocks as the modern Nero, when Rearick began to come down with an idea. Nowadays people pay him five thousand dollars apiece for ideas, but he used to fork them out to us gratis — and they had twice the candle-power. As soon as we saw Rearick begin to perspire we just knocked off and sat around, and it was n't two minutes before he was making a speech.

" Fellows," he said, " we 're due for a cleaning to-morrow. It 's official. The Faculty has ordered it. If I had a Faculty I 'd put kerosene on it and call the health department; but that 's neither here nor there. We 've got to lose. We 've got to let Kiowa roll us all over the field; and if we back out we 've got to give up football. Now some of you want to resign from college and some of you want to burn the chapel, but these things will not do you any good. Kiowa will beat us just the same. Therefore I propose that if we have to be beaten we make it so emphatic that no one will ever forget it. Let 's make it picturesque and instructive. Let 's show the Faculty that we can obey orders. Let 's play a game of football the way Sillcocks and his tools would like to see it. You let me pick the team now, and give me to-night and to-morrow morning to drill them, and I 'll bet Kiowa will never burn any property celebrating."

Bost was there with his head down between his knees and he said he did n't care — Rearick or Sillcocks or his satanic majesty could pick the team. As for himself, he was going to leave college and go to herding hens somewhere over two thousand miles from the Faculty. So we left it to Rearick and went home to sleep and dream murderous dreams about meeting profs in lonesome places.

The first thing I saw next morning when I went out of the house was a handbill on a telegraph pole. It was printed in red ink. It implored every Siwash student to turn out to the game that afternoon. "New team — new rules — new results!" it read. "The celebrated Sillcocks system of football will be played by the Siwash team. Attendance at this game counts five chapel cuts after Thanksgiving. Admission free. Tea will be served. You are requested to be present."

Were we present? We were — every one of us that was n't tied down to a bed. There was something promising in that announcement. Besides, the greenest of us were taken in by that chapel-cut business. Besides, it was free! College students are just like the rest of the world. They 'd go to their great-grandmother's funeral if the admission was free. Our gang put on big crêpe bows, just to be doing something, and marched into the stadium that afternoon with hats off. It was packed. Talk about promotion work. Rearick had pasted up bills until all Jonesville was red in the face. And the Faculty was there, too. Every member was present. They sat in a big special box and Sillcocks had the seat of honor. He looked as pleased as though he had just reformed a cannibal tribe. I suppose the programs did it. They announced once more that the celebrated Sillcocks system of football as worked out by the coach and Mr. Keg Rearick would be played in this game by the Siwash team. The whole town was there too,

congested with curiosity. In one big bunch sat all
the Siwash men who had ever played football, in their
best clothes and with their best girls. They were the
guests of honor at their own funeral.

The Kiowa team came trotting out — behemoths,
all of them — ready to get revenge for three painful
years. They had heard all about the massacre and
regarded it as the joke of the century on Siwash.
They also regarded it as their providential duty to
emphasize the joke — to sharpen up the point by scoring about a hundred and ten points on the scared
young greenhorns who would have to play for us. All
our ex-players stood up and gave them a big cheer
when they came. So did everybody else. It's always
a matter of policy to grin and joke while you're being
dissected. Nothing like cheerfulness. Cheerfulness
saved many a martyr from worry while he was being
eaten by a lion.

Then our gymnasium doors opened and the brand-
new and totally innocent Siwash football team came
forth. When we saw it we forgot all about Kiowa,
the Faculty, defeat, dishonor, the black future and
the disgusting present. We stood up and yelled
ourselves hoarse. Then we sat down and prepared
to enjoy ourselves something frabjous.

Rearick had used nothing less than genius in
picking that team. First in line came Blakely, a
mandolin and girl specialist, who had never done
anything more daring than buck the line at a soda
fountain. He had on football armor and a baseball

mask. Then came Andrews. Andrews specialized in poetry for the Lit magazine and commonly went by the name of Birdie, because of. an unfortunate sonnet that he had once written. Andrews wore evening dress, and carried a football in a shawl strap. Then came McMurty and Boggs, sofa-pillow punishers. They roomed together and you could have tied them both up in Ole Skjarsen's belt and had enough of it left for a handle. James, the champion featherweight fusser of the school, followed. He carried a campchair and a hot-water bottle. Petey Simmons, five feet four in his pajamas, and Jiggs Jarley, champion catch-as-catch-can-and-hold-on-tight waltzer in college, came next. Then came Bain, who weighed two hundred and seventeen pounds, had been a preacher, and was so mild that if you stood on his corns he would only ask you to get off when it was time to go to class. He was followed by Skeeter Wilson, the human dumpling, and Billings, who always carried an umbrella to classes and who had it with him then. Behind these came a great mob of camp-followers with chairs, books, rugs, flowers, lunch tables, tea-urns and guitars. It was the most sensational parade ever held at Siwash; and how we yelled and gibbered with delight when we got the full aroma of Rearick's plan!

The Kiowa men looked a little dazed, but they did n't have time to comment. The toss-up was rushed through and the two teams lined up, our team with the ball. It would have done your eyes good to see Rearick adjust it carefully on a small doily in the exact center of the field, mince up to it and kick it like an old lady urging a setting hen off the nest. A Kiowa halfback caught it and started up the field. Right at him came Birdie Andrews, hat in hand, and when the halfback arrived he bowed and asked him to stop. The runner declined. McMurty was right behind and he also begged the runner to stop. Boggs tried to buttonhole him. Skeeter Wilson, who was as fast as a trolley car, ran along with him for twenty-five yards, pleading with him to listen to reason and consent to be downed. It was no use. The halfback went over the goal line. The Kiowa delegation did n't know whether to go crazy with joy or disgust. Our end of the grandstand clapped its hands pleasantly. Down in the Faculty box one or two of the professors, who had n't forgotten every-thing this side of the Fall of Rome, wiggled uneasily and got a little bit red behind the ears.

The teams changed goals and Rearick kicked off again. This time he washed the ball carefully and changed his necktie, which had become slightly soiled. The other Kiowa half caught the ball this time; he plowed into our boys so hard that McMurty could n't get out of the way and was knocked over. Our whole team held up their hands in horror and rushed to his aid. They picked him up, washed his face, re-arranged his clothes and powdered his nose. He cried a little and wanted them to telegraph his mother to come, but a big nurse with ribbons in her cap — it was Maxwell — came out and comforted him and gave him a stick of candy half as large as a barber-pole.

By this time you could tell the Faculty a mile off. It was a bright red glow. Every root-digger in the bunch had caught on except Sillcocks. He was intensely interested and extremely grieved because the Kiowa men did not enter into the spirit of the occasion. As for the rest of the crowd, it sounded like drowning men gasping for breath. Such shrieks of pure unadulterated joy had n't been heard on the campus in years. When the teams lined up again Kiowa had got thoroughly wise. They had held a five-minute session together, had taken off their shin, nose and ear guards, had combed their hair and had put on their hats. The result was what you might call picturesque. You could hear ripping diaphragms · all over the stadium when they tripped out on the field. The two teams lined up and Rearick kicked off again. This time he had tied a big loop of ribbon around the ball; when it landed a Kiowa man stuck his forefinger through the loop and began to sidle up toward our goal, holding an imaginary skirt. Our team rushed eagerly at him, Billings and his umbrella in the lead. On every side the Kiowa players bowed to them and shook hands with them. The critical moment arrived. Billings reached the runner and promptly raised his umbrella over him and marched placidly on toward our goal. Hysterics from the bleachers. The Kiowa man did n't propose to be outdone. He stopped, removed his derby and presented the ball to Billings. Billings put his hand on his heart and declined. The Kiowa man bowed still lower and insisted. Billings bumped the ground with his forehead and would n't think of it. The Kiowa man offered the ball a third time, and we found afterward that he threatened to punch Billings' head then and there if he did n't take it. Billings gave in and took the ball.

"Siwash's ball!" we yelled joyfully. The two teams lined up for a scrimmage. Right here a difficulty arose that threatened to end the game. The opposing players insisted on gossiping with their arms around each other's necks. They would not get down to business. The referee raved — he was an imported product, with no sense of humor, and was rapidly getting congestion of the brain. "Don't hit in the clinches!" yelled some joker. For five minutes the teams gossiped. Then our quarter gave his signal — the first two bars of "Oh Promise Me" — and passed the ball to Wilson, who was fullbacking.

It was twice as interesting as an ordinary game because nobody knew what Wilson would do; in fact, he did n't seem to know himself. He stood a minute dusting off the ball carefully and manicuring his soiled nails. The Kiowa team and our boys strolled up, arm in arm. Wilson still hesitated. The Kiowa captain offered to send one of his men to carry the ball. Wilson would n't think of causing so much trouble. Our captain suggested that the ball be taken to our goal. The Kiowa captain protested that it had been there twice already. Some one suggested that they flip for goals. The captains did it. Siwash won. Calling a messenger boy, our captain sent him over to Kiowa's goal with the ball, while the two teams sat down in the middle of the field and the Kiowa captain set 'em up to gum.

By this time people were being removed from the stadium in all directions. There was a sort of purple aurora over the Faculty box that suggested apoplexy. The learned exponents of revised football looked about as comfortable as a collection of expiring beetles mounted on large steel pins — that is, all but Professor Sillcocks. He was beaming with pleasure. I never saw a man so entirely wrapped up in manly sports as he was just then. Evidently the new football suited him right down to the ground. He clapped his hands at every new atrocity; and whenever some Siwash man put his arm around a Kiowan and helped him tenderly on with the ball, he turned around to the populace behind him and nodded his head as if to say: "There, I told you so. It can be done. See?"

When the Kiowa center kicked off for the next scrimmage he introduced a novelty. He produced a large beanbag, which I presume Rearick had slipped him, kicked it about four feet and then hurriedly picked it up and presented it to one of our men. All of our boys thanked him profoundly and then lined up for the scrimmage. Immediately the Kiowa captain put his right hand behind him. Our captain guessed "thumbs up." He was right and we took the ball forward five yards. Deafening applause from the stadium. Then our captain guessed a number between one and three. Another five yards. Shrieks of joy from Siwash and desperate cries of "Hold 'em!" from the Kiowa gang. Then the Kiowa captain demanded that our captain name the English king who came after Edward VI. That was a stonewall defense, because Rearick had flunked two years running in English history. Kiowa took the ball, but the umpire butted in. It was an offside play, he declared, because it wasn't a king at all. It was a queen and it was Siwash's ball and ten yards. That made an awful row. The Kiowa captain declared that the whole incident was "very regrettable," but the umpire was firm. He gave us the ball; and on the very next down Rearick conjugated a French verb perfectly for a touchdown.

All of this was duly announced to the stadium and the excitement was intense. I guess there were as many as two hundred Chautauqua salutes after that touchdown. Both teams had tea together and our rooters' chorus sang "Juanita," while old Professor Grubb got up, with rage printed all over his face in display type, and went home. He never went near the stadium again as long as he lived, I understand.

It was a most successful occasion up to this point, but somehow college boys always overdo a thing. The strain was telling on the two teams; for, when you

come right down to it, no Siwash man loves a Kiowa
man any more fervently than a bull pup loves a cat.
The teams lined up again and began playing " ring-
around-a-rosy " to find who should make the next
touchdown, when something happened. Klingel, the
two-hundred-and-ten-pound Kiowan guard, started
it. He was just about as good a fellow as a white
rhinoceros, and an hour of entire civilization was
about all he could possibly stand. He had the beanbag and he was tired of it. Beanbags meant nothing
to him. He could n't grasp their solemn beauty. He
offered it to Petey Simmons. Petey declined, with
profuse thanks. Klingel insisted. Petey bowed very
low and swore that rather than make another touchdown on Kiowa he would suffer wild horses to tear
him into little bits. Then Klingel began to get
offside.

" You hear what I say, you little shrimp! " he said
politely. " If you don't take this thing and quit
your yawping I 'm going to make you do it."

" Listen, you overfed mountain of pork! " said
Petey, with equal cordiality. " If you don't like that
beanbag eat it. It would do you good. You don't
know beans anyway."

Then Klingel, without further argument, hit Petey
in the eye and laid him out.

Wow! Talk about irritating a hornet convention.
Klingel was a great little irritator. The whole game
had been torture for our real team, cooped up among
the ruffles in the stadium; and when they saw little

" If you don't like that bean bag eat it "

Page 220

Petey go down they gave one simultaneous roar and vaulted over the railing. It was a close race, but Ole Skjarsen beat Hogboom out by a foot. He hit Klingel first. Hogboom hit him second, third, fifth and thirty-fourth. Then the two teams closed together and for five minutes a cyclone of dust, dirt, sweaters, collars, arms, legs, hair and bright red noses swept up and down the field. The grandstand went crazy. The five hundred Kiowa rooters grabbed their canes and started in. They met about seven hundred Siwash patriots and then the whole universe exploded.

The police interfered and about half an hour later the last Siwash student was pried off the last Kiowan. It was the most disgraceful riot in the history of the college. I don't think there was a whole suit of clothes on the field when it was over; and the Siwash man who did n't have two or three knobs on his head was n't considered loyal. The girls all cried. The Faculty went home in cabs, the mayor declared martial law and the Kiowa gang walked out of town to the crossing and took the train there to avoid further hard feelings. We were all ashamed of ourselves and I think the two schools liked each other a little better after that. Anyway, we regarded the whole affair as only logical.

The Faculty held a meeting that lasted all the next day. Then it adjourned and did absolutely nothing at all except to pile upon us more theses, themes and special outrages that semester than any body of students had ever been inflicted with in a like period. The profs would n't speak to us. They regarded us as beneath notice. But when the real Kiowa game was scheduled by mutual consent, two weeks afterward, there was n't a remark from head-quarters. We played Kiowa and spread them all over the map — and not a Faculty member was in town that day.

I understand Professor Sillcocks is not yet thor-oughly persuaded that his style of football was n't a success. " But for that unfortunate riot, which comes from playing with less cultured colleges," he remarked to a Senior the next spring, " that would have been the most successful exhibition of mental control and inherent gentility ever seen at Siwash."

True, very true.

CHAPTER IX

CUPID — THAT OLD COLLEGE CHUM

WELL! Well! Well! Here's another magazine investigator who has made a great discovery. Listen to this, Sam: "Co-education, as found in American colleges, is amazingly productive of romance, and the great number of marriages resulting between the men and women in co-educational schools indicates all too plainly that love-making occupies an important part of the courses of study."

Those are his very words. Isn't he the Christopher Columbus, though! Who would have thought it? Who would have dreamt that there were any mutual admiration societies in co-educational colleges? I am amazed. What won't these investigators discover next? Why, one of them is just as likely as not to get wise to the fact that there is a hired-girl problem. You can't keep anything away from these gimlet-eyed scientists.

Oh, sure! I knew it was just about time for some kind of an off-key noise from you, you grouchy old leftover. Just because you graduated from one of those paradises in pants, where they import a car-

load of girls from all over the country to one dance a
year and worry along the rest of the time with chorus
girls and sweet young town girls who began bringing
students up by hand about the time Wm. H. Taft
was a Freshman, you think you are qualified to toss
in a few hoots about co-education. Back away, Sam!
That subject is loaded. I've had palpitations on a
college campus myself; and I want to tell you right
here that it beats having them at a stage door, or at
a summer resort, or in a parlor just around the corner from nine relatives, or in one of those short-story
conservatories, or in the United States mails, forty
ways for Sunday; and, besides, it's educational. We
co-educationalists get a four years' course in close-
coupled conversation and girl classification while you
fellows in the skirtless schools are getting the club
habit and are saving up for the privilege of dancing
with other fellows' fiancées at the proms once a
year.

Honestly, I never could see just why a fellow should
wait until he is through college before he begins
to study the science of how to make some particular
girl believe that if Adam came back he would look
at him and say: " Gee, it swells me all up to think
that chap is a descendant of mine! "

And I may be thick in my thought dome, but I
never could see any objection to marrying a classmate,
either, even though I didn't do it myself. I admit
co-educational schools are strong on matrimony.
Haven't I dug up for thirty-nine wedding presents

for old Siwash students already? And don't I get
a shiver that reaches from my collar-button down to
my heels every time I get one of those thick, stiff,
double-barreled envelopes, with "Kindly dig," or
words to that effect, on the inside? Usually they
come in pairs — the bid to the next wedding and the
bill for the last present. Why, out of sixty-five
ninety-umpters with whom I graduated, six couples
are already holding class reunions every evening;
and just the other day another of the boys, who
thought he would look farther, came back after having made a pretty thorough inspection all over the
civilized world, and camped outside of the home of
a girl in our class until she admitted that he looked
better to her than any of the rising young business
men who had bisected her orbit in the last ten years.
They're to be married this spring and I'm going
back to the wedding. Incidentally I'm going to help
pay for three more silver cups. We give a silver cup
to each class baby and each frat baby, and I've been
looking around this past year for a place where we
can buy them by the dozen.

Weddings! Why, man, a co-educational college is
a wedding factory. What of it? As far as I can
see, Old Siwash produces as many governors, congressmen and captains of industry to the graduate
as any of the single-track schools. And I notice one
thing more. You don't find any of our college couples
hanging around the divorce courts. There is a
peculiar sort of stickiness about college marriages.

They are for keeps. When a Siwash couple does n't
have anything else agreeable to talk about it can
sit down and have a lovely three months' conversation
on the good old times. It takes a mighty acrimonious
quarrel to stand a college reunion around a breakfast
table. Take it from me, you lonesome old space-
waster, with nothing but a hatrack to give you an
affectionate welcome when you come home at night,
there is no better place on earth to find good wife
material than a college campus. Of course I don't
think a man should go to college to find a wife; but
if his foot should slip, and he should marry a girl
whose sofa pillows have the same reading matter on
them as there is on his, there 's nothing to yell for
help about. Ten to one he 's drawn a prize. Girls
who go through co-educational colleges are extra fine,
hand-picked, sun-ripened, carefully wrapped-up
peaches — and I know what I 'm talking about.

How do I know? Heavens, man! did n't I go
through the Siwash peach orchard for four years?
Don't I know the game from candy to carriages?
Did n't I spend every spring in a light pink haze of
perfect bliss? And was n't all the Latin and Greek
and trigonometry and athletic junk crowded out of
my memory at the end of every college year by the
face of the most utterly, superlatively marvelous girl
in the world? And was n't it a different face every
spring? Oh, I took the entire course in girlology,
Sam! I never skipped a single recitation. I got a
Summa Cum Laudissimus in strolling, losing frat

pins, talking futures and acquiring hand-made pennants. And the only bitter thought I 've got is that' I can't come back.

You 'll never realize, my boy, how old Pa Time roller-skates by until you go back to a co-ed college ten years afterward. Here, in the busy mart of trade, I 'm a promising young infant who has got to " Yes, sir " and " No, sir " to the big ones, and be good and get to work on time for thirty years before I will be trusted to run a monopoly alone on a quiet day; but back on the Siwash Campus, Sam, I 'm a patriarch. That 's one reason why I don't go back. I 'm married and I don't care to be madly sought after, but also I don't care to make a hit as a fine old antique for a while yet, thank you. When I am forty, and have gummed up my digestion in the dollar-herding game until I wheeze for breath when I run up a column of figures, I 'll go back and have a nice comfy time in the grandpa class. But not now. The only difference between a thirty-year-old alumnus and the mummy of Rameses, to a college girl, is in favor of the mummy. It does n't come around and ask for dances.

I suppose, Sam, you think you 've been all lit up under the upper left-hand vest pocket over one or two girls in your time, but I don't believe a fellow can fall in love so far over his ears anywhere in the world as he can in Siwash College. That 's only natural, for the finest girls in the world go to Siwash — except one girl who went to another school by acci-

dent and whom I ran across about three years ago
wearing an Alfalfa Delt pin. I'll take you up to
the house to see her some time. She was too nice a
girl to wear an Alfalfa Delt pin and I just naturally
had to take it off and put on an Eta Bita Pie pin;
and somehow in the proceedings we got married —
and all I have to say about it is three cheers for the
universe!

'Anyway, as I was saying, it was as easy to fall in
love at Siwash as it was to forget to go to chapel. We
got along all right in the fall. We liked the girls
enormously and were always smashing up some football team just to please them. And, of course, we
kept ourselves all stove up financially during the winter hauling them to parties and things in Jonesville's
nine varnished cabs. It took about as much money to
support those cabs as it does to run a fleet of battleships. But it was in the spring that the real fireworks
began. Suddenly, about the first Wednesday after
the third Friday in April, the ordinary Siwash man
discovers that some girl whom he has known all year
isn't a girl at all, but a peachblow angel who is
just stopping on earth to make a better man of him
and show him what a dull, pifflish thing Paradise
would be without her. Life becomes a series of awful
blank spots, with walks on the campus between them.
He can't get his calculus because he is busy figuring
on a much more difficult problem; he is trying to
figure whether three dances with some other fellow
mean anything more to Her than charity. He gets

cold chills every time he reflects that at any minute
a member of some royal family may pass by and
notice Her, and that he will have to promote international spasms by hashing him. He realizes that
he has misspent his life; that football is a boy business; that frats are foolish, and that there ought to
be a law giving every college graduate a job paying
at least two thousand dollars a year on graduation.
He is nervous, feverish, depressed, inspired, anxious,
oblivious, glorified, annihilated, encouraged and all
cluttered up with emotion. The planet was invented
for the purpose of letting Her dig Her number three
heels into it on spring afternoons. Sunshine is important because Her hair looks better with the light
on it. Every time She frowns the weather bureau
hangs out a tornado signal, and every time She smiles
somebody puts a light-blue sash around the horizon
and a double row of million-candle-power calcium
lights clear down the future, as far as he can see.

That's what love does to a college boy in spring.
It's a kind of rose-colored brainstorm, but it very
seldom has complications. By the next fall, the
ozone is out of the air; and after a couple has gone
strolling about twice, football and the sorority rushes
butt in — and it's all over. Freshman girls are a
help, too. Beats all how much assistance a Freshman
girl can be in forgetting a Senior girl who isn't on
the premises! Even in the spring-fever period we
didn't get engaged to any extent. The nearest I
ever came to it was to ask the light of my life for

ninety-several if she would wear my frat pin forever and ever until next fall. And, let me tell you, there was n't any local of the Handholders' Union on the Siwash Campus. That's another place where you soubrette worriers have us figured out wrong. Rushing a Siwash girl was about as distant a proposition for us as trying to snuggle up to the planets in the telescopic astronomy course. For cool, pleasant and skillful unapproachability, a co-ed girl breaks all records. We just worshiped them as higher beings, and I find that a lot of Siwash boys who have married Siwash girls are still a little bit dazed about the whole affair. They can't figure how they ever had the nerve to start real businesslike negotiations.

This very high-class insulation in our love affairs caused us fellows a lot of woe once in a while. You never could tell whether or not a girl was engaged to some fellow back home. We did n't get impertinent enough to ask. I think there ought to be a law compelling a girl who comes to college engaged to some rising young merchant prince in the country store back home to wear an engagement ring around her neck, where it can be easily seen. More than once, a Siwash man who had been conservative enough to worship the same girl right through his college course and who had proposed to her on the last night of school, when the open season for thou-beside-me talk began, has found that all the time some chap has been writing her a letter a day and that she has only regarded the Siwash man as a

kind friend, and so on. Never will I forget when
Frankling got stung that way! Of course we did n't
generally know when a tragedy of this sort happened,
but in his case he brought it on himself. If he
had n't made a furry-eared songbird out of himself
when Ole Skjarsen drew his girl at the Senior class
party —

You want to know about this girl lottery business,
you say? Well, it 's plain that I shall have to begin
right back at the beginning of the Siwash social system and educate you a little at a time. Now this
class party drawing is an institution which has been
handed down at Siwash ever since the ancients went
to school before the war. You see, at Siwash, as at
most colleges, there is the fraternity problem. The
frat men give parties to the sorority girls as often as
the Dean of Women will stand for it, and every one
gets gorgeously acquainted and extremely sociable.
The non-fratters go to the Y. M. C. A. reception at
the beginning of each year and to the Commencement
exercises, and that 's about all. Of course they pick
up lots of friends among the non-sorority girls; and
I guess D. Cupid solders up about as many jobs among
them as he does among the others. But there is n't
much chance for these two tribes to mix. That was
why the class lottery was invented. It has been a
custom at Siwash, ever since there has been a Siwash,
for each class to hold a party each year. Now class
parties are held in order that pure and perfect
democracy may be promoted, and it is necessary to

take violent measures to shuffle up the people and get every one interested.   So they draw for partners. The class which is about to effervesce socially holds a meeting.   At this meeting the names of all the men are put in one hat and the names of all the girls in another.   Then two judges of impregnable honesty draw out a name from each hat simultaneously and read them to the class.

When I was at Siwash a class party was the most exciting event in college.   For uncertainty and breath-grabbing anxiety they made the football games seem as tame as a church election.   Of course everybody can't be a Venus de Milo or an Apollo with a Beveled Ear, as Petey Simmons used to call him.   Every class has its middle-aged young ladies, who are attending college to rest up from ten or fifteen years of school-teaching, and its tall young agriculturalists with restless Adam's apples, whose idea of being socially interesting is to sit all evening in the same chair making a noise like one of those $7.78-suit dummies.   That's what made the class lotteries so interesting.   The plow-chasers drew the prettiest girls in the class and the most accomplished fusser among the fellows usually drew a girl who would make the manager of a beauty parlor utter a sad shriek and throw up his job.   Of course every one was bound in honor to take what came out of the hat.   Nobody flinched and nobody renigged, but there was a lot of suppressed excitement and well-modulated regret.

I have been reasonably wicked since I left college.

Once or twice I have slapped down a silver dollar or thereabout and have watched the little ball roll round and round a pocket that meant a wagon-load of tainted tin for me; and once in a while I have placed five dollars on a pony of uncertain ability and have watched him go from ninth to second before he blew up. But I never got half the heart-ripping suspense out of these pastimes that I did out of a certain few party drawings, when I waited for my name to come out and wondered, while I looked across the hall at the girl section, whether I was going to draw the one girl in the world, any one of four or five mighty interesting runners-up, or the fat little girl in the corner with ropy hair and the general look of a person who had had a bright idea a few years before and had been convalescing from it ever since.

Talk about excitement and consequences! Those drawings kept us on the jump until the parties were pulled off. Generally the proud beauties who had been drawn by the midnight-oil destroyers did not know them, and some one had to steer the said destroyers around to be introduced. What with dragging bashful young chaps out to call and then seeing that they did n't freeze up below the ankles and get sick on the night of the party; and what with teaching them the rudiments of waltzing and giving them pointers on lawn ties; or how to charter a good seaworthy hack in case the girl lived on an unpaved street; and bracing up the fellows who had drawn blanks, and going to call on the blanks we had drawn and getting gloriously snubbed — give me a wallflower for thorns! — well, it was no cinch to run a class party. But they were grand affairs, just the same, and promoted true fellowship, besides furnishing amusement for the whole college in the off season. And, besides, I always remember them with gratitude for what they did to Frankling.

You know there are two kinds of fussers in college. There is the chap like Petey Simmons, for instance, whose heart was a directory of Siwash girls; and there is the fellow who grabs one girl and stakes out claim boards all around her for the whole four years. That was Frankling's style. He was what we always called a married man. He and Pauline Spencer were the closest corporation in college. They entered school in the same class, and he called on her every Friday night at Browning Hall and took her to every party and lecture and entertainment for the next three and a half years — except, of course, the class parties. It was one of our chief delights to watch Frankling grind his teeth when some lowbrow — as he called them — drew her name. She always had rotten luck — you never saw such luck! Once Ettleson drew her. He was a tall, silent farmer, who wore boots and a look of gloom; and he marched her through a mile of mud to the hall without saying a word, handed her to the reception committee and went over to a corner, where he sat all evening. But that wasn't so bad as the Junior she drew. His name was Slaughter. His father had a dairy at the edge of Jonesville and Slaughter decided that, as the night was cold and rainy, a carriage would be appropriate. So he scrubbed up the milk wagon thoroughly, put a lot of nice, clean straw on the floor, hung a lantern from the top for heat and drove her down to the party in state. She was game and did n't make a murmur, but Frankling made a pale-gray ass of himself. As I said, I never liked Frankling. He had a nasty, sneering way of looking at the whole school, except his own crowd. His father owned the locomotive works and he always went to Europe for his summers. He was one of those unnecessary individuals who are solemnly convinced that if you don't do things just as they do something is lacking in your mind; and, though he was perfectly bred, he was only about half as pleasant to have around as a well-behaved hyena.

I never could see what Miss Spencer saw in him, unless it was the locomotives. As far as we could tell — we never got much chance to judge — she was a real nice girl. She was a little haughty and never had much to say, and always acted as if she was a princess temporarily off the job. But she was a good scout, and proved it at the class parties by making it as pleasant as she could for the nervous nobodies who took her; while the yellow streak in Frankling was so broad there was n't enough white in him to look like a collar. That's why the whole college went crazy with delight over the Ole Skjarsen

affair. — Last station, ladies and gents. Story begins here.

   When we were Seniors Ole Skjarsen was the chief
embarrassment of the class. As a football player he
was a wonder, but as a society fritterling he was one
long catastrophe. He just could n't possibly get hep
— that was all. He was as companionable and as
good-natured as a St. Bernard pup and just as incon-
venient to have around. He dressed like a vaudeville
sketch, and the number of things he could do in an
hour, which are not generally done in low-vest and
low-neck circles, was appalling. However we all
loved Ole because of his grand and historic deeds
on the team, and we took him to our parties and
never so much as fell out of our chairs when he took
off his coat in order to dance with more comfort
and energy. The girls were as loyal as we were and
danced with him as long as their feet held out, and
we made them leather hero medals and really had a
lot of fun out of the whole business — all except
Frankling. It just about killed him to have to
mingle with Ole socially; and when the time for the
Senior class party drew near he got so nervous that
he called a meeting of a few of us fellows and made
a big kick.

   " I tell you, fellows, this has got to stop! " he declared. " We 've encouraged this lumber-jack until
he has gotten too fresh for any use. Why, he 'll ask
any girl in the college to dance with him, and he
goes and calls on them, too. Now, it 's up to us to

show him his place. I'm dead against putting his
name in the hat for the party. He'll be sure to
draw a girl who will be humiliated by having to go
with him; and I have a little too much regard for
chivalry and courtesy to allow him to do it. We'll
just have to hint to him that he'd better have another engagement the night of the class party, that's
all."

Thereupon we all rose joyously up and told Frankling to go jump in the creek. And he called us
muckers and declared we were ignorant of the first
principles of social ethics. He said that Skjarsen
might be near enough our level to be inoffensive, but
as for him he declined to have anything to do with
the class party. Thereupon we gave three cheers,
and that made him so mad that he left the meeting
and fell over three chairs trying to do it with speed
and dignity. Altogether it was a most enjoyable
occasion. We'd never gotten quite so much satisfaction out of him before.

The drawing took place the next week and, sure
enough, Frankling declined to allow his name to be
put in the hat. We put Ole's name in and were
prepared to have him draw a Class A girl; but what
happened knocked the props out from under us. His
name came fourth and he drew the mortgaged and
unapproachable Miss Spencer.

We didn't know whether to celebrate or prepare
for trouble. It seemed reasonable that Miss Spencer
would back up Frankling and reduce Ole to an icicle

when he asked her to go with him. But the next morning, when we saw Frankling, we were so happy that we forgot to worry. He was one large paroxysm. I never saw so much righteous indignation done up in one bundle. He cornered the class officers and declared in passionate tones that they had committed the outrage of the century. They had insulted one of the finest young women in the college. They had made it advisable for all persons of culture to remain away from Siwash. The disgrace must not be allowed. He did n't speak as a friend, but as a disinterested party who wanted justice done; and he proposed to secure it.

We took all this quite humbly and asked him why he did n't see Ole himself and order him to unhand the lady. From the way he turned pale, we guessed he had done that already. Ole weighed two-twenty in his summer hair-cut and was quick-tempered. We then asked him why he did n't buy Ole off. We also asked him why he did n't shut down the college, and why he did n't have Congress pass a law or something, and if his head had ever pained him before. He was tearing off his collar in order to answer more calmly and collectedly when Ole came into the room. Ole had combed his hair and shined his shoes, and he had on the pink-and-blue necktie that he had worn the month before to the annual promenade with a rented dress suit. He seemed very cheerful.

"Vell, fallers," says he, "das leetle Spencer gal ban all rite. She say she go by me to das party.

Ve ban goin' stylish tu, Aye bet yu." Then he saw
Frankling and went over to him with his hand out.
"Don't yu care, Master Frankling," he said, with
one of his transcontinental smiles. "Aye tak yust
sum good care by her lak Aye ban her steddy faller."

Phew!

.   .   .   .

Ole took Miss Spencer to the party. There isn't
a bit of doubt but that he took her in style. He put
more care and exertion into the job than any of the
rest of us and he got more impressive results. Ole
has his ideas about dress. Ordinarily he wore one
of those canned suits that you buy in the coat-and-
pants emporiums, giving your age and waist measure
in order to get a perfect fit. He wore a celluloid
collar with it and a necktie that must have been an
heirloom in the family; and he wore a straw hat
most of the year. He wore each one till it blew away
and then got another. This rig was good enough for
Ole in ordinary little social affairs, but when it came
to dances and receptions he blossomed out in evening
clothes. He had made a bargain with a second-hand
clothes-man downtown — split his wood all winter
for the use of a dress suit that had lost its position
in a prominent family and was going downhill fast.
You know how the tailors work the dress-suit racket.
They can't exactly change the style of a suit — it's
got to be open-faced and have tails — but they work
in some little improvement like a braid on or off,
or an extra buttonhole, or a flare in the vest each

year; so that a really bang-up-to-date chap would blush all over if he had to wear a last year's model. I notice the automobile makers are doing the same stunt. They can't improve their cars any more, so they put fore doors on one year, cut 'em in two the next and take them off the year after.

This hasn't anything to do with Ole except that that dress suit of his was behind the times one hundred and two counts. It had been a fat man's suit in the first place. It fitted him magnificently at the shoulders. He and the suit began to leave each other from that point down. At the waist it looked like a deflated balloon. The top of the trousers fitted him about as snugly as a round manhole in the street. The legs flapped like the mainsail of a catboat that's coming about. They ended some time before his own legs did and there was quite a little stretch of yarn sock visible before the big tan shoes began. Ole had two acres of feet and he polished his shoes himself, with great care. They were not so large as an ordinary ballroom, but somehow he used them so skillfully that they gave the effect of covering the entire space. Four times around Ole's feet constituted a pretty fair encore at our dances; and I've seen him pen up as many as three couples in a corner with them when he got those feet tangled.

That was Ole's formal costume. But he didn't regard it with awe. Any one could wear a dress suit. It seemed to him that a Senior party to which he was to escort Miss Spencer was too important to pass

airily off with the same old suit.   He had another
card up his sleeve.

" Aye ent tal yu," he explained when we asked
him anxiously what it was he proposed to wear.
" Yust vait.   Aye ban de hull show, Aye tank.   Yu
fallers yust put on your yumpin'-yack suits.   Aye
mak yu look lak torta cent."

Of course we waited.   We did n't have anything
else to do.   We worried a little, but we had gotten
used to Ole, anyway — and what was the difference?
It would be a little hard on Miss Spencer, but it
would be magnificently horrible to Frankling, who
considered that a collar of the wrong cut might en-
danger a man's whole future career.   So we resigned
ourselves and attended to our own troubles.

The night of the party was a cold, clear January
evening.   There was snow on the ground and it was
packed hard on the sidewalks.   This was nuts for
the oil-burners.   They walked their girls to the hall.
Four of the reckless ones clubbed together and hired
a big closed carriage affair from the livery stable.
It happened to be a pallbearers' carriage during the
daytime, but they did n't know the difference and
the girls did n't tell them; and what you don't know
will never cause your poor old brain to ache.   We
frat fellows blew our hard-worked allowances for
varnished cabs and thereby proved ourselves the biggest suckers in the bunch.   To this day I can't see
why a girl who can dance all night, and can stroll
all afternoon of a winter's day, has to be hauled three

blocks in a two-horse rig every time she goes to a party. The money we spent on cabs while I was at Siwash would have built a new stadium, painted every frat house in town and endowed a chair of United States languages. But, there! — I'm on my pet hobby again. How it did hurt to pay for those hacks!

I got there late with my girl — she was a shy little conservatory student, who evidently regarded conversation as against the rules — and I found the usual complications that had to be sorted out at the beginning of every class party. Stiffy Short was sore. He was short five dances for his girl — had been working on her program for a week — and he accused the fellows of dodging because she could n't dance; and was threatening to be taken sick and spend the evening in the dressing room smoking cigarettes. Miss Worthington, one of our Class A girls, did n't have a dance, because Tullings, who had drawn her, had presumed that she was to sit and talk with him all evening. Petey Simmons was in even worse. His girl could n't dance, but insisted on doing so. She had done it the year before, too. Petey had been training up for two weeks by tugging his dresser around the room. Then there was Glenallen. We always had to form a committee of national defense against Glenallen. He could n't dance, either, and he would insist on hitching his chair out towards the middle of the room. I've seen him throw as many as four couples in a night. And there was a telephone call

from Miss Morse, class secretary and first-magnitude
star. Her escort had n't shown up. He never did
show up. When we went around to lynch him the
next day he explained desperately that at the last
minute he found he had forgotten to get a lawn
necktie. You know how a little thing like a lawn
necktie that ain't can wreck an evening dress, unless
you are an old enough head to cut up a handkerchief
and fold the ends under.

We had gotten things pretty well straightened out
before we discovered that Ole was missing. That
would never do. If Miss Spencer needed rescuing
we were the boys to do it. Three of us rushed down
the stairs to send a carriage over to Browning Hall,
and that minute Ole arrived at the party.

He had worn his very best — the suit he was
proudest of and the one he knew could n't be dupli-
cated. It was his lumber-camp rig — corduroy trousers, big boots and overshoes, red flannel shirt, canvas
pea-jacket and fur cap. He came marching up the
walk like the hero in a moving-picture show and we
thought he was alone till he reached the door. Then
we saw Miss Spencer. She was seated in state behind him on one of those hand-sledges the farmers
use for hauling cordwood. There were evergreen
boughs behind her and all around her, and she was
so wrapped up in a huge camp blanket that all we
could see of her was her eyes.

We gave Ole three cheers and carried Miss Spencer
upstairs on the evergreen boughs. The two were

the hits of the party. We never had a better one.
The incident broke more ice than we could have
chopped out in a month with all the dull-edged talk
we had been handing around. Every one had a good
laugh by way of a general introduction and then we
all turned in and made things hum. The wallflowers
got plucked. Somebody taught the president of the
Y. M. C. A. how to waltz and poor Henry Boggs forgot for two hours that he had hands and feet, and
that they were beyond his control. It was a tremendous success; we were so enthusiastic by the time
things broke up that we told the cabmen to go hang
and all walked home to the Hall, the men fighting
for a chance to pull on the sledge-rope with Ole.

Hold on, Sam. Put down your hat. This is n't
the end, thank you. It 's just the prologue. Of course
we all expected, when Ole unloaded Miss Spencer
at the Hall and she bade him good evening, and
thanked him for her delightful time and so on, that
the incident would be closed. Never dreamed of anything else. Lumber-jack suits and cordwood sledges
are fine for novelties, but they can't come back, you
know — once is enough. And that 's why we fell
dead in rows when Ole, straw hat and all, walked
over to Lab. from chapel with Miss Spencer the next
day — and she did n't call for the police. We
could n't have stared any harder if the college chapel
had bowed and walked off with her. And we had n't
recovered from the blow when Friday night rolled
around and those of us who went to call at the Hall

found Ole seated in Frankling's particular corner, entertaining Miss Spencer with an average of one remark a minute, which, so far as we could hear, consisted generally of " Aye tank so " and " No, ma'am."

By this time we had decided that Frankling was sulking and that Miss Spencer was showing him that if she wanted to be friendly with Ole, or the town pump, or the plaster statue of Victory in the college library, she had a perfect right to. I guess she showed him all right, too, for after a couple of weeks he surrendered and then the queerest rivalry Siwash had ever seen began. Frankling, son of the locomotive works, authority on speckled vests and cotillons, was scrapping with Ole Skjarsen, the cuffless wonder from the lumber camps, for the affections of the prettiest girl in college. No wonder we got so interested that spring that most of us forgot to fall in love ourselves.

I don't to this day believe that Miss Spencer meant a word of it. I think that she was simply good-natured, in the first place, and that, when Frankling began to bite little semicircular pieces out of the air, she began mixing her drinks, so to speak, just for the excitement of the thing. Anyway, Frankling walked over to chapel with her and Ole lumbered back. Frankling took her to the basketball games and Ole took her to the Kiowa debate and slept peacefully through most of it. Frankling bought a beautiful little trotting horse and sleigh and took Miss Spencer on long rides. In Siwash, young people do not have chaperons, guards, nurses nor conservators. That was a knockout, we all thought; but it never feazed Ole. He invited Miss Spencer to go street-car riding with him and she did it. Some of us found them bumping over the line in one of the flat-wheeled catastrophes that the Jonesville Company called cars — and Miss Spencer didn't even blush. She bowed to us just as unconcernedly as if she wasn't breaking all long-distance records for eccentricity in Siwash history.

Frankling dodged the whole college and got wild in the eyes. He looked like an eminent statesman who was being compelled to act as barker in a circus against his will. It must have churned up his vitals to do his sketch act with Ole; but when you have had one of those four-year cases, and it has gotten tangled up in your past and future, you can't always dictate just what you are going to do. It was plain to see that Miss Spencer had Frankling hooked, haltered, hobbled, staked out, Spanish-bitted, wrapped up and stamped with her name and laid on the shelf to be called for; and it was just as evident that she considered he would be all the nicer if she walked around on him for a while and massaged his disposition a little with her little French heels.

So Frankling continued to divide time with Ole, and all the fellows whom he had insulted about their neckties and all the girls whom he had forgotten to dance with sat around in perfect content and watched the show.

He invited Miss Spencer to go street-car
riding with him

Page 246

We all thought it would wear out after a few weeks. But it did n't. The semester recess came and, when college assembled again, Ole cut Frankling out for the athletic ball as neatly as if he had been in the girl game all his life. Frankling countered with the promenade two weeks later, but he went clear to the ropes when Miss Spencer came out one fine morning at chapel with Ole's football charm — the one he had won the year the team had annihilated two universities and seven assorted colleges. He came back gamely and decorated her with fraternity hat-pins, cuff buttons, belt buckles and side combs; and on the strength of it he got three Friday evenings in a row. That might have jarred any one but Ole. But he came up smiling and took Miss Spencer to a Y. M. C. A. social, where he bought her four dishes of ice cream and had to be almost violently restrained from offering her the whole freezer.

Winter wore out and spring came. Frankling brought the whole resources of the locomotive works into play. He got a private car and took a party off to the Kiowa baseball game, with Miss Spencer as guest of honor. He bombarded her with imported candy and American beauties, and cluttered up the spring with a series of whist parties, which butted into the social calendar something frabjous. Ole plowed right along with his own peculiar style of argument. He met the private-car business with a straw ride and his prize offering was a hunk of spruce gum from his pine woods, as big as your two fists;

and, so far as we could see, the gum got exactly the same warmth of reception as the candy — though it did n't disappear with anywhere near the rapidity.

As April went by, we Seniors got busy with the first awful preliminaries of Commencement. It began to be considered around college that Senior Day would settle the affair one way or the other. Senior Day is the last event of Commencement Week at Siwash and more engagements have been announced formally or otherwise that day than at any other time. If a Senior man and girl, who had been making a rather close study of each other, walked out on the campus together after the exercises and took in the corporation dinner at noon side by side, no one hesitated about offering congratulations. They might not be exactly due, but it was a sign that there was going to be an awful lot of nice-looking stationery spoiled by the two after the sad partings were said. Now we did n't have a doubt that either Frankling or Ole would amble proudly down between the lilac rows on Class Day with Miss Spencer, under the good old pretense of helping her locate the dinner-tables a hundred yards away; and betting on the affair got pretty energetic. Day after day the odds varied. When Frankling broke closing-time rules at Browning Hall by a good thirty minutes some two-to-one money was placed on him. When Ole and Miss Spencer cut chapel the next day the odds promptly switched. You could get takers on either side at any time, but I think the odds favored Ole a little. You can't help boosting your preferences with your good money. It's like betting on your college team.

Commencement Week came and, although we were Seniors, we went through it without hardly noticing the scenery. We watched Ole and Frankling all through Baccalaureate, and when Ole won a twenty-yard dash across the church and over several of us, and marched down the street with Miss Spencer, it looked as if all was over but the Mendelssohn business. But Frankling had her in a box at the class play the next night. How could you pay any attention to the glorious threshold of life and the expiring gasps of dear college days with a race like that on!

Commencement was on Wednesday and Senior Day was Thursday. Up to Wednesday night it was an even break — steen points all. One of the two had won. We hadn't a doubt of it. But, if both men had been born poker players, drawing to fill, in a jack-pot that had been sweetened nine times, you couldn't have told less to look at them. Frankling was as glum as ever and Ole had the same reënforced-concrete expression of innocence that he used to wear while he was getting off the ball behind somebody's goal line, after having carried it the length of the field. We were discussing the thing that night on the porch of the Eta Bita Pie house and were putting up a few final bets when Ole came up, carpet-bag in hand and his diploma under his arm, and bade us good-by. He was going out on the midnight train — going away for good.

For a minute you could have heard the grass growing. If Ole was going away that night it meant just one thing: the cruel Miss Spencer had tossed him over and he was bumping the bumps downward into a cold and cheerless future. We were so sorry we could hardly speak for a minute. Then Allie Bangs got up and put his arm as far across Ole's shoulder as it would go.

"By thunder, I'm sorry, old chap!" he said huskily.

For a man who had just had an air-castle fall on his neck, Ole did n't talk very dejectedly. "Vy yu ban sorry?" he demanded. "Aye got gude yob St. Paul vay. De boss write me Aye skoll come Friday. Aye ent care to be late first t'ing."

"But, Ole —" Bangs began. Then he stopped. You can't bawl out a question about another man's love affairs before a whole mob.

"Yu fallers ban fine tu me," Ole began again. "Aye lak yu bully! Ven yu come by St. Paul, take Yim Hill's railroad and come to Sven Akerson's camp, femt'n mile above Lars Hjellersen's gang. Aye ban boss of Sven's camp now. Aye gat yu gude time and plenty flapyack."

He turned to go. Allie and I got up and walked firmly down the walk with him. We were going to be relieved of our suspense if we had to buy the information.

"Now, Ole," said Allie, grabbing his carpet-bag, "you know we're not going to let you go down to the train alone. Besides, we want to know if everything is all right with you. You know we love you. We're for you, Ole. You — you and Miss Spencer parting good friends?"

"Yu bet!" said Ole enthusiastically. "She ban fine gur'rl, Aye tal yu. Sum day Aye ban sending her deerskin from lumber camp."

Bangs braced up again. "Er — you and Miss Spencer — er — not engaged, are you?" he said, the way a fellow goes at it when he is diving into cold water. Ole looked around in perfect good humor. "Get married by each odder?" he said. "Yee whiz! no, Master Bangs. She ban nice gur'rl. It ent any nicer in Siwash College. But she kent cook. She kent build fire in woodstove. She kent wash. She kent bake flatbrot. She kent make close. She yust ban purty, like picture. Vat for Aye vant to marry picture gallery? Aye ban tu poor faller fur picture gallery, Aye tank."

"But, Ole," says I, jumping in, "you've been rushing the girl all winter as if your life depended on it. What did you mean by that?"

Ole turned around patiently and sat down on the steps of the First Methodist Church, which happened to be passing just then. "Vell, Aye tal yu," he explained. "Miss Spencer she ban nice tu me. She go tu class party 'nd ent give dam vat das Frankling faller say. Aye ent forget dat, Aye tal yu; 'nd, by yimmuny Christmas! Aye show her gude time all right."

We took Ole to the station and sat down to rest three times on the way back. So all that terrific performance was a reward for Miss Spencer! " O gratitude! " says the poet, " how many crimes are committed in thy name! "

We were so dazed that night that it did n't occur to us to wonder why Miss Spencer stood for all the gratitude. But the next day, when the exercises were over, that young lady stepped down from the platform and was met by a tall chap whom she later introduced to us as a friend of the family from her home town. You can always spot these family friends by the way the girl blushes when she introduces them. Miss Spencer wore a fine new diamond ring and we knew what it meant. It was just another case where the girl came to school and the man stayed at home and built a seven-room house on a prominent corner four blocks from his hardware store and waited — and tried not to get any more jealous than possible. I suppose Miss Spencer used Ole as a sort of parachute to let Frankling down easily at the last. Anyway, we wiped the whole affair off the slate after that. She was n't one of us, anyway. Made us shiver to think of her. What if one of us had sailed in the Freshman year and cut Frankling out!

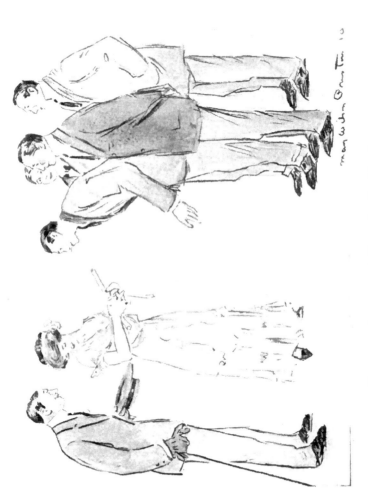

You can always spot these family friends

Page 252

CHAPTER X

DO I BELIEVE in woman's suffrage? Certainly, if you do, Miss Allstairs. As I sit here, where I could n't help seeing you frown if I did n't please you, I favor anything you favor. If you want the women to vote just hand me the ax and show me the man who would prevent them. If you think the women should play the baseball of our country it's all right with me. I 'll help pass a law making it illegal for Hans Wagner to hang around a ball park except as water-boy. If you believe that women ought to wear three-story hats in theaters —

No, I 'm not making fun of you. I hope I may never be allowed to lug a box of Frangipangi's best up your front steps again if I am. If you want the women to vote, Miss Allstairs, just breathe the word, and I 'll go out and start a suffragette mob as soon as ever I can find a brick. And I would be a powerful advocate, too. You can't tell me that women would n't be able to handle the ballot. You can't tell me they would get their party issues mixed up with their party gowns. I 've seen them vote and I 've seen them play politics. And let me tell you, when woman gets the vote man will totter right back to the kitchen and prepare the asparagus for supper, just to be out of harm's way. His good old arguments about the glory of the nation, the rising price of wheat and the grand record of those sterling patriots who have succeeded in getting their names on the government payroll won't get him to first base when women vote. He'll have to learn the game all over again, and the first ninety-nine years' course of study will be that famous subject, " Woman."

How do I know so much about it? Just as I told you. I've been through the mill. I've seen women vote. I've tried to get them to vote my way. I've never herded humming birds or drilled goldfishes in close formation, but I'd take the job cheerfully. It would be just a rest cure after four years' experience in persuading a large voting body of beautiful and fascinating young women to vote the ticket straight and to let me name the ticket.

Oh, no! I never lived in Colorado, and I never was a polygamist in Utah, thank you. I'm nothing but an alumnus of Siwash College, which, as you know, is co-educational to a heavenly degree. I'm just a young alumnus with about eighty-nine gray hairs scattered around in my thatch. Each one of those gray hairs represents a vote gathered by me from some Siwash co-ed in the cause of liberty and progress and personal friends. Eighty-nine was my total score. Took me four years to get 'em, working seven days in the week and forty weeks in the year. I'm no brass-

finished and splash-lubricated politician, but I 'll bet
I could go out in any election and cord up that many
votes with whiskers on them in three days. "Votes
for Women" is a fine sentiment and very appropriate,
Miss Allstairs, but "Votes from Women" has always
been the motto under which I have fought and been
bled — I beg your pardon; that just slipped out accidentally. Of course there was nothing of the sort
possible. Now there is n't the slightest use of your
getting angry and making me feel like an Arctic explorer in a linen suit. If you insist I 'll go out on
the front porch and sit there a few weeks until you
forgive me, but that 's the very best I can do for you.
I will positively not erase myself from your list of
acquaintances. When a man has been hanging around
the world in a bored way for thirty-two years, just
waiting for Fate to catch up with its assignments and
trundle you along within my range in order to give
the sun a rest —

Oh, well — if you forgive me of course I 'll stop
anything you say. Though really, now, that was n't
joshing. It came from the depths. Anyway, as I
was saying, "Votes from Women" — excuse me,
please; I fell off there once and I 'm going to go
slow — "Votes from Women" was the burning question back at Siwash when I infested the campus. The
women had the votes already — no use agitating that.
The big question was getting 'em back when we needed
them. You see, the Faculty always insisted on regulating athletics more or less and on organizing things

for us — did n't believe we mere college youths could get an organization together according to Hoyle, or whoever drew up the rules of disorder in college societies, without the help of some skyscraper-browed professor. So they saw fit to organize what they called a general athletic association. Every student who paid a dollar was enrolled as a member, with a vote and the privilege of blowing a horn in a lady or gentleman like manner at all college games. And just to assure a large membership, the faculty made a rule that the dollar must be paid by all students with their tuition at the beginning of the year. That, of course, enrolled the whole college, girls and all, in the Athletic Association. And it was the Athletic Association that raised the money to pay for the college teams and hired the coaches and greased old Siwash's way to glory every fall during the football season.

Now this did n't bother any for a few years. The men went to the meetings and voted, and the girls stayed at home and made banners for the games. Everything was lovely and comfortable. Then one day, in my Freshman year just before the election, there was a crack in the slate and the Shi Delts saw a chance to elect one of their men president — it was n't their turn that year, but you never could trust the Shi Delts politically any farther than you could kick a steam roller. They put up their man and there was a little campaign for about three hours that got up to eleven hundred revolutions a minute.

We clawed and scratched and dug for votes and were still short when Reilly got an idea and rushed over to Browning Hall. Five minutes before the polls closed he appeared, leading twenty-seven Siwash girls, and the trouble was over. They voted for our man and he was elected by four votes. But, incidentally, we tipped over a can of — no, wait a minute. I've simply got to be more classical. What's the use of a college diploma if you have to tell all you know in baseball language? Let's see — you remember that beautiful Greek lady who opened a box under the impression that there was a pound of assorted chocolate creams in it and let loose a whole international museum of trouble? Dora Somebody — eh? Oh, yes, Pandora. I always did fall down on that name. Anyway, the box we opened in that election would have made Pandora's little grief repository look like a box of pink powder. The kind you girls — oh, very well. I take it back. Honestly, Miss Allstairs, you'll get me so afraid of the cars in a minute that I'll have to ditch this train of thought and talk about art. Ever hear me talk about art? Well, it would serve you right if you did. I talked about art with a kalsominer once, and he wanted to fight me for the honor of his profession.

However, as I was saying, the women voted at Siwash that fall and I guess they must have liked the taste, for the first thing we knew we had the woman vote to take care of all the time. The next fall pretty nearly every girl in the college turned out to class meetings, and the way they voted pretty nearly drove us mad. They seemed to regard it as a game. They fussed about whether to vote on pink paper or blue paper; voted for members of the Faculty for class president; one of them voted for the President of the United States for president of the Sophomore class; wanted to vote twice; came up to the ballot box and demanded their votes back because they had changed their minds; went away before election and left word with a friend to vote for them. Took us an hour, right in football practice time, to get the ticket through in our class; and what with lending pencils and chasing girls who carried their ballots away with them, and getting called down for trying to see that everything went along proper and shipshape and according to program, we boys were half crazy when it was all over.

But the girls liked it enormously. It was a novelty for them, and we saw right there that it was a case of organize the female vote or have things hopelessly muddled up before the end of the year. In the interests of harmony things had to be done in a businesslike manner. Certain candidates had to be put through and certain factions had to be gently but firmly stepped on. Harmony, you know, Miss Allstairs, is a most important thing in politics. Without harmony you can't do a thing. Harmony in politics consists of giving the insurgents not what they ask for, but something that you don't want. I was a grand little harmonizer in my day too. I ran

the oratorical league the year before it went broke
and then traded the presidency to the Chi Yi-Delta
Whoop crowd for the editorship of the Student
Weekly. That's harmony. They were happy and
so was I. When I saw how hard they had to hustle
to pay the association debts the next fall I was so
happy I could hardly stand it.

No, Miss Allstairs, that was not meanness on my
part. It was politics. There is a great deal of
difference between meanness and politics. One
is low-down and contemptible and nasty, and the
other is expedient. See? Why, some of the most
generous men in the world are politicians. Time
and again I've seen Andy Hoople, the big politician
of our town, pay a man's fare to Chicago so that
he could go up there and rest during the last week
of a political campaign and not bother himself and
get all worried over the way things were going —
and the man would be on the other side too.

Anyway, to — wait a minute; I'm going to hook
over some French now. Look out, low bridge — to
rendezvous to our muttons — how's that? In a good
many ways there are worse jobs than that of persuading a pretty girl to vote the right way. Sometimes I
liked the job so well that I was sorry when election
came. But, on the whole, it was hard, hard work.
We tried arguments and exhortation and politics,
and you might as well have shot cheese balls at
the moon. Never touched 'em. I talked straight
logic to a girl for an hour once, showing her con-

clusively that it was her duty as a patriotic Siwash student to vote for a man who could give a strong mind and a lot of money to the debating cause; and then she remarked quite placidly that she would always vote for the other man for whatever office he wanted, because he wore his dress suit with such an air. I had to take her clear downtown and buy her ice cream and things before she could understand the gravity of the case at all —

No, indeed, Miss Allstairs, I did n't bribe her. You must be very careful about charging people with bribery. Bribery is a very serious offense. It's so serious that nowadays it's a very grave thing to charge a politician with it. I think it will be made a crime soon. I bought ice cream for this girl because she could understand things better while she was eating ice cream. It made her think better. Of course, you can't do that with a man in real politics. You have to give him an office or a contract or something in order to get his mind into a cheerful condition. You can argue so much better with a man when he is cheerful. No, indeed. I would n't bribe a fly. Nobody would. There is n't any bribing any more anyway. Illinois has taught the world that.

But that was the least of our troubles. After you had persuaded a girl to vote right you had to keep her persuaded. Now most any man might be able to keep one vote in line, but that was n't enough. Some of us had to keep four or five votes all ready for use,

for competition was pretty swift and there were a
tremendous number of co-eds in school. You
never saw such a job as it was. No sooner would
I have Miss A. entirely friendly to my candidate
for the editorship of the Weekly than Miss B. would
flop over and show marked signs of frost — and then
I would have to drop everything and walk over from
chapel with her three mornings hand-running, and
take her to a play, and make a wild pass about not
knowing whether any one would go to the prom with
me or not. And then just as she would begin to
smile when she saw me Miss A. would pass me on
the street and look at me as if I had robbed a hen-
roost. And just as I was entirely friendly with
both of them it would occur to me that I had n't
called on Miss C. for three weeks and that Bannister,
of the Alfalfa Delts, was waiting for Miss D. after
chapel every morning and would doubtless make a
low-down, underhanded attempt to talk politics to
her in the spring. For a month before each election
I felt like a giddy young squirrel running races
with myself around a wheel. Some college boys
can keep on terms of desperate and exclusive friendliness with a dozen girls at a time — Petey Simmons got up to eighteen one spring when we won the
big athletic election — but four or five were as many
as I could manage by any means, and it kept me
busted, conditioned and all out of training to accomplish this. And when election-time approached and
it came to talking real politics, and the girl you had

counted on all winter to swing her wing of the third
floor in Browning Hall for your candidate would
suddenly remember in the midst of a businesslike
talk on candidates and things that you had cut two
dances with her at the prom, and you could n't explain that you simply had to do it because you had
to keep your stand-in with a girl on the first floor
who had the music-club vote in her pocket-book —
well, I may get out over Niagara Falls some day
on a rotten old tight-rope, with a sprained ankle
and a fellow on my shoulders who is drunk and
wants to make a speech standing up — but if I do
I won't feel any more wobbly and uncertain about
the future than I used to feel on those occasions.

Of course it was entirely impossible for the few
dozen college politicians to make personal friends
and supporters of all the girls in Siwash. We did n't
want to. There are girls and girls at Siwash, just
as there are everywhere else. Maybe a third of the
Siwash girls were pretty and fascinating and wise and
loyal, and nine or ten other exceedingly pleasant
adjectives. And perhaps another third were —
well, nice enough to dance with at a class party and
not remember it with terror. And then there was
another third which — oh, well, you know how it
goes everywhere. They were grand young women,
and they were there for educational purposes.
They took prizes and learned a lot, and this was
partly because there were no swarms of bumptious
young collegians hanging around them and wasting

their time. Far be it from me, Miss Allstairs, to speak disparagingly of a single member of your sex — you are all too good for us — but, if you will force me to admit it, there were girls at Siwash — ex-girls — who would have made a true and loyal student of art and beauty climb a high board — certainly, I said I was n't going to say anything against them, and I 'm not. Anyway, it 's no great compliment to be admired for your youth and beauty alone. Age has its claims to respect too — oh, very well; I 'll change the subject.

As I was saying, we could n't influence all the co-ed vote personally, but we handled it very systematically. Every popular girl in the school had her following, of course, at Browning Hall. So we just fought it out among the popular girls. Before elections they 'd line up on their respective sides, and then they 'd line up the rest of the co-ed vote. On a close election we 'd get out every vote, and we 'd have it accounted for, too, beforehand. The real precinct leaders had nothing on us. It took a lot of time and worry; but it was all very pleasant at the end. The popular girls would each lead over her collection of slaves of Horace and Trig, and Counterpoint and Rhetoric, and we 'd cheer politely while they voted 'em. Then we 'd take off our hats and bow low to said slaves, and they would go back to their galleys after having done their duty as freeborn college girls, and that would be over for another year. Everything would have continued lovely and comfortable and darned expensive if it had n't been for Mary Jane Hicks, of Carruthers' Corners, Missouri.

No, I 've never told you of Mary Jane Hicks. Why? The real reason is because when we fellows of that period mention her name we usually cuss a little in a hopeless and irritable sort of way It 's painful to think of her. It 's humiliating to think that twenty-five of the case-hardened and time-seasoned politicians of Siwash should have been double-crossed, checkmated, outwitted, out-generaled, sewed up into sacks and dumped into Salt Creek by a red-headed, freckled-nosed exile from a Missouri clay farm; and a Sophomore at that — say, what am I telling you this for, Miss Allstairs? Honestly, it hurts. It 's nice for a woman to hear, I know, but I may have to take gas to get through this story.

This Mary Jane Hicks came to Siwash the year before it all happened and was elected to the un-noticeables on the spot. She was a dumpy little girl, with about as much style as a cornplanter; and I suspect that she bade her pet calf a fond good-by when she left the dear old farm to come and play tag with knowledge on the Siwash campus. Nobody saw her in particular the first year, except that you could n't help noticing her hair any more than you can help noticing a barn that 's burning on a damp, dark night. It was explosively red and she did n't seem to care. She always had her nose turned up a little — just on principle, I guess. And when

It was a blow between the eyes

See page 268

you see a red-headed girl with a freckled nose that turns up just locate the cyclone cellars in your immediate vicinity, say I.

Well, Mary Jane Hicks went through her Freshman year without causing any more excitement than you could make by throwing a clamshell into the Atlantic Ocean. She drew a couple of classy men for the class parties and they reported that she towed unusually hard when dancing. She voted in the various elections under the protecting care of Miss Willoughby, who was a particular friend of mine just before the Athletic election, and that's how I happened to meet her. I was considerably grand at that time — being a Junior who had had a rib smashed playing football and was going to edit the college paper the next year — but the way she looked at me you would have thought that I was the fractional part of a peeled cipher. She just nodded at me and said "Howdedo," and then asked if the vest-pocket vote was being successfully extracted that day. That was nervy of her and I frowned; after which she remarked that she objected to voting without being told in advance that the cause of liberty was trembling in the voter's palm. I remember wondering at the time where she had dug up all that rot.

Miss Hicks voted at all the elections along with the rest of the herd, and as far as I know no rude collegian came around and broke into her studies by taking her anywhere. Commencement came and we all went home, and I forgot all about her. The next fall was a critical time with the Eta Bita Pie-Fly Gam-Sigh Whoopsilon combination, because we had graduated a large number of men and we had to pull down the fall elections with a small voting strength. So I went down to college a day early to confer with some of the other patriotic leaders regarding slates and other matters concerning the good of the college.

I had n't more than stepped off the train until I met Frankling, the president of the Alfalfa Delts, and Randolph, of the Delta Kappa Sonofaguns, and Chickering, of the Mu Kow Moos, in close consultation. It was very evident that they were going to do a little high-class voting too. And before night I discovered that the Shi Delts and the Delta Flushes and the Omega Salves had formed a coalition with the independents, and that there was going to be more politics to the square inch in old Siwash that year than there had been since the year of the big wind — that 's what we called the year when Maxwell was boss of the college and swept every election with his eloquence.

There were any number of important elections coming off that fall. There were all the class elections, of course, and the Oratorical election, and a couple of vacancies to fill in the Athletic Association, and a college marshal to elect, and goodness knows what all else to nail down and tuck away before we could get down to the serious job of fighting con-

ditions that fall. I was so busy for the first three
days, wiring up the new students and putting
through a trade on the Athletic secretaryship with
the Delta Kap gang, that I could n't pay any attention to the class elections. But they were pretty
safe anyway. It was only about a day's job to put
through a class slate. The Junior election came
first, and we had arranged to give it to Miss Willoughby. We always elected women presidents of
the Junior class at Siwash. Little Willoughby had
a cinch because, of course, our crowd backed her
hard — and we were strong in Juniors — and, besides she had a good following among the girls. So
we just turned the whole thing over to the girls to
manage and thought no more about it, being mighty
hard pressed by the miserable and un-American bi-
partisan combination on the Athletic offices.

School opened on Tuesday. The Junior class
election came off on Thursday afternoon and a Miss
Hamthrick was elected president. I would have bet
on the college bell against her. It was the shock-
ingest thing that had happened in politics for five
years. Miss Hamthrick was a conservatory student.
Even when you shut your eyes and listened to her
singing she did n't sound good-looking. Davis drew
her for the Sophomore class party the year before
and exposed himself to the mumps to get out of
going. Not only was she elected president, but the
rest of the offices went to — no, I 'll not describe
them. I 'm sort of prejudiced anyway. They made

Miss Hamthrick seem beautiful and clever by comparison.

It was a blow between the eyes. The worst of it was we could n't understand it. I went over to see Miss Willoughby about it, and she came down all powdery and beautiful about the eyes and nose and talked to me as haughtily as if I had done it myself. She said she had trusted us, but it was evident that all a woman could hope for in politics was the privilege of being fooled by a man. She even accused me of helping elect the Hamthrick lady, said she wished me joy, and asked if it had been a pretty romance. That made me tired, and I said — oh, well, no use remembering what I said. It was the last thing I ever had a chance to say to Miss Willoughby anyway. I was pretty miserable over it — politically, of course, I mean, Miss Allstairs. You understand. Now there 's no use saying that. It was n't so. College girls are all very well, and one must be entertained while getting gorged with knowledge; but really, when it comes to more serious things, I never —

All right, I 'll go on with my story. The next day we got a harder blow than ever. The Freshman class election came off on a snap call, and about half the class, mostly girls, elected a lean young lady with spectacles and a wasp-like conversation to the presidency. We raised a storm of indignation, but they blandly told us to go hence. There was nothing in the Constitution of the United States to prevent a woman from being president of the Freshman class, and there did n't seem to be any other laws on the subject. Besides, the Freshman class was a brand-new republic and did n't need the advice of such an effete monarchy as the Senior class. While we were talking it all over the next day the Sophomores met, and after a terrific struggle between the Eta Bita Pies, the Alfalfa Delts and the Shi Delts, Miss Hicks was elected president by what Shorty Gamble was pleased to term " the gargoyle vote." I would n't say that myself of any girl, but Shorty had been working for the place for a year, and when the twenty girls who had never known what it was to have a sassy cab rumble up to Browning Hall and wait for them cast their votes solidly and elected the Missouri Prairie Fire he felt justified in making comments.

By this time it was a case of save the pieces. The whole thing had been as mysterious as the plague. We were getting mortal blows, we could n't tell from whom. All political signs were failing. The game was going backward. A lot of the leaders got together and held a meeting, and some of them were for declaring a constitutional monarchy and then losing the constitution. My! But they were bitter. Everybody accused everybody else of double-crossing, underhandedness, gum-shoeing, back-biting, trading, pilfering and horse-stealing. I think there was a window or two broken during the discussion. But we did n't get anywhere. The

next day the Senior class elected officers, and every
frat went out with a knife for its neighbor.   A
quiet lady by the name of Simpkins, who was one
of the finest old wartime relics in school, was elected
president.

That night I began putting two and two and fractional numbers together and called in calculus and
second sight on the problem.   I remembered what
the Hicks girl had said to me the year before.   That
was more than the ordinary girl ought to know about
politics.   I remembered seeing her doing more or
less close-harmony work with the other midnight-oil
consumers — and the upshot was I went over to
Browning Hall that night and called on her.

She came down in due time — kept me waiting
as long as if she had been the belle of the prom —
and she shook hands all over me.

"My dear boy," she said, sitting down on the
sofa with me, "I'm so delighted to renew our old
friendship."

Now, I don't like to be "my dear boyed" by a
Sophomore, and there never had been any old friendship.   I started to stiffen up — and then did n't.
I did n't because I did n't know what she would do
if I did.

"How are all the other good old chaps?" she said
as cordially as could be.   "My, but those were grand
days."

I did n't see any terminus in that conversation.
Besides, she looked like one of those most uncom-

" How are all the other good old chaps?" she said

fortable girls who can guy you in such an innocent and friendly manner that you don't know what to say back. So I brushed the preliminaries aside and jumped right into the middle of things. "Miss Hicks," says I, "why are you doing all this?"

"Singular or plural you?" she asked. "And why am I or are we doing what, and why should n't we?"

"Help," said I, feeling that way. "Do you deny that you have n't been instrumental in upsetting the whole college with those fool elections?"

"I am a modest young lady," said she, "so, of course, I deny it. Besides, this college is n't upset at all. I went over this morning and every professor was right side up with care where he belonged. And, moreover, you must not call an election a fool because it does n't do what you want it to. It can't help itself."

"Miss Hicks," says I, feeling like a fly in an acre of web, "I am a plain and simple man and not handy with my tongue. What I mean is this, and I hope you'll excuse me for living — do you admit that you had a hand in those class elections?"

Miss Hicks looked at me in the friendliest way possible. "It is more modest to admit it than to declare it, is n't it?" she asked.

"Certainly," says I; "and this leads right back to question Number One — Why did you do it?"

"And this leads back to answer Number One — Why should n't I?" she asked again.

"Why, don't you see, Miss Hicks," says I, "that you've elected a lot of girls that never have been active in college work, and that don't represent the student body, and —"

"Don't go to the proms?" she suggested.

"I didn't say it and I'd die before I did," said I virtuously. "But what's your object?"

"Education," said Miss Hicks mildly. "I'm paying full tuition and I want to get all there is out of college. I think politics is a fascinating study. I didn't get a chance to do much at it last year, but I'm learning something about it every day now."

"But what's the good of it all?" I protested. "You'll just get the college affairs hopelessly mixed up —"

"Like the Oratorical Association was last year?" she inquired gently.

"Oh, pshaw!" said I, getting entirely red. "Let's not get personal. What can we do to satisfy you?"

"You've been satisfying us beautifully so far," said Miss Hicks.

"Who's us?" I asked.

"I don't in the least mind telling you," said Miss Hicks. "It's the Blanks."

"The Blanks!" I repeated fretfully. "Never heard of 'em."

"I know it," said Miss Hicks, "but you named them yourselves. What do you say you've drawn when you draw a homely girl's name out of the hat as a partner for a class party?"

"Oh!" said I.

"We're the Blanks," said Miss Hicks, "and we feel that we haven't been getting our full share of college atmosphere. So we're going into politics. In this way we can mingle with the students and help run things and have a very enjoyable time. It's most fascinating. All of us are dippy over it."

"Oh," said I again. "You mean you're going to ruin things for your own selfish interests?"

"My dear boy," said Miss Hicks — my, but that grated — "we're not going to ruin anything. And we may build up the Oratorical Association."

That was too much. I got up and stood as nearly ten feet as I could. "Very well," said I. "If there's no use of arguing on a reasonable basis we may as well terminate this interview. But I'll just tell you there's no use of your going any further. Now we know what we have to fight, we'll take precious good care that you do not do any more mischief."

"Oh, very well," said Miss Hicks — she was infuriatingly good-natured — "but I might as well tell you that we're going to get the Athletic offices, the prom committee, the Oratorical offices and the Athletic election next spring."

"Ha, ha!" said I loudly and rudely. Then I took my hat and went away. Miss Hicks asked me very eagerly to drop in again. Me? I'd as soon have dropped on a Mexican cactus. It couldn't be any more uncomfortable.

I went away and called our gang together and
we seethed over the situation most all night. They
voted me campaign leader on the strength of my service, and the next day we got the rest of the frats
together, buried the hatchet and doped out the campaign. It was the pride and strength of Siwash
against a red-headed Missouri girl, weight about
ninety-five pounds; and we could n't help feeling
sorry for her. But she had brought it on herself.
Insurgency, Miss Allstairs, is a very wicked thing.
It 's a despicable attempt on the part of the minority
to become the majority, and no true patriot will desert the majority in his time of need.

I 'm not going to linger over the next month. I 'll
get it over in a few words. We started out to ex-
terminate Miss Hicks. We put up our candidate
for the Oratorical Association presidency. The hall
was jammed when the time came, and before anything could be done Miss Hicks demanded that no
one be allowed to vote who had n't paid his or her
dues. Half the fellows we had there never had
any intention of getting that far into Oratorical
work, and backed out; but the rest of us paid up.
There had never been so much money in the treasury since the association began. Then the Blanks
nominated a candidate and skinned us by three votes.
When we thought of all that money gone to waste
we almost went crazy.

But that was just a starter. We were determined
to have our own way about the Junior prom. What

do wall-flowers know about running a prom? We
worked up an absolute majority in the Junior class,
only to have a snap meeting called on us over in
Browning Hall, in which three middle-aged young
ladies who had never danced a step were named.
The roar we raised was terrific, but the presiden'
sweetly informed us that they had only followea
precedent — we'd had to do the same thing the
year before to keep out the Mu Kow Moos. We
appealed to the Faculty, and it laughed at us. Unfortunately, we did n't stand any too well there
anyway, while most of the Blanks were the pride
and joy of the professors. Anyway, they told us
to fight our own battles and they'd see that there
was fair play. Oh, yes. They saw it. They
passed a rule that no student who was conditioned
in any study could vote in any college election.
That disenfranchised about half of us right on the
spot. If ever anarchy breaks out in this country,
Miss Allstairs, it will be because of college Faculties.

We made a last stand on the Athletic Association
treasurership. It looked for a while as if it was
going to be easy. We threw all the rules away and
gave a magnificent party for all the girls we thought
we could count on. It was the most gorgeous affair
on record, and half the dress suits in college went
into hock afterward for the whole semester. The
result was most encouraging. The girls were delighted. They pledged their votes and support
and we counted up that we had a clear majority.

We went to bed that night happy and woke up to find that Miss Hicks had entertained the non-fraternity men in the gymnasium that night and had served lemonade and wafers. She had alluded to them playfully as slaves, and they had broken up about fifty chairs demonstrating that they were not. When the election came off she had the unattached vote solid, and we lost out by a comfortable majority. An estimable lady, who did n't know athletics from croquet, was elected. And when the reception committee of the prom was announced the next day it was composed exclusively of men who would have had to be led through the grand march on wheels.

After that we gave up. I tried to resign as campaign manager, but the boys would n't let me. They admitted that no one else could have done any better, and, besides, they wanted me to go over and see Miss Hicks again. They wanted me to ask her what her crowd wanted. When I thought of her pleasant conversational hatpin work I felt like resigning from college; but there always have to be martyrs, and in the end I went.

Miss Hicks received me rapturously. You would have thought we had been boy and girl friends. She insisted on asking how all the folks were at home, and how my health had been, and had n't it been a gay winter, and was I going to the prom, and how did I like her new gown? While I was at it I thought I might as well amuse myself, too, so I asked her to marry me. That was the only time I ever got ahead of her. She refused indignantly, and I laughed at her for getting so fussed up over a little thing.

"Marriage is a sacred subject," she said very soberly.

"So was politics," said I, "until you came along. If you won't talk marriage let's talk politics. What do you girls want?"

"Oh, I told you a while ago," she said.

"But, Great Scott!" said I. "Are n't you going to leave a thing for us fellows who have done our best for the college?"

"Now you put it that way," she said quite kindly, "I'll think it over. We might find something for you to do. There's a couple of janitorships loose."

"Hicksey," says I.

"Miss Hicks," says she.

"I beg your pardon — my dear girl, then," said I. "I've come over to the bunch to confess. You've busted us. We're on the mat nine points down and yelling for help. We don't want to run things. We only want to be allowed to live. We surrender. We give up. We humbly ask that you prepare the crow and let us eat the neck. Is n't there any way by which we can get a little something to keep us busy and happy? We're in a horrible situation. Are n't you even going to let us have the Athletic Association next spring?"

"I was thinking of running that myself," said Miss Hicks thoughtfully.

I let out an impolite groan.

"But I'll tell you what you might do," said Miss Hicks. "You boys might try to win my crowd away from me. You see, you've played right into my hand so far. You haven't paid any attention to my supporters. Now, if you were to go after them the way you do the other girls in the college I shudder to think what might happen to me."

"You mean take them to parties and theaters?"

"Why not?" asked Miss Hicks. "You see, they're only human. I'll bet you could land every vote in the bunch if you went at it scientifically."

"But —"

"Oh, I know they're not pretty," said Miss Hicks. "But they cast the most bee-you-ti-ful votes you ever saw."

"What you mean," I said, "is that if we don't show those girls a superlatively good time this winter we won't get a look at the election next spring?"

"They'd be awfully shocked if you put it that way," said Miss Hicks; "and I wouldn't advise you to talk to them about it. Their notions of honor are so high that I had to pay for the lemonade for the independent men myself at the last election."

"Oh, very well," says I, taking my hat, "we'll think it over."

"You might wear blinders, you know," she suggested.

"Oh, go to thunder!" said I as earnestly as I could.

"Come again," she said when she closed the door after me. "I do so enjoy these little confidences."

Honestly, Miss Allstairs, when I think of that girl I shrink up until I'm afraid I'll fall into my own hat. It ought not to be legal for a girl to talk to a man like that. It's inhuman.

We thought matters over for two weeks and tried one or two little raids on the enemy with most horrible results to ourselves. Then we gave in. We put our pride and our devotion to art in cold storage and took up the politicians' burden. We gave those girls the time of their young-to-middle-aged lives. We got up dances and crokinole parties and concerts for them. We took them to see Hamlet. We had sleighing parties. We helped every lecture course in the college do a rushing business. We just backed into the shafts and took the bit without a murmur. And maybe you think those girls did n't drive us. They seemed determined to make up for the drought of all the past. They were as coy and uncertain and as infernally hard to please as if they'd been used to getting one proposal a day and two on Sunday. Let one of us so much as drop over to Browning Hall to pass the time of day with one of the real heart-disturbers, and the particular vote that he was courting would go off the reservation for a week. It would take a pair of theater tickets at the least to square things.

We gave dances that winter at which only one in five girls could dance. We took moonlight strolls with ladies who could remember the moon of seventy-six, and we gave strawrides to girls who insisted on talking history of art and missionary work to us all the way. When I think of the tons of candy and the mountains of flowers and the wagonloads of latest books that we lavished, and of the hard feelings it made in other quarters, and of our loneliness amid all this gayety, and of our frantic efforts to make the prom a success, with ten couples dancing and the rest decorating the walls, I sometimes wonder whether the college was worth our great love for it after all.

But we were winning out. By April it was easy to see this. The Blanks thawed with the snow-drifts. They got real friendly and sociable, and after the warm weather came on we simply had to entertain them all the time, they liked it so. When I think of those beautiful spring days, with us saun-tering with our political fates about the campus, and the nicest girls in the world walking two and two all by themselves — Oh, gee! Why, they even made us cut chapel to go walking with them, just as if it was a genuine case of " Oh, those eyes! " and " Shut up, you thumping heart."

All this time Miss Hicks would n't accept any invitation at all. She just flocked by herself as usual, and watched us taking her votes away from her without any concern apparently. I always felt that she had something saved up for us, but I could n't

Why, they even made us cut chapel to go walking
with them

Page 280

tell what it was; and anyway, we had those votes.
By the time the Athletic election came around there
was n't a doubt of it.

I must say the women did pretty well during the
year. They 'd cleaned up the Oratorical debt, and
somehow there was about three times as much money
in the Athletic treasury after the football season as
there had ever been before. But they 'd raised a lot
of trouble too. No passes. Dues had to be paid up.
Nobody got any fun out of the class affairs. They got
up lectures and teas and made the class pay for them.
And, anyway, we wanted to run things again.
We 'd felt all year like a bunch of last year's sun-
flowers. Besides, we 'd earned it. We 'd earned a
starry crown as a matter of fact, but all we asked
was that they give our little old Athletic Association
back and let us run it once more.

Miss Hicks announced herself as a candidate, and
we felt sorry for her. Not one of her gang was with
her. They were enthusiastically for us. We 'd
planned the biggest party of the year right after the
election in celebration, and had invited them already.
Election day came and we hardly worried a bit.
The result was 189 to 197 in favor of Miss Hicks.
Every independent man and every bang-up-to-date
girl in college voted for her.

Of course it looks simple enough now, but why
could n't we see it then? We supposed the real girls
knew that it was a case of college patriotism. And, of
course, it was a low-lived trick for Miss Hicks to

float around the last day and spread the impression that we 'd never loved them except for their votes. She simply traded constituencies with us, that 's all. Take it coming or going, year in or year out, you could n't beat that girl. I 'll bet she goes out to Washington state and gets elected governor some day.

I went over to Browning Hall the night after the election, ready to tell Miss Hicks just what everybody thought of her. I was prepared to tell her that every athletic team in college was going to disband and that anarchy would be declared in the morning. She came down as pleasant as ever and held out her hand.

"Don't say it, please," she said, "because I 'm going to tell you something. I 'm not coming back next year."

"Not coming back!" said I, gulping down a piece of relief as big as an apple.

"No," she said, "I 'm — I 'm going to be married this summer. I 've — I 've been engaged all this year to a man back home, but I wanted to come back and learn something about politics. He 's a lawyer."

"Well, you learned enough to suit you, did n't you?" I asked.

"Oh, yes," she said with a giggle. "Was n't it fun, though! My father will be so pleased. He 's the chairman of the congressional committee out at home and he 's always told me an awful lot about politics. I 've enjoyed this year so much."

" Well, I have n't," I said; " but I hope to enjoy next year." And then I took half an hour to tell her that, in spite of the fact that she was the most arrant, deceitful, unreliable, two-faced and scuttling politician in the world, she was almost incredibly nice. She listened quite patiently, and at the end she held up her fingers. They 'd been crossed all the time.

No, that 's the last I ever saw of her, Miss Allstairs. She left before Commencement. She sent me an invitation to the wedding. I 'll bet she did n't quite get the significance of the magnificent silver set we Siwash boys sent. We sent it to the groom.

That was the end of women dominion at Siwash. There was n't a rag of the movement left next fall. But we boys never entirely forgot what happened to us, and it 's still the custom to elect a co-ed to some Athletic office. They do say that the only way to teach a politician what the people want is to bore a shaft in his head and shout it in, but our experience ought to be proof to the contrary. Why, all we needed was the gentle little hint that Mary Jane Hicks gave us.

CHAPTER XI

HOW did the Siwash game come out Saturday?
Forget it, my boy. You'll never know in this
oversized, ingrowing, fenced-off, insulated metropolis
till some one writes and tells you. Every fall I
ask myself that same question all day Saturday and
Sunday, and do you suppose I ever find a Siwash
score in one of those muddy-faced, red-headed, ward-
gossip parties that they call newspapers in New York?
Never, not at all, you hopeful tenderfoot from the
unimportant West. After you've existed in this
secluded portion of the universe a few years you'll
get over trying to find anything that looks like news
from home in the daily disturbances here. And I
don't care whether your home is in Buffalo, Chicago
or Strawberry Point, Iowa, either. Go down on the
East Side and beat up a policeman, and you'll get
immortalized in ten-inch type. Go back West and get
elected governor, and ten to one if you're mentioned
at all they'll slip you the wrong state to preside over.

Excuse me, but I'm considerably sore, just as I
am every Sunday during the football season. Here
I am, eating my heart out with longing to know

whether good old Siwash has dusted off half a township with Muggledorfer again, and what do I get to read? Four yards of Gale; five yards of Jarhard; two yards of Ohell; and a page of Quincetown, Hardmouth, Jamhurst, Saint Mikes, Holy Moses College and the Connecticut Institute of Etymology. Nice fodder for a loyal alumnus eleven hundred and then some miles from home, is n't it? Honest, when I first hit this seething burg I used to go down to the Grand Central station on Sunday afternoon and look at the people coming in from the trains, just because some of them were from the West. Once I took a New Yorker up to Riverside Park, pointed him west and asked him what he saw. He said he saw a ferryboat coming to New York. That was all he had ever seen of the other shore. He called it Hinterland. That made me mad and I called him an electric-light bug. We had a lovely row.

But we 're blasting out a corner for the old coll., even back here. We 've got things fixed pretty nicely here now, we Siwash men. Down near Gramercy Park there 's an old-fashioned city dwelling house, four stories high and elbow-room wide. It 's the Siwash Alumni Club. There are half a hundred Siwash men in New York, gradually getting into the king row in various lines of business, and we pay enough rent each year for that house to buy a pretty fair little cottage out in Jonesville. Whenever a Siwash man drops in there he 's pretty sure to find another Siwash man who smokes the same brand of

tobacco and knows the same brand of college songs.
We 've got one legislator, four magazine publishers,
two railroad officials, a city prosecutor and three
bankers on the membership roll, and maybe some
day we 'll have a mayor. Then we 'll pass a law
requiring the boys and girls of New York to spend
at least one hour a day learning about Siwash College, Jonesville, the big team of naughty-nix and
the formula for getting credit at the Horseshoe Café.
We 'll make it obligatory for every newspaper to publish a full page about each Siwash game in the fall,
with pictures of the captain, the coach and the fullback's right leg. Hurrah for revenge! I see it
coming.

Join the club? Why, you don't have to ask to join
it. You 've got to join it. Ten dollars, please, and
sign here. When we get a little huskier financially
we won't charge new-fledged graduates anything for
a year or two, but we 've got to now. The soulless
landlord wants his rent in advance. You 'll find the
whole gang there Saturday nights. Just butt right
in if I 'm not around. You 're a Siwash man, and
if you want to borrow the doorknob to throw at a
hackman you 've a perfect right to do it.

I 'll tell you, old man, you don't know how nice
it is to have a hole that you can hunt in this hurri-
cane town, when you 're a bright young chap with a
glorious college past and a business future that you
can't hock for a plate of beans a day! Leaving college and going into business in a big city is like

taking a high dive from the hall of fame into an
ice-water tank.   Think of that and be cheerful.
You've got a nice time coming.   Just now you're
Rudolph Weedon Burlingame, Siwash Naughty-
several, late captain of the baseball team, prize
orator, manager of two proms and president of the
Senior class.   To-morrow you'll be a nameless cum-
berer of busy streets, useful only to the street-car
companies to shake down for nickels.   To-morrow
you're going around to the manager of some firm
or other with a letter from some customer of his, and
you're going to put your hand on your college diploma so as to have it handy, and you're going to
hand him the letter and prepare to tell the story of
your strong young life.   But just before you begin
you'll go away, because the manager will tell you
he's sorry, but he's busy, and there are fourteen
applicants ahead of you, and anyway he'll not be
hiring any more men until 1918, and will you please
come around then, and shut the door behind you, if
you don't mind.

Yep, that's what will happen to you.   You'll
spend your first three days trying to haul that
diploma out.   The fourth day you'll put it in your
trunk.   I've known men to cut 'em up for shaving
paper.   You'll stop trying to tell the story of your
life and in about a week you'll be wondering why
you have been allowed to live so long.   In two weeks
a clerk will look as big as a senator to you and
you'll begin to get bashful before elevator men.

You'll get off the sidewalk when you see a man who looks as if he had a job and was in a hurry. You'll envy a messenger boy with a job and a future; you'll wonder if managers are really carnivorous or only pretend to be. You feel as tall as the Singer Building to-day, but you'll shrink before long. You'll shrink until, after a long, hard day, with about nine turndowns in it, you'll have to climb up on top of the dresser to look at yourself in the glass.

That's what you're going up against. Then the Siwash Club will be your hole and you'll hunt it every evening. You'll be a big man there, for we judge our members not by what they are, but by what they were at school. You'll sit around with the boys after dinner, and the man on your right, who is running a railroad, will be interested in that home run you made against Muggledorfer, and the man on your left, who won't touch a law case for less than five thousand dollars, will tell you that he, too, won the Perkins debate once. And he'll treat you as if you were a real life-sized human being instead of a job hunter, knee high to a copying clerk. You'll be back in the old college atmosphere, as big as the best of 'em, and after you've swapped yarns all evening you'll go to bed full of tabasco and pepper, and you'll tackle the first manager the next morning as if he were a Kiowa man and had the ball. And sooner or later you'll get old Mr. Opportunity where he can't give you the straight arm, and if you don't put a knee in his chest and tame him for life you have n't got the real Siwash spirit, that's all.

Funny thing about college. It is n't merely an education. It's a whole life in itself. You enter it unknown and tiny — just a Freshman with no rights on earth. You work and toil and suffer — and fall in love — and climb and rise to fame. When you are a Senior, if you have good luck, you are one of the biggest things in the whole world — for there is n't any world but the campus at college. Freshmen look up to you and admire men who are big enough to talk with you. The Sophomores may sneer at faculties and kings, but they would n't think of sassing you. The papers publish your picture in your football clothes. You dine with the professors, and prominent alumni come back and shake you by the hand. Of course, you know that somewhere in the dim nebulous outside there is a President of the United States who is quite a party in his way, but none of the girls mention it when they tell you how grand you looked after they had hauled the other team off of you and sewed on your ear. They talk about you exclusively because you 're really the only thing worth talking about, you know.

When Commencement comes you move about the campus like some tall mountain peak on legs. The students bring their young brothers up to meet you and you try to be kind and approachable. They give you a tremendous cheer when you go down the aisle in the chapel to get your prizes. You are referred to on all sides as one of the reasons why America is great. The professors when they bid you good-by ask you anxiously not to forget them. Then Commencement is over and college life is past, and there is nothing left in life but to become a senator or run a darned old trust. You leave the campus, taking care not to step on any of the buildings, and go out into the world pretty blue because you're through with about everything worth while; and you wonder if you can stand it to toil away making history eleven months in the year with only time to hang around college a few weeks in spring or fall. You're done with the real life. You're an old man, you've seen it all; and it sometimes takes you two weeks or more to recover and decide that after all a great career may be almost as interesting in a way as college itself. So you buck up and decide to accept the career — and that's where you begin to catch on to the general drift of the universe in dead earnest.

Take a man of sixty, with a permanent place in Who's Who and a large circle of people who believe that he has some influence with the sunrise and sunset. Then let him suddenly find himself a ten-year-old boy with two empty pockets and an appetite for assets, and let him learn that it isn't considered even an impertinence to spank him whenever he tries to mix in and air his opinions. I don't believe he would be much more shocked than the college man who finds, at the conclusion of a glorious four-year slosh in fame, that he is really just about to begin life, and

that the first thing he must learn is to keep out from
under foot and say " Yes, sir," when the boss barks at
him.   It's a painful thing, Burlingame.   Took me
about a year to think of it without saying " ouch."

The saddest thing about it all is that the two
careers don't always mesh.   The college athlete may
discover that the only use the world has for talented
shoulder muscles is for hod-carrying purposes.   The
society fashion plate may never get the hang of how
to earn anything but last year's model pants; and
the fishy-eyed nonentity, who never did anything
more glorious in college than pay his class tax, may
be doing a brokerage business in skyscrapers within
ten years.

When I left Siwash and came to New York I
guess I was as big as the next graduate.   Of course
I had n't been the one best bet on the campus, but I
knew all the college celebrities well enough to slap
them on the backs and call them by pet names and
lend them money.   That of course should be a great
assistance in knowing just how to approach the president of a big city bank and touch him for a cigar
in a red-and-gold corset, while he is telling you to
make yourself at home around the place until a job
turns up.   Allie Bangs, my chum, went on East with
me.   We had decided to rise side by side and to buy
the same make of yachts.   Of course we were sensible.
We did n't expect to crowd out any magnates the first
week or two.   We intended to rise by honest worth,
if it took a whole year.   All we asked was that the

fellows ahead should take care of themselves and not
hold it against us if we ran over them from behind.
We did n't think we were the biggest men on earth
— not yet. That's where we fell down. We've
never had a chance to since. You've got to seize
the opportunity for having a swelled head just as you
have for everything else.

It took us just six weeks to get a toe-hold on the
earth and establish our right to breathe our fair share
of New York air. At the end of that time neither
one of us would have been surprised if we had been
charged rent while waiting in the ante-rooms of New
York offices to be told that no one had time to tell
us that there was no use of our waiting to get a
chance to ask for anything. Talk about a come-
down! It was worse than coming down a bump-the-
bumps with nails in it. It was three months before
we got jobs. They were microscopic jobs in the same
company, with wages that were so small that it
seemed a shame to make out our weekly checks on
nice engraved bank paper — jobs where any one from
the proprietor down could yell " Here, you! " and
the office boy could have fired us and got away with
it. If I had been hanging on to a rope trailing
behind a fifty-thousand-ton ocean liner I don't believe I should have felt more inconsequential and
totally superfluous.

But they were jobs just the same and we were
game. I think most college graduates are after they
get their feelings reduced to normal size. We hung

on and dug in, and sneaked more work into our
positions, and did n't quarrel with any one except the
window-washer's little boy who brought meat for the
cats in the basement. We drew the line at letting
him boss us. And how we did enjoy being part of
the big rumpus on Manhattan Island. We had a
room — it was n't so much of a room as it was a sort
of stationary vest — and we ate at those hunger cures
where a girl punches out your bill on a little ticket
and you don't dare eat up above the third figure
from the bottom or you 'll go broke on Friday. By
hook or crook we always managed to save a dollar from
the wreckage each week for Sunday, and say, did you
ever conduct a scientific investigation into just how far
a dollar will go providing a day's pleasure in a big
city? We did that for six months, and if I do say
it myself we stretched some of those dollars until the
eagle's neck reached from Tarrytown to Coney Island.
We saw New York from roofgarden to subcellar. We
even got to doing fancy stunts. We 'd dig out our
dress suits, go over to one of those cafés where you
begin owing money as soon as you see the head waiter,
and put on a bored and haughty front for two hours
on a dollar and twenty cents, including tips. And
what we did n't know about the Subway, the Snubway
and the Grubway, the Clubway, and the various Dub-
ways of New York was n't worth discovering or even
imagining.

We had n't been conducting our explorations for
more than a week when a most tremendous thing

happened to us. You know how you are always running up against mastodons in the big town. You see
about every one who is big enough to die in scare-
heads. Taking a stroll down Fifth Avenue with an
old residenter and having him tell about the people
you pass is like having the hall of fame directory read
off to you. Well, one Sunday night when we were
blowing in our little fifty cents apiece on one of those
Italian table d'hôte dinners with red varnish free,
Allie looked across the room and began to tremble.
" Look at that chap," says he.

" Who is he? " I asked, getting interested.
" Roosevelt ? "

" Roosevelt nothing," he says scornfully. " Man
alive, that's Jarvis! "

I just dropped my jaw and stared. Of course you
remember Jarvis, the great football player. At that
time I guess most of the college boys in America said
their prayers to him. Out West we students used to
read of his terrific line plunges on the eastern fields
and of his titanic defense when his team was hard
pushed, and wonder if any of us would ever become
great enough to meet him and shake him by the hand.
What did we care for the achievements of Achilles
and Hector and Hercules and other eminent hasbeens,
which we had to soak up at the rate of forty lines of
Greek a day? They had old Homer to write them up
— the best man ever in the business. But they were
too tame for us. I've caught myself speculating more
than once on what Achilles would have done if Jarvis

had tried to make a gain thróugh him.   Achilles was
probably a pretty good spear artist, and all that,
but if Jarvis had put his leather-helmeted head down
and hit the line low — about two points south of the
solar plexus — they would have carted Ac. away in
a cab right there, invulnerability and all.

That's about what we thought of Jarvis.   We had
his pictures pasted all over our training quarters
along with those of the other super-dreadnoughts
from the colleges that break into literature, and I
imagine that if he had suddenly appeared back in
Jonesville we should have put our heads right down
and kow-towed until he gave us permission to get up.
And here we were, sitting in the same café with him.
I'll tell you, I had never felt the glory of living in
the metropolis and prowling around the ankles of the
big chiefs more vividly than right there in that room
the night we first saw him.

We sat and watched Jarvis while our meat course
got cold.   There was no mistaking him — some people have their looks copyrighted and Jarvis was one
of them.   We would have known it was he if we
had seen him in a Roman mob.   After a while Bangs,
who always did have a triple reënforced Harveyized
steel cheek, straightened up.   "I'm going over to
speak to him," he said.

"Sit still, you fool," says I; "don't annoy him."

"Watch me," says Bangs; "I'm going over to
introduce myself.   He can't any more than freeze me.
And after I've spoken to him they can take my little

old job away from me and ship me back to the hay-
fields whenever they please. I 'll be satisfied."

" You ought to bottle that nerve of yours and sell
it to the lightning-rod pedlers," says I, getting all
sweaty. " Just because you introduced yourself to
a governor once you think you can go as far as you
like. You stay right here — " But Bangs had gone
over to Jarvis.

I sat there and blushed for him, and suffered the
tortures of a man who is watching his friend making
a furry-eared nuisance of himself. There was the
greatest football player in the world being pestered
by a frying-sized sprig of a ninth assistant shipping
clerk. It was preposterous. I waited to see Bangs
wilt and come slinking back. Then I was going to
put on my hat and walk out as if I did n't belong
with him at all. But instead of that Bangs shook
hands with Jarvis, talked a minute and then sat down
with him. When Bangs is routed out by the Angel
Gabriel he 'll sit down on the edge of his grave and
delay the whole procession, trying to find a mutual
acquaintance or two. That 's the kind of a leather-
skin he is.

Presently Bangs turned around and beckoned to
me to come over. More colossal impudence. I was n't
going to do it, but Jarvis turned, too, and smiled at
me. Like a hypnotized man I went over to their
table. " I want you to meet Mr. Jarvis," said Bangs,
with the air of a man who is giving away his aeroplane to a personal friend.

"Glad to meet you," said Jarvis kindly.

"M-m-m-mrugh," says I easily and naturally. Then I sat down on the edge of a chair.

Well, sir, Jarvis — it was the real Jarvis all right — was as pleasant a fellow as you would ever care to meet. There he was talking away to us fishworms just as cordially as if he enjoyed it. He did n't seem to be a bit better than we were. I 've often noticed that when you meet the very greatest people they are that way. It 's only the fellows who are n't sure they 're great and who are pretty sure you are n't sure either, who have to put up a haughty front. Jarvis offered us cigarettes and put us so much at our ease that we stayed there an hour. It was a dazzling experience. He told us a lot about the city, and asked us about ourselves and laughed at our experiences. And he told us that he often dined there and hoped to see us again. When we got safely outside, after having bade him good-by without any sort of a break, I mopped my forehead. Then I took off my hat. "Bangs," said I, " you 're the world's champion. Some day you 'll get killed for impudence in the first degree, but just now I 've got ten cents and I 'm going to buy you a big cigar and walk home to pay for it."

Incredible as it may sound, that was the beginning of a real friendship between the three of us. Jarvis seemed to take a positive pleasure in being democratic. And he was wonderfully thoughtful, too. He realized instinctively that we had about nine cents

apiece in our clothes as a rule, and he did n't offer
to be gorgeous and buy things we could n't buy back.
We got to dropping in at the café once a week or
so and eating at the same table with him. Why on
earth he fancied eating around with grubs like us,
when he could have been tucking away classy fare
up on Fifth Avenue, we could n't imagine. Some
people are naturally Bohemian, however. It seemed
to delight Jarvis to hear us tell about our team, and
our college, and our prospects, and how lucky we
had been up to date, not getting stepped on by any
financial magnate or other tall city monument. He
was n't a talkative man himself. It was especially
hard to pry any football talk out of him, probably
because he was so modest. When we insisted he
would finally open up, and tell us the inside facts
about some great college game that we knew by
heart from the newspaper accounts. And he would
mention all the famous players by their first names
— you can't imagine how much more alarming it
sounded than calling a president " Teddy " — and
we would just sit there and drink it in, and watch
history from behind the scenes until suddenly he
would stop, look absent and shut up like a clam.
No use trying to turn him on again. Presently he
would bid us good night and go away. The first
time we thought we had offended him and we were
miserable for a week. But when we ran across him
again he seemed as pleased as ever to see us. It
was just moods, after all, we finally decided, and

thought no more about it. Great men have a right
to have moods if they want to. We admired his
moods as much as the rest of him, and were only
glad they were n't violent.

It was a couple of months before we got up courage
enough to ask him to drop in at our room. Even
Allie got timid. He explained that he did n't want
to break the spell. But finally I braced up myself
and invited him to drop around with us, and he consented as kindly as you please. Came right up to our
little three by twice and would n't even sit in the
one chair. Sat on the bed and looked over our college pictures, and chatted until Allie asked him if he
was going back for the big game that fall. Then he
said sort of abruptly that he could n't get away, and
a few minutes afterward he went home. We thought
we 'd offended him again, but a week afterward he
turned up and called on us — we 'd asked him to
drop in any time. We decided that he did n't like
to have too much familiarity about his football career
and we respected him for it. It 's all right for a
man like that to be affable and democratic, but he
must n't let you crawl all over him. He 's got his
dignity to maintain.

As the winter came on Jarvis dropped up to see
us quite frequently. He never asked us to come and
see him and we were really a little grateful — for I
don't believe I should have had the nerve to go
bouncing into the apartments of a national hero and
hobnob with the mile-a-minute class. Anyway we

did n't expect it or dream of it. And we did n't ask him any more questions about himself. We did n't care to try to elbow into his circle. If he chose to come slumming and sit around with us, we were more than content. We had seen enough of him already to keep us busy paralyzing Siwash fellows for a week when we went back to Commencement. "Jarvis? Oh, yes. Fact is, he 's a friend of ours. Comes up to our rooms right along. We happened to meet him in a café. And say, he tells us that when he made that fifty-yard run — and so on." We used to practise saying things like this naturally and easily. We could just see the undergrads at the frat house sitting around in circles and lapping it up.

All this time we were plugging away down at the plant, early and late, with every ounce of steam we had. There 's one good thing about business in this Bedlam — when you break in you keep right on going. By the time Commencement rolled around we were getting checks with two figures on them, and had a better job treed and ready to drop. Ask for a vacation? Why, we would n't have asked for four days off to go home and help bury our worst enemy. That 's what business does to the dear old college days when it gets a good bite at them. There we were, one year out of Siwash, breaking forty-five reunion dates, and never even sitting around with our heads in our hands over it. This business bug is a bad, bad biter all right. Just let it get its tooth into you, and what do you care if some other fellow is smoking your two-quart pipe back in the old chapter house? And for that matter, what do you care about anything else until you get up far enough to take breath and look around? Sometimes, after a couple of weeks of extra hard work, I've taken my mind off invoices long enough to wag it around a bit and I've felt like a swimmer coming up after a long dive.

We landed those promotions in July and went right after another pair. I got mine in August — Allie in September. And along in December they called us both up in the office, where the big crash was. He said nice things to us about getting a chance to fire our own chauffeurs if we kept on tending to business, and first thing we knew we had offices of our own in the back of the building, with our names painted on the doors, and call-bells that brought stenographers and the same old brand of office boys that used to blow us out of the other offices along with their cigarette smoke. And we realized then that if we worked like thunder for thirty years more and saved our money and made it earn one hundred per cent, perhaps some of the real business kings would notice us on the street some day. That's about the way the college swelling goes down.

All this time we hadn't seen much of Jarvis. He'd stopped coming to the café and we'd really been so busy that we almost forgot about him. It's simply wonderful the things business will drive out

of your mind. It was n't until late in the winter
that we realized that we 'd probably lost track of
Jarvis for good — that is, until we climbed up into
his set and discovered him at some dinner that was
a page out of the social register. We mixed around
a lot more now. We went to the million-candle-power
restaurants every now and then, and ate a good deal
more than sixty-five cents' worth apiece without batting
an eye; and we went to see a play occasionally and
did n't climb up into the rarefied atmosphere to find
our seats, either. And whenever we broke in with the
limousine crowd we kept a bright lookout for Jarvis.
We wanted to see him and show him that we were
coming along. We wanted him to be proud of us.
I 'd have given all my small bank balance to hear
him say: " Fine work, old man; keep it up." I 'll
tell you when a big chap like that takes an interest
in you, it 's just as bracing as a hypodermic of
ginger. Baccalaureates and inspirational editorials
can't touch it.

I was holding down the proud position of shipping
clerk and Allie was my assistant the next spring, and
it seemed as if we had to empty that warehouse every
twenty-four hours and find the men to load the stuff
with search-warrants. Help was scandalously scarce.
We could n't have worked harder if we had been
standing off grizzly bears with brickbats. I 'd just
fired the fourth loafer in one day for trying to roll
barrels by mental suggestion, when the boss came into
my office.

"Can you use an extra man?" he asked me.

"Use him?" says I, swabbing off my forehead — I'd been hustling a few barrels myself. "Use him? Say, I'll give him a whole car to load all by himself, and if he can get the job finished by yesterday he can have another to load for to-day."

"Now, see here," said the boss, sitting down; "this is a peculiar case. This chap's been at me for a job for months. There's nothing in the office. He's a fine fellow and well educated, but he's on his uppers. He can't seem to land anywhere. I'm sorry for him. He looks as if he was headed for the bread line. He's too good to roll barrels, but it won't hurt him. If you'll take him in and use him I'll give him a place as soon as I get it; let me know how he pans out."

"Just ask him to run all the way here," I said, and put my nose down in a bill of lading. After a while the door opened and some one said, "Is this the shipping clerk?" It was the ghost of a voice I used to know and I turned around in a hurry. It was Jarvis.

I don't suppose it is strictly business to cry while you are shaking hands with a husky you're just putting into harness at one-fifty per. I didn't intend to do it, but somehow when your whole conception of fame and glory comes clattering down about your ears, and you find you've got to order your star and idol to get a hustle on him and load the car at door four damquick, you are likely to do something foolish. I just stood and sniveled and let my mouth hang open. Neither of us said a word, but presently I put my arm around his shoulders and led him out into the shipping room. "There's the foreman," I said, in a voice like a wet sponge. "And you report here at six o'clock sharp." Then I went and hunted up Allie and for once we let business go hang in business hours. We could n't work. We kept clawing for the solid ground and trying to readjust society and the universe and the beacon lights of progress all afternoon.

When quitting time came we waited for Jarvis. We did n't say anything, but we loaded him into a cab and took him up to the old café. Then he told us his story, while we learned a lot of things about glory we had n't even vaguely suspected before. He was one of the greatest football players who ever carried a ball, Jarvis was. Of that there was no doubt. He admitted it himself then. I might say he confessed it. He'd come to his university without any real preparation — you know even in the best regulated institutions of learning they sometimes get your marks on tackling mixed with your grades on entrance algebra. He'd spent two hours a day on football and the rest of his time being a college hero. He'd had to work at it like a dog, he said. How he got by the exams. he never knew. It seemed to him as if he must have studied in his sleep. By the time he graduated he'd had about every honor that has been invented for campus consumption. He belonged to the exclusive societies.   All kinds of big people had shaken hands with him — asked for the privilege. He had a scrapbook of newspaper stories about his career that weighed four pounds.   He knew the differences between eight kinds of wine by the taste and he had a perfect education in forkology, waltz-ology, necktiematics, and all the other branches of social science.

He would never forget, he said, how he felt when he was graduated and the university moved off behind him and left him alone.   It was up to him to keep on being a famous character, he felt.   His college demanded it.   He had to make good.   But there he was with a magnificent football education and no more football to play.   His financial training consisted in knowing when his bank account was overdrawn.   His folks had pretty nearly paralyzed themselves putting him through and he wasn't going to draw on them any further.   He went to New York because it seemed to be almost as big as the university, and he started all alone on the job of shouldering his way past the captains of finance up to the place where his college mates might feel proud of him some more.

The result was so ridiculous that he had to laugh at it himself.   He lost five yards every time he bucked an office boy.   His college friends kept inviting him out and he went until they began offering him help.   Then he cut the whole bunch.   He didn't care to have them watch the struggle.   He'd been in

New York two years when he met us, he said, and he had n't earned enough money to pay his room-rent in that time. There were times when he might have got a decent little job at twelve dollars per, or so, but he would have had to meet the boys who had looked up to him as a world-beater and somehow he just could n't tackle it. When we had come over and paid homage to him he saw we had taken him for a successful man of the world, as well as a member of the All-America team, and he had n't been able to resist the desire to let two human beings look up to him again. He had n't invited us to his room, he said, because part of the time he did n't have a room; and he even confessed that once or twice he 'd walked up to our rooms from downtown because he was crazy for a smoke and did n't have the price.

I guess there never was a more peculiar dinner party in New York. Part of the time I sniveled and part of the time Allie sniveled, and once or twice we were all three all balled up in our throats. But after a while we braced up and I told Jarvis what the Boss had told me, and we drank a toast to the glad new days, and another to success, and another to Jarvis, the coming business pillar, and some more to our private yachts and country homes, and to Commencement reunions, and this and that. Then we chartered a sea-going cab and took Jarvis home with us. We made him sleep in the bed while we slept on the floor, and the next morning we loaned him a pair of overalls that we had honorably retired and we all went down to work together.

The next three months were perfectly ridiculous. We simply could n't order Jarvis around. Suppose you had to ask the Statue of Liberty to get a move on and scrub the floors? We could n't get our ingrained awe of that freight hustler out of our systems. Of course when any one was around we had to keep up appearances, but when I was alone and I had something for Jarvis to do I'd call him in and get at it about this way: "Er — say, Jarvis, could you help me out on a little matter, if you have the time? You know there's a shipment for Pittsburgh that's got to go out by noon. I think the car is at door 6. Those barrels ought to be put into the car right away, and if you'd see that they get in there I'd be very much obliged to you. I'd attend to it myself, but they've given me a lot of stuff to go over here."

Then Jarvis would grin cheerfully and hustle those barrels in before I could get over blushing. If you don't believe football has its advantages in after life you ought to watch a prize tackle waltzing a three-hundred-pound barrel through a car door.

By day we ordered Jarvis about in this fashion, and made him earn his one-fifty with the rest of the red-shirted gang. But at six o'clock we dropped all that like a hot poker. Nights we were his adoring young friends again. We sat together in restaurants and said "sir" to him to his infinite disgust, and made him tell over and over again the stories of

the big games and the grand doings of the old days.
When his promotion came, three months later, and
he went into a small job in the office, with a traveling
job looming up in the offing, we held a celebration
that set us back about half the price of a railroad
ticket home. It meant more to us than it did to him.
To him it was three dollars more a week, congenial
work and a chance. But to us it was the release of
a great man from grinding captivity — a racehorse
rescued from the shafts of a garbage cart; a Richard
the Lion-hearted hauled from the gloomy dungeon,
where he had had to peel his own potatoes, and set
on the road to kingly pomp and circumstance again.
Excuse me for this frightful mess of language. I
can't help getting a little squashy with my adjectives
when I think of that glorious banquet night.

I 'm glad to say that Jarvis kept coming along after
that. He developed into a first-class salesman, and in
a couple of years he came in from the road and took
a desk in the house with his name on the side in
gilt letters. When this happened we made him look
up every one of his old college friends again. He
hesitated a little, but we got behind him and pushed.
We pushed him into his college club and back to Commencement, and we really pushed him out of our life
— for every one was glad to see him, of course, and
to his amazement he found that he was still a grand
old college institution among the alumni. So he
trained with his own crowd after that, but even now
we go over to his club and dine with him at least once

a year — always on some anniversary or other.   And for the last two years he has been sending his machine around for us.

Oh, no, you don't!   I'm paying for this lunch, young fellow.   Don't fight any one about paying for your lunch just because you still have the price.   It's a privilege we older chaps insist on with you newcomers anyway.   And remember, there is always a bunch of us before the fire at the club Saturday evenings, and we don't talk business.   While you're waiting for that job, don't you dare miss a meeting. And say — one thing more.   Don't be afraid of those blamed office boys.   They're all a bluff.   I'm getting so I can fire them without even getting pale.

CPSIA information can be obtained
at www.ICGtesting.com
Printed in the USA
LVHW082151170520
655881LV00014B/283